Programmed Learning Aid for

THE BASIC ACCOUNTING CYCLE

Programmed Learning Aid for

THE BASIC ACCOUNTING CYCLE

JAMES DON EDWARDS
Professor of Accounting
University of Georgia

ROGER H. HERMANSON
Professor of Accounting
Georgia State University

ROLAND F. SALMONSON
Professor of Accounting
Michigan State University

Coordinating Editor
ROGER H. HERMANSON

LEARNING SYSTEMS COMPANY

A division of
RICHARD D. IRWIN, INC. Homewood, Illinois 60430

Also available through

IRWIN-DORSEY LIMITED Georgetown, Ontario L7G 4B3

ISBN 0-256-01707-7

Printed in the United States of America

567890K43210

FOREWORD

Each of the books comprising the Programmed Learning Aid Series is in programmed learning format to provide the reader with a quick, efficient and effective means of grasping the essential subject matter.

The specific benefits of the programmed method of presentation are as follows:

1. It keeps the reader *active* in the learning process and increases his comprehension level.
2. Incorrect responses are *corrected immediately*.
3. Correct responses are *reinforced immediately*.
4. The method is *flexible*. Those who need more "tutoring" receive it because they are encouraged to reread frames in which they have missed any of the questions asked.
5. The method makes learning seem like a game.

The method of programming used in this PLAID on the Basic Accounting Cycle and in most of the other PLAIDS is unique and simple to use. The reader begins by reading Frame 1^1 in Chapter 1. At the end of that frame he will answer the question(s) given. To determine the correctness of his responses he merely turns the page and examines the answers in Answer Frame 1^1. He is told *why* each answer is correct. He should use his performance on the questions given as a measure of his understanding of all the materials in Frame 1^1. If he misses any of the questions asked, he is encouraged to reread Frame 1^1 before continuing to Frame 2^1. This same procedure should be used throughout the book. Specific instructions are given throughout as to where to turn next to continue working the program.

The reader may desire to go through the PLAID a second time leaving out the programmed questions and answers. Or, he may desire to further test his understanding by going through it a second time answering all of the questions once again and rereading only those frames in which his comprehension is unsatisfactory.

My two coauthors of this PLAID are prominent leaders in the field of accounting. James Don Edwards has held the position of Chairman of the Department of Accounting and Finance at Michigan State University, Dean of the College of Business at the University of Minnesota, and is currently Research Professor of Accounting at University of Georgia. He has also served as President of the American Accounting Association and is a Trustee of the Financial Accounting Foundation. Roland F. Salmonson is a Professor of Accounting at Michigan State University, has held the position of Vice President of the American Accounting Association, is a member of the Board of Examiners of the American Institute of Certified Public Accountants, and chairman of the Theory Committee, and has gained recognition as an accounting theoretician. They are both known as outstanding teachers with students as their primary interest. I hope you will find that this PLAID reflects that dedicated interest.

Roger H. Hermanson
Coordinating Editor

PREFACE

This Programmed Learning Aid offers a self-review and a thorough coverage of the basic accounting cycle. It may be used as a *preview* before taking a first course in accounting or as a *review* of the cycle before taking more advanced courses.

The PLAID consists of eight chapters which should be read in order. Each chapter will take from 1–1/2 to 2 hours to work through. The steps you should go through in studying each chapter are as follows:

1. Study the *Learning Objectives* given at the beginning of the chapter.
2. Work through the *chapter,* answering the programming questions which are contained within the chapter and following the instructions given.
3. Read the *Summary* given at the end of the chapter.
4. Study the *Glossary* to learn the meaning of new terms presented in the chapter.
5. Work the *Student Review Quiz* at the end of the chapter.
6. Check your answers against the *Solutions to the Student Review Quiz* given in the back of the book.

This book has many uses. By working through this book on the accounting cycle persons who have had no exposure to accounting could determine whether they have the ability and aptitude to study accounting further. Also, those who are intending to take a course in introductory accounting may desire to study this PLAID to get a head start on the course requirements. Students who have had a course in introductory accounting may have forgotten some of the subject matter over the summer. If so, they may want to brush up on the accounting cycle by studying this PLAID before beginning intermediate accounting. Business executives who have never had a course in accounting may wish to study this PLAID to gain an understanding of the fundamentals of data accumulation in accounting so they can better communicate with accounting personnel.

JAMES DON EDWARDS
ROGER H. HERMANSON
ROLAND F. SALMONSON

CONTENTS

chapter 1

THE NATURE AND USES OF ACCOUNTING INFORMATION

LEARNING OBJECTIVES

Study of the material presented in this chapter is designed to achieve a number of objectives. These include an introductory level comprehension of—

1. Why accounting information is likely to be of some value to almost every person in our society.
2. The nature of accounting and the various actions undertaken by the accountant in accounting for the economic activity of an organization.
3. The major career areas where accountants are employed—public accounting, private or industrial accounting, and accounting in the not-for-profit sector—and the areas of specialization within each.
4. The type of accounting information that is needed and used in decision making by persons within and outside a business organization.
5. The statement of financial position, the earnings statement, and the statement of retained earnings as the basic financial statements prepared for a business organization and the accounting process undertaken that yields these statements.
6. Some of the basic concepts or notions relied upon in the practice of accountancy—entity, transaction, duality, money measurement, cost basis of measurement, periodicity, continuity, and accrual basis.

Note: When undertaking initial study of any discipline, new terms are encountered. To assist in the process of becoming familiar with the language of accounting, a glossary of the important terms introduced in each chapter is presented at the end of the chapter.

Frame 1[1]

Individuals in all walks of life must make decisions that consist of choosing among several alternatives that have different expected outcomes or consequences and costs. These decisions may be of an economic, social, or intimately personal nature. But often doubt exists as to the preferred course of action to be followed in achieving a known objective. It is the purpose of information to reduce this doubt, this uncertainty, with the result that a rational, informed decision will be made.

Accounting, because it is the primary source of information on economic activity, seeks to reduce doubt in the minds of those charged with conducting or those seeking to profit from such activity. Because it includes the production, exchange, and consumption of scarce goods, economic activity is found everywhere in our society. Accounting is nearly as extensive. Where-ever economic resources are employed, an accounting is likely to be required to show what was accomplished, at what cost or sacrifice. And this follows whether the resources are employed by individuals, employers, churches, a unit of government, or not-for-profit organizations, such as a hospital.

From this it follows that the welfare of nearly every individual in our society is affected, directly or indirectly, by accounting information. This is sufficient reason for maintaining that some knowledge of accounting is essential to every person who seeks to function intelligently and efficiently in our society.

ACCOUNTING DEFINED

A measurement and communication system. Accounting is a systematic process of measuring and reporting to various users relevant financial information for decision making regarding the economic activity of an organization or unit. While not ignoring other kinds of information completely, it is financial information—that is, information capable of being expressed in money terms—with which accounting is primarily concerned.

Measurement. Although described as a measurement and reporting system or process, accounting for economic activity consists of a number of more or less distinct actions or functions. Before measurement can take place, a decision must be made as to what is to be measured. Since they are reporting upon economic activity, it follows logically that accountants must *observe* the economic scene and *select* (or identify) those happenings, events, or transactions that may be considered evidence of economic activity. (The purchase and sale of goods and services are examples.) Accountants then through the use of natural numbers, a monetary scale, and certain other principles and procedures (to be discussed in this text) seek to attach a money amount to the selected events. Accountants *record* these money amounts in order to provide a permanent, historical record or account of the financial activities of the organization. Together, all of the above functions enable the accountant to build a store or data bank of money measurements of economic activity.

Communication. As was true for measurement, before communication (reporting) can take place a decision must be made as to what to communicate or report. Here knowledge of the decisions to be made by users of accounting information helps the accountant to provide relevant information. Since it would be meaningless to present an almost endless diary-like narrative of money measurements of recorded events, accountants seek to *classify* them into meaningful groups through use of a logical framework, as will be illustrated and discussed later. The next steps are to *summarize* the recorded data and *present* them in financial statements and other accounting reports. Frequently, accountants are asked to *interpret* these statements and reports. Interpretation may involve explanation of the uses, meaning, and limitations of accounting information as well as the drawing of attention to significant items through percentage and ratio analysis. Together, the above functions or actions describe rather loosely the communication function of accounting.

Accounting distinguished from bookkeeping. Many uninformed persons fail to perceive the difference between accounting and bookkeeping and between accountants and bookkeepers. Even though persons referred to as bookkeepers do prepare financial statements, bookkeeping is but a minor part of the accounting function or process and is concerned largely with procedural matters and the development and maintenance of accounting records. Accounting, on the other hand, is more conceptual in nature, dealing with matters such as why a given measurement is preferable in certain circumstances and what uses are made of accounting information and why. In addition to financial statement preparation, accounting is concerned with income tax returns, budgets, audits, managerial cost studies, financial advising, and the design of accounting systems.

Indicate whether each of the following statements is true or false by writing "T" or "F" in the space provided.

______ 1. The welfare of a prisoner in a state penitentiary is quite likely to be affected by decisions made that are based in part on accounting information.

______ 2. Accounting is primarily concerned with providing financial information on the economic activities of an organization.

______ 3. Accounting could be briefly defined as a measurement and communication process or system.

______ 4. Accounting and bookkeeping are essentially the same.

To check the correctness of your answers, turn to Answer Frame 1[1] on page 4.

Frame 2[1]

ACCOUNTANCY AS A PROFESSION

In our society accountants typically are employed in (1) public accounting, (2) private industry, or (3) the not-for-profit sector. Within each of these areas, specialization is possible; an accountant may, for example, be considered an expert in auditing, systems development, budgeting, or cost or tax accounting.

Public accounting. Accountants may offer their services, individually or as members of a firm, to the general public for a fee in much the same manner as do attorneys and doctors. Although the business organization is the primary client, individuals and not-for-profit organizations are included. If an accountant has passed a rigorous examination prepared and graded by the American Institute of Certified Public Accountants (AICPA)—the accounting equivalent of the American Bar Association or the American Medical Association—and has met certain other requirements, such as having a certain number of years of experience, he or she may be licensed by the state to practice as a certified public accountant (CPA). As an independent, professional person, a CPA may offer clients auditing, management advisory, and tax services.

Auditing. When a business seeks a loan from a financial institution or seeks to have its securities (stocks and bonds) traded on an exchange, it is usually required to provide financial statements containing information on its financial affairs. Users of these statements may accept them much more readily and be more willing to rely upon them when they are accompanied by an *auditor's report.* This auditor's report contains the professional opinion of the CPA as to whether the management of a business has presented a fair report on its financial affairs. In order to have the knowledge necessary for an informed opinion, the CPA conducts an examination or investigation (called an audit) of the underlying accounting and related records and seeks supporting evidence from external sources (such as the company's bank).

Management advisory services. As a result of knowledge gained in an audit, CPAs typically offer suggestions to their clients on how to improve their operations. From these as well as other direct contacts, CPAs may be engaged to provide a wide range of what are called management advisory services. Although such services may include, for example, executive recruiting and production scheduling, they are more likely to involve services related to the accounting process—the design and installation of an accounting system, electronic processing of accounting data, development of an inventory control system, budgeting, or financial planning.

Tax services. CPAs are often called upon for expert advice regarding the preparation and filing of federal, state, and local tax returns. The objective here is to use legal means to minimize the amount of taxes paid. But of equal importance, because of high tax rates and complex tax laws, is the area known as tax planning. Proper

Answer frame 1[1]

1. True. The amount of money given to prison authorities for food and medical care of prisoners will undoubtedly be determined, in part at least, by information in accounting reports on the amount of money available to the state for a variety of purposes.
2. True. Briefly stated, this is the function of accounting.
3. True. Accounting has been so defined in this text.
4. False. Bookkeeping is but a minor part of the accounting process being concerned largely with the routine, clerical, repetitive, and relatively uncomplicated aspects of accounting.

If you missed any of the above, you should read Frame 1[1] again before going to Frame 2[1] on page 3. You should follow this same procedure throughout this text.

Frame 2[1] continued

tax planning requires that the tax effects, if any, of every business decision be known fully and understood before the decision is made, as there may be little opportunity to alter its tax effects after it has been made.

Private or industrial accounting. Accountants employed by a single business organization are often referred to as private or industrial accountants; they may be the employer's only accountant, or one of several hundred. They may or may not be CPAs. If they have passed a rigorous examination prepared and administered by the National Association of Accountants—an organization composed primarily of accountants employed in private industry—they will possess a Certificate in Management Accounting (CMA). As in public accounting, they may be recognized as specialists in providing certain types of services.

They may, for example, be primarily concerned with the recording of events and transactions involving outsiders and in the preparation of financial statements that are, for the most part, issued to external parties. Or they may be engaged primarily in accumulating and controlling the costs of producing goods manufactured by their employer. They may be specialists in budgeting—that is, in the development of plans relating to future operations. Many private accountants (as well as public accountants) become specialists in the design and installation of systems for the accumulation and processing of accounting data. Others are called internal auditors because they are employed by a firm to see that its policies and procedures are being adhered to in its various departments and divisions.

Accounting in the not-for-profit sector. Many accountants, including CPAs, are employed by not-for-profit organizations, including governmental agencies at the federal, state, and local levels. Here again specialization is possible as, for example, in budgeting or systems design, although the governmental accountant is likely to be concerned with the accounting for and control of tax revenues and their appropriation and expenditure. Accountants are also employed by governmental agencies whose main function is the regulation of business activity—for example, the regulation by a state public service commission of public utilities. As might be expected, many accountants are employed by the federal government in its administration of our income tax laws and regulations.

It should also be noted that many accountants (including CPAs) are employed in the academic arm of the profession. Here attention is directed toward the teaching of accounting and to research into the uses, limitations, and improvement of accounting information and of the theories and procedures under which it is accumulated and communicated.

Indicate whether each of the following statements is true or false by writing "T" or "F" in the space provided.

_______ 1. An accountant may be an expert auditor and not a CPA.

_______ 2. To become a CPA, an accountant must be an expert in providing management advisory services.

_______ 3. A CPA may practice as an independent professional person, or may be employed as an accountant by a manufacturing company.

_______ 4. A CPA employed by a mining company would be permitted to express a professional opinion on the fairness of the company's financial statements.

Check your answers in Answer Frame 2[1] on page 6.

Frame 3[1]

THE NEED FOR ACCOUNTING INFORMATION

The objective of accounting to provide information on economic activity that is relevant to decision makers has already been noted. But little has been said about the specific users of accounting information and the uses made of this information. It has become customary to divide the users of accounting information into two major classes—internal users and external users. Attention is directed first at the types of decisions made within a business organization.

Internal decisions. In all but the smallest of companies, internal decisions will be made at various levels of management (shop foreman, crew chief, branch manager, plant manager, divisional vice president, and so on) with each level requiring different accounting information. But the decisions to be made can be classified roughly into four categories even though not every level of management will be concerned with the same type of decision. These categories and examples of the types of decisions made in each are:

1. Financing decisions—deciding what amount of capital (money) is needed and whether it is to be obtained from owner investment or by borrowing from creditors; and if it is to come from owner's, whether it is to be obtained by new investment or by "plowing back profits."

2. Resource allocation decisions—deciding how the total investment in or capital of a business is to be distributed among various types of productive resources such as buildings, machinery, and equipment.

3. Production decisions—determining what products are to be produced, by what means, when, and in what quantities in a given run; deciding whether new product lines considered desirable should be added and whether old lines are to be discontinued.

4. Marketing decisions—establishing selling prices and advertising budgets; determining markets and choosing the appropriate means or channels of distribution for the products sold.

But, although divided into four categories, internal decisions seldom fall solely within one category. For example, a decision to add a new product line requires knowledge that the product can be produced economically, that the proper equipment is available, that money will be available to acquire the equipment, and that the product can be sold in quantities and prices sufficient to yield a profit.

Managerial accounting. That part of the accounting discipline asked to provide accounting information for such internal decisions is called managerial (or management) accounting. Managerial accounting varies from the very broad (long-range planning budgets covering several years or more) to the quite detailed (determining the reasons why individual costs varied from their planned or budgeted amounts). Typically, the information must meet two tests: (1) it must be useful, and (2) it must not cost more to accumulate than it is worth. The information

Answer frame 2[1]

1. True. Many expert auditors employed by large companies as internal auditors are not CPAs and have little reason to seek the CPA certificate.
2. False. It is the demonstrated ability in expressing a professional opinion based upon evidence as to the fairness of the information contained in financial statements (the attest function as it is called) not in providing management advisory services that is required before an accountant can become a CPA.
3. True. When properly licensed by the state, CPAs may practice as independent, professional persons. But if they believe their personal prospects for success (however defined) are greater, they may be employed as accountants by a manufacturing company.
4. False. An accountant, even though a CPA, is not practicing as a CPA when in the employ of a mining company. He or she would not be considered an independent professional accountant and, as a consequence, would not be permitted to express an opinion on the fairness of the employer's financial statements. In order to express such an opinion, the CPA must, in addition to being licensed to practice as a CPA, be *independent*.

If you answered incorrectly, read Frame 2[1] again before beginning Frame 3[1] on page 5.

Frame 3[1] continued

generally relates to a part of an enterprise—a certain plant, division, or department—because these are the levels at which decisions are made. Management accounting information often is used to measure the success of managers and to motivate them to help a firm achieve its goals. It is forward-looking, often involving short-range and long-range planning.

Indicate whether each of the following statements is true or false by writing "T" or "F" in the space provided.

______ 1. The same information is likely to be needed at various levels of management decision making within a business.

______ 2. Management accounting information generally relates to some part rather than the whole of an enterprise.

______ 3. In any situation requiring a decision, the decision maker may forego securing information if it is not worth its cost.

______ 4. In general, the purpose of information is to reduce doubt.

Check your responses in Answer Frame 3[1] on page 8.

Frame 4[1]

External users and their decisions. The many external users of accounting information relative to business enterprises can be classified broadly into six major categories. These categories and examples of the questions to which accounting information helps to provide answers are:

1. Owners and prospective owners (stockholders in the case of a corporation) and their advisers—financial analysts and investment counselors. Should an ownership interest be acquired in this particular business? Or, if one is now held, should it be increased, decreased, disposed of entirely, or simply retained at its

present level? Has the management of the firm earned a satisfactory level of profits in the past year? (Note that in the case of a small business organization, its owners may also function as managers and thus not be outsiders.)

2. Creditors and lenders. Should the business firm be permitted to buy on a credit rather than a cash-only basis? Should a long-term loan be granted the firm? Will the firm be able to pay its debts as they become due?

3. Employees and the unions representing them. Does the business have the ability to pay increased wages and other benefits without raising prices? Does the firm appear financially able to provide permanent employment?

4. Customers and consumers. Will the company remain in operation so that its product warranties will be honored, if necessary? Can the business install costly pollution control equipment and still remain profitable? Is it financially able to install such equipment? Are its profit margins reasonable?

5. Governmental units and agencies. Is this business, a public utility supplying gas and electricity, earning a fair profit on its capital investment? How much federal and state income taxes does the firm owe? Should the Department of Justice file suit to block a proposed merger between two business firms? In the aggregate, is total business activity at the desired level for sound growth without inflation?

6. The general public. What might be the possible effects of raising the legal minimum wage? Are profits too high? Do they represent an increasing or decreasing proportion of the national income? Are the firms in this industry contributing to inflation? To what extent do tax laws favor the firms in a certain industry?

Although some governmental agencies have the power to prescribe in detail the information to be provided to them, the information needs of the above users typically are met by providing a single set of general-purpose financial statements. These statements are the end products of a process known as financial accounting.

Financial accounting. In general, in a business setting, financial accounting provides reports or statements on a firm's financial condition, the changes in its financial condition, and on the results of its operations—its profitability. These statements usually are published in a document containing 20 to 50 pages known as an *annual report*. The annual report also contains the CPA's auditor's report or opinion as to the fairness of the financial statements, as well as considerable other information about the reporting company's activities, plans, and expectations.

Financial accounting information generally relates to the company as a whole since outsiders typically do not participate in internal decisions and can make decisions only on matters pertaining to the enterprise in its entirety, such as a decision to extend credit. Such information is usually historical in nature, being a report of what has happened. Because it is used externally and often compared as between companies, the information supplied must conform to certain standards or principles.

But it would be a mistake to assume that a clear-cut distinction can be drawn between financial accounting information and managerial accounting information. Key management officials often are keenly aware of the fact that their jobs may depend upon how the figures come out in the annual report. Also, much of what is called managerial accounting information is first accumulated in an accounting system designed with financial reporting in mind.

Recycling. Whether financial or managerial accounting information is involved, the role of the accountant and of accounting information in what might be called a recycling process should be noted. The accountant observes economic activity, selects certain aspects for measurement, records these measurements, and then classifies, summarizes, and reports these measurements in financial statements or reports. The recipients of these reports use this information as well as information obtained from other sources in making further decisions. These decisions cause new economic activity to be generated for the accountant to observe, measure, record, and report upon. Thus, accounting information plays an important role in the continuous chain of events that constitutes economic activity.

Answer frame 3[1]

1. False. It is quite unlikely that the general manager of a large manufacturing plant would need the same information as the foreman of one of the producing departments in that plant.
2. True. Management accounting information is most widely used by internal management personnel who are responsible for a part rather than the whole of an organization.
3. True. As is true in any situation involving a purchasable commodity, the cost of information may exceed its value to some user.
4. True. In brief, this is the purpose of all information.

If you missed any of the above answers, you should read Frame 3[1] again before proceeding to Frame 4[1] on page 6.

Frame 4[1] continued

Indicate whether each of the following statements is true or false.

_______ 1. The annual report of a company contains a statement showing the financial condition of the reporting company.

_______ 2. Financial accounting information is often called general-purpose information because it is believed that the same information can satisfy the information needs of various external users.

_______ 3. As part of the management advisory services rendered, the CPA will express a professional opinion on the fairness of the bulk of the managerial accounting information accumulated by a company.

_______ 4. Basically, and in very broad terms, managerial accounting information is used internally while financial accounting information is used by external parties.

Check your responses in Answer Frame 4[1] on page 10.

Frame 5[1]

Types of business organizations. Although accounting information is absolutely essential in the successful management of a not-for-profit organization, primary attention in this text is devoted to business firms, of which there are three major types:

1. The single proprietorship. This is a business owned by one individual who provides the capital of the business and usually directs its activities. The owner has unlimited liability for the debts of the business—that is, if the business cannot pay its debts, the owner will be called upon to do so from his personal resources.

2. The partnership. This is a business owned by two or more individuals who provide the capital of the partnership and usually direct its activities. The partners, like single proprietors, generally have unlimited liability for the debts of the business.

3. The corporation. This is a creation of the law, ownership in which is evidenced by shares of capital stock. The capital of the business is usually provided by many stockholders, with hired managers often employed to direct the corporation's activities. A corporation's owners (stockholders) usually are not personally liable for the debts of the corporation.

Because the corporation is the dominant form of business organization and because much of the management accounting information needed is developed from data accumulated for financial reporting, the discussion in this text will focus upon the financial accounting for business corporations.

FINANCIAL STATEMENTS OF BUSINESS ENTERPRISES

Current literature discusses at length the fact that a modern business firm may have a number of objectives or goals. Among those mentioned are earning a satisfactory profit, providing good-paying jobs and comfortable working conditions for employees, being a good citizen, controlling pollution, providing equal employment opportunities for minority groups, and maintaining a sound financial position. But the two primary objectives of every business firm are *profitability* and *solvency*. Unless a firm can earn a reasonable profit and pay its debts as they become due, the other objectives it may have will never be realized simply because the firm will not survive.

Whether a business is reaching these objectives can be determined, in part, from its financial statements. The *statement of financial position* can be used in appraising a firm's ability to pay its maturing debts, while its *earnings statement* is clearly intended to provide information on profitability. The discussion of financial accounting which follows begins with financial statements, even though these statements are the end products of the process. Knowledge of what is sought by engaging in the process may aid considerably in understanding the process itself.

The statement of financial position. The statement of financial position (often called a balance sheet) presents measures of the assets, liabilities, and owners' equity in a business firm as of a specific moment in time. Assets are things of value; they constitute the *resources* of the firm. They have value to the firm because of the uses to which they can be put or the things that can be acquired by exchanging them. In Figure 1.1, the assets of the Bond Company amount to $36,670 and consist of current assets of cash and accounts receivable (amounts due from customers) and property, plant, and equipment consisting of delivery equipment and office equipment. Current assets consist of cash and other short-lived assets that are reasonably expected to be converted into cash or to be consumed or used up in the operations of a business within a short period, usually one year. (Technically speaking, the time period is one operating cycle or one year, whichever is longer. An operating cycle is the length of time that it takes cash spent for merchandise to be sold to come back to the selling company in the form of collections from its customers. Thus, in some industries—distilling, for example—the operating cycle extends for a number of years.) Property, plant, and equipment refers to relatively long-lived assets that are to be used in the production or sale of other assets or services rather than being sold.

Liabilities are the debts owed by a firm. Typically, they must be paid at certain known moments in time. The liabilities of the Bond Company are both relatively short-lived liabili-

FIGURE 1.1
A statement of financial position

BOND COMPANY
Statement of Financial Position
July 31, 1975

Assets			*Liabilities and Stockholders' Equity*		
Current Assets			Current Liabilities		
Cash	$13,470		Accounts payable	$ 1,600	
Accounts receivable	700	$14,170	Notes payable	3,000	$ 4,600
Property, Plant, and Equipment			Stockholders' Equity		
Delivery equipment	$20,000		Capital stock	$30,000	
Office equipment	2,500	22,500	Retained earnings	2,070	32,070
Total Assets		$36,670	Total Liabilities and Stockholders' Equity		$36,670

Answer frame 4[1]

1. True. One of the important statements in the annual report is one showing financial position.
2. True. Many classes of external users are provided with the same general financial information about a company.
3. False. The purpose of securing the professional opinion of a CPA as to the fairness of the information contained in a financial statement is to increase its reliability to *outsiders.* The management of a firm might wish to color the information it reports externally to make management appear more efficient and effective to outsiders. But management would only be deceiving itself if it sought to manipulate or somehow distort managerial accounting information. Hence, there is little need, if any, for a CPA to attest to managerial accounting information.
4. True. As a broad generalization, the statement is true, although some of the information released to outsiders may very well be used at the top levels of management where decisions are made relating to the company as a single whole.

If you answered incorrectly, restudy Frame 4[1] before going to Frame 5[1] on page 8.

Frame 5[1] continued

ties, consisting of accounts payable (amounts owed to suppliers or vendors) and notes payable (written promises to pay) totaling $4,600.

The Bond Company is a corporation, and it is customary to refer to the owners' interest in a corporation as stockholders' (or shareholders') equity. Bond Company's stockholders' equity consists of $30,000 paid in for shares of capital stock and retained earnings (earnings not paid out to stockholders) of $2,070. All of these items will be discussed further below. At this point, simply note that the statement of financial position heading includes the name of the organization, the title of the statement, and the date of the statement.

The earnings statement. The purpose of the earnings statement (often called the income statement) is to report upon the profitability of a business organization for a *stated period* of time. In accounting, profitability is measured by comparing the revenues generated in a period with the expenses incurred to produce those revenues. Revenue is defined as the flow of goods or services from an enterprise to its customers and is usually measured by the assets these customers are willing to surrender for the products or services. Expense is defined as the sacrifice made or the cost incurred to produce revenue. It is measured by the assets surrendered or consumed in serving customers. If revenues exceed expenses, net earnings result. If the reverse is true, the business is said to be operating at a loss. Figure 1.2 contains the earnings statement of the Bond Company for the month of July, 1975. This statement shows that revenues were generated by serving customers in the amount of $4,700. Expenses (the cost of producing the revenues) for the month amounted to $2,630 resulting in net earnings for the month of $2,070. Or, looked at another way, the assets secured in serving customers in July exceeded the cost of the assets surrendered or consumed in serving customers in July by $2,070.

FIGURE 1.2
An earnings statement

BOND COMPANY
Earnings Statement
For the Month of July, 1975

Service revenues		$4,700
Expenses:		
Wages	$1,600	
Gas and oil	400	
Rent	300	
Advertising	200	
Utilities	100	
Interest	30	2,630
Net Earnings		$2,070

Note that the heading of an earnings statement specifies the name of the company on which it reports, the type of statement involved, and the time period covered by the statement. Failure to specify the time period covered would render an earnings statement useless, or nearly so.

Indicate whether each of the following statements is true or false.

_______ 1. The basic elements of accounting are assets, liabilities, owners' equity, revenues, and expenses.

_______ 2. A statement of financial position reports upon the financial position of an organization as of a stated moment in time.

_______ 3. The solvency of a business organization can be appraised through study of its earnings statement.

_______ 4. Broadly speaking, revenue represents accomplishment and expense represents sacrifice.

Check your responses in Answer Frame 5[1] on page 12.

Frame 6[1]

THE FINANCIAL ACCOUNTING PROCESS

Having briefly introduced two of the principal financial statements, attention is now directed to the process that yields the data for such statements.

The accounting equation. As shown in the statement of financial position in Figure 1.1, the total assets of the Bond Company are equal to its liabilities plus its stockholders' equity. This equality results inevitably from the basic assumption in accounting that the assets of a business (or of any organization) are equal to the equities in those assets; that is, Assets = Equities. Assets have already been defined as things of value. In a more sophisticated sense, the accountant designates and records as assets all those economic resources owned by a business that he can measure. And all desired things, except those available in unlimited quantity without cost or effort, are economic resources.

Equities are interests in or claims upon assets. If, for example, you purchase a new automobile for $4,000 by withdrawing $400 from your savings account and borrowing the balance of $3,600 from your credit union, your equity in the automobile is $400 and that of your credit union is $3,600. The $3,600 can be further described as a liability, while your $400 equity is often described as the owner's equity or the residual equity or interest in the asset. Since, in the case of a corporation, the owners are the stockholders, the basic equation becomes:

Assets = Liabilities + Stockholders' Equity

This equation must always be in balance because the sum of the interests in assets must always be equal to the assets themselves. It is intuitively logical to hold that everything of value belongs to someone or to some organization.

The right side of the equation is also looked upon in yet another manner—namely, it shows the sources of the existing stock of assets. Thus, liabilities are not only claims to assets but they also are sources of assets. And, in a corporation, all of the assets are provided either by creditors (liability holders) or owners (stockholders).

As a business engages in economic activity, the dollar amounts and the composition of its assets, liabilities, and stockholders' equity change. But the equality of the basic equation always holds.

Transaction analysis. Our society is characterized by exchange. That is, the bulk of the goods and services produced are exchanged rather than consumed by their producers. From this it follows that much of the economic activity of our society can be observed from the exchanges that take place. In accounting, these exchanges (as well as other changes) are called *transactions* and provide much of the raw data entered in the accounting system. There are several reasons why this is so. First, an exchange is a readily observable event providing good evidence that economic activity has occurred. Second, an exchange usually takes place at an agreed-upon price, and this price provides a highly objective measure of the economic activity that has transpired. Thus, the analysis of

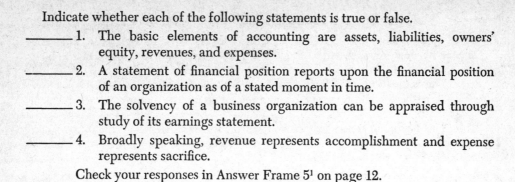

Answer frame 5[1]

1. True. Accounting is indeed concerned with these elements, as well as with the difference between revenues and expenses—the net earnings or net losses of the business for a period.
2. True. This is the function of the statement of financial position.
3. False. A business could be profitable and unable to pay its maturing debts due to a lack of cash.
4. True. This is a broad generalization well worth remembering.

If you responded incorrectly to any of the above questions, read Frame 5[1] again before proceeding to Frame 6[1] on page 11.

Frame 6[1] continued

transactions is a most important part of the financial accounting process.

To illustrate the analysis of transactions and their effects upon the basic accounting equation, the activities of the Bond Company that led to the statements in Figures 1.1 and 1.2 are presented and discussed below. Assume that the Bond Company was organized as a corporation on July 1, 1975, and that in its first transaction it issued shares of capital stock to Lee Bond, his wife, and their son. Analyzed, the transaction increased the assets (cash) of the Bond Company by $30,000 and simultaneously also increased its equities (the capital stock element of stockholders' equity) by $30,000. In other words, the only claim to the company's only asset, cash, is the claim of its owners—the stockholders. Consequently, the transaction yields a basic accounting equation containing the following:

Assets	=	Liabilities	+	Stockholders' Equity
(Cash, $30,000)		($0)		(Capital stock, $30,000)

Assume that as its second transaction, the company borrowed $6,000 from Mrs. Bond's father, giving its written promise to repay the amount in one year. Which of the following analyses properly describes the effects of this transaction upon the accounting equation of the company? Place a check by the correct answer.

_____ 1. Assets would increase by $6,000, and stockholders' equity would decrease by $6,000.

_____ 2. Assets would increase by $6,000, and liabilities would increase by $6,000.

_____ 3. Both assets and stockholders' equity would increase by $6,000.

_____ 4. Both assets and liabilities would decrease by $6,000.

Check your response in Answer Frame 6[1] on page 14.

Frame 7[1]

The basic equation depicting the financial position of the Bond Company now is:

Assets	=	Liabilities	+	Stockholders' Equity
(Cash, $36,000)		(Notes payable, $6,000)		(Capital stock, $30,000)

As its third transaction, the Bond Company spent $20,000 of its cash for three delivery trucks and $1,500 of cash for some office equipment. In this transaction, the company received delivery equipment (an asset) priced at $20,000 and office equipment (also an asset) priced at $1,500. It gave in exchange $21,500 of cash (an asset). This transaction thus does not change the totals in the basic equation, it merely changes the composition of the assets. The equation is as follows:

Assets		=	Liabilities		+	Stockholders' Equity	
Cash	$14,500						
Delivery equipment	20,000		Notes payable	$6,000		Capital stock	$30,000
Office equipment	1,500						
	$36,000	=		$6,000	+		$30,000

Assume that as its fourth transaction in the month of July, the company purchased an additional $1,000 of office equipment, agreeing to pay for it within 10 days after it received a bill for it from the supplier. Note carefully that this transaction (called a purchase on account) would have an effect on the accounting equation of the company even though it does not involve cash. The transaction increases office equipment (an asset) by $1,000. It also increases liabilities in the form of accounts payable (which are amounts owed to suppliers or vendors for items purchased from them for which payment has not been made) by $1,000. The items making up the totals in the accounting equation now appear as follows:

Assets		=	Liabilities		+	Stockholders' Equity	
Cash	$14,500		Accounts payable	$1,000			
Delivery equipment	20,000		Notes payable	6,000		Capital stock	$30,000
Office equipment	2,500						
	$37,000	=		$7,000	+		$30,000

Revenue and expense transactions. Thus far the transactions presented have consisted of the acquisition of assets either by borrowing or by stockholder investment. But a business is not formed merely to acquire assets. Rather, it seeks to use the assets entrusted to it as a means of securing still greater amounts of assets. This is accomplished by providing customers with goods or services, with the expectation that the value of the assets received will exceed the cost of the assets consumed or surrendered in serving them. Thus, a retailer of men's suits may purchase suits for $80 each and sell them at $125 each. Or the service-rendering organization expects that the assets received for the services rendered will be sufficient to cover all of the costs incurred in rendering these services and to provide an income, a net earnings. This total flow of services rendered or goods delivered (as measured by assets received from customers) has already been defined as revenue. Thus, revenue is a source of assets. The cost of serving customers is called expense and is measured by the cost of the assets surrendered or consumed. Expenses thus drain assets out of a business. If revenues exceed expenses, net earnings exist and the assets provided by customers exceed the assets consumed in serving them. If expenses exceed revenues, a net loss has been suffered in that the cost of the assets consumed in serving customers exceeded the value of the assets received from them.

Answer frame 6[1]

Statement 2 is the correct response. The company received an additional $6,000 in cash and gave in exchange a written promise to pay this sum at a later date. This written promise to pay is a note payable and is a liability. Thus, the company now has a creditor interest in its assets which it did not have previously. When properly analyzed, the effects of the transaction then are to increase assets in the form of cash by $6,000 and to increase equities in the form of liabilities (notes payable) by $6,000, thus keeping the equation in balance.

If you answered incorrectly, be sure that you understand why the second statement is correct before going on to Frame 7[1] on page 12.

Frame 7[1] continued

To illustrate a revenue transaction, assume that as its fifth transaction in July the Bond Company rendered delivery services for some of its customers for $3,800 cash. It is evident that the asset, cash, has increased by $3,800. But what other change has occurred, which, if properly included in the company's accounting equation, would reflect the appropriate analysis of this transaction? Place a check by the correct answer.

_______ 1. Liabilities increased by $3,800.

_______ 2. Stockholders' equity increased by $3,800.

_______ 3. Other assets decreased by $3,800.

_______ 4. Some combination of liability increase and stockholders' equity increase occurred.

Check your response in Answer Frame 7[1] on page 16.

Frame 8[1]

Incorporating the effects of the revenue transaction upon the financial position of the company yields the following basic equation:

Assets		=	Liabilities		+	Stockholders' Equity	
Cash	$18,300		Accounts payable	$1,000		Capital stock	$30,000
Delivery equipment	20,000		Notes payable	6,000		Retained earnings	3,800 (Service revenue)
Office equipment	2,500						
	$40,800	=		$7,000	+		$33,800

Note that the increase in stockholders' equity brought about by the revenue transaction is recorded in the equation as a separate item, "Retained earnings." The growth in stockholders' equity cannot be recorded as capital stock since no additional shares of stock were issued. Furthermore, the $3,800 did not represent a direct capital investment by the stockholders. Rather, it is an indirect stockholder investment. The expectation is that revenue transactions will yield net earnings. If net earnings are not distributed to the stockholders, they are in fact retained, and the title "retained earnings" is quite descriptive. Subsequent chapters will show that because of complexities in handling large numbers of transactions, revenues will be shown as affecting retained earnings only at the end of an accounting period. The procedure presented above is a shortcut used to explain why the accounting equation remains in balance when a revenue transaction occurs.

Assume that as its sixth transaction in July

the company performs services for customers who agree to pay $900 at a later date. The transaction consists of an exchange of services for a promise by the customer to pay later. It is similar to the preceding transaction in that stockholders' equity is increased because revenues have been earned. It differs because cash has not been received. But a thing of value, an asset, has been received, and this is the claim upon the customer, the right to collect from him at a later date. Technically, such claims are called *accounts receivable,* but the important point is that accounting does recognize them as assets and does record them. The accounting equation, including this item, is as follows:

Assets		=	Liabilities		+	Stockholders' Equity	
Cash	$18,300						
Accounts receivable	900		Accounts payable	$1,000		Capital stock	$30,000
Delivery equipment	20,000		Notes payable	6,000		Retained earnings	4,700 (Service revenue)
Office equipment	2,500						
	$41,700	=		$7,000	+		$34,700

To illustrate one more step regarding accounts receivable, assume that as its seventh transaction, the company collects $200 from its customers "on account," to use accounting terminology. The transaction consists of the receipt of an asset, cash, in exchange for an asset, the surrender of the claim upon the customer. The effect of the transaction is to increase cash from $18,300 as shown above to $18,500 and to decrease accounts receivable from $900 to $700, with all other items in the equation remaining unchanged. Note that the transaction consists of an exchange of assets—an increase in one, a decrease in another—not an increase in assets resulting from the generation of revenue. Transactions involving the collection of cash from customers must be analyzed carefully to determine whether they consist of a cash sale of goods or services or merely the collection of an account recorded when a previous revenue transaction was recorded.

Attention may now be directed toward expenses, which are the sacrifices made, the assets surrendered or consumed, in serving customers. Suppose (transaction 8) that the Bond Company paid its employees $1,600 for services received from them in conducting business operations during July. The transaction consists of an exchange of cash for employee services. But what is its effect on the accounting equation? Place a check by the correct answer.

______ 1. There would be no effect upon the totals of the two sides of the equation.

______ 2. Assets would decrease and liabilities would decrease.

______ 3. Assets would decrease and stockholders' equity would decrease.

______ 4. The effects cannot be determined.

Check your response in Answer Frame 8[1] on page 16.

Frame 9[1]

As already noted, the payment of wages consists of an exchange of cash for employee services, and a proper analysis of such a transaction would appear to indicate an exchange of one form of asset for another. This seems especially true when one recognizes that business corporations generally will surrender assets only for other things of value, for other assets. But, because the value of the services received typically has expired by the time payment is made, the account-

Answer frame 7[1]

The second response is correct. Stockholders' equity would increase by $3,800. The correctness of this answer can be arrived at by a process of elimination by noting that there is no increase in liabilities brought about by the rendering of the services. Furthermore, no specific assets have been surrendered, yielding the conclusion that stockholders' equity must have increased. And, it can be further noted that the very purpose for the existence of a business corporation is to bring about an increase in stockholder wealth through its operations.

If you answered incorrectly, you should study the first part of Frame 7[1] again before proceeding to Frame 8[1] on page 14.

Answer frame 8[1]

Statement 3 is the correct answer. Accountants typically, as is explained further in Frame 9[1], treat transactions such as this as expense transactions. Expenses indirectly reduce stockholders' equity in that their incurrence prevents stockholders' equity from increasing by the full amount of the revenue earned. Thus, if an asset was purchased for $10 and sold for $15, the net increase in stockholders' equity would be $5 even though recorded as an increase of $15 and a decrease of $10.

Even if you answered incorrectly, continue on in Frame 9[1] on page 15 for additional explanation of expense transactions.

Frame 9[1] continued

ant engages in a short-cut and treats the transaction as a decrease in an asset and in stockholders' equity. From a purely theoretical point of view, the transaction should be regarded as involving an increase in one asset (labor services) and a decrease in another asset (cash), and then a decrease in an asset (labor services) and a decrease in stockholders' equity (retained earnings) because of the recognition of an expense —wages.

Let us assume further that (as transaction 9) the company paid cash of $300 as rent for truck storage space and office space and that (as transaction 10) it paid its utilities bill for July in the amount of $100. These transactions will be treated by the accountant as having the same effect upon the financial position of the company, namely, a decrease in the asset, cash, of $400 and a decrease in stockholders' equity, retained earnings, of $400 because of the incurrence of rent expense of $300 and utilities expense of $100. Incorporating these two items and the wages of $1,600 cumulatively into our accounting equation, it now reads:

Assets		=	Liabilities		+	Stockholders' Equity			
Cash	$16,500		Notes payable	$6,000		Capital stock	$30,000		
Accounts receivable	700		Accounts payable	1,000		Retained earnings	2,700	Service revenue	$4,700
Delivery equipment	20,000							Less expenses:	
Office equipment	2,500							Wages	1,600
								Rent	300
	$39,700	=		$7,000	+		$32,700	Utilities	100

Because of their similar effects, transactions 11 and 12 of the Bond Company may be treated simultaneously. Assume that the company received a bill for gasoline, oil, and other delivery equipment supplies consumed during the month in the amount of $400 and a bill for $200 for advertising in July. Both transactions would be treated by the accountant as involving an increase in a liability, accounts payable, and a decrease in stockholders' equity because of the incurrence of an expense. Here again, in each instance, an asset was actually acquired. But, because it has been consumed in producing revenue during the month, the accountant treats it as an expense—a reduction in retained earnings. Note also that to wait until the bills were paid before recognizing the expenses incurred would be to assign the expenses to the wrong month, presumably August, assuming the bills are paid in August. The accounting equation depicting the financial position of the Bond Company now reads:

Assets		=	Liabilities		+	Stockholders' Equity			
Cash	$16,500		Notes			Capital			
Accounts			payable	$6,000		stock	$30,000		
receivable	700		Accounts			Retained			
Delivery			payable	1,600		earnings	2,100	Service	
equipment	20,000							revenue	$4,700
Office								Less expenses:	
equipment	2,500							Wages	1,600
	$39,700 =			$7,600 +			$32,100	Rent	300
								Utilities	100
								Gas and oil	400
								Advertising	200

In reviewing his needs for cash at the end of the month of July, Mr. Bond decided that he would not need as much cash as he now holds. Consequently, he paid $3,000 on the note owed to his father-in-law, plus interest for the month of $30. The recording of this transaction would have what effects upon the accounting equation? Place a check by the correct answer.

———— 1. Assets and liabilities would both decrease by $3,030.

———— 2. Assets and stockholders' equity would both decrease by $3,030.

———— 3. Assets would decrease by $3,030, liabilities would decrease by $3,000, and stockholders' equity would decrease by $30.

———— 4. Assets would decrease by $3,030 and liabilities would decrease by $3,000.

Check your answer in Answer Frame 9[1] on page 18.

Frame 10[1]

Summary of transactions. The effects of all transactions entered into by the Bond Company in the first month of its existence upon its assets, liabilities, and stockholders' equity are summarized in Figure 1.3 on page 18.

The ending balances in each of the columns are the dollar amounts reported in the statement of financial position in Figure 1.1, page 9. The itemized data in the retained earnings column are the revenue and expense items reported in the earnings statement in Figure 1.2, page 10.

From this summary, it can be easily seen how transactions affect the basic equation of accounting, Assets = Liabilities + Stockholders' Equity, and how one element of stockholders' equity—retained earnings—is affected by expense and revenue transactions. While such a summary could be prepared as the means of accounting for any business, we shall see in later chapters that it would be basically a very inefficient means of gathering accounting data.

Answer frame 9[1]

Statement 3 is the correct answer. The transaction decreased cash by the total amount paid out, $3,030. Of this amount, $3,000 was applied to reduce the principal amount owed on notes payable (a liability was reduced) and the remaining $30 consisted of the payment of interest expense—an element that reduces retained earnings. Note that answer 4 would automatically be wrong simply because it would leave the accounting equation out of balance.

This transaction serves to illustrate that any given transaction may affect assets, liabilities, and stockholders' equity simultaneously.

If you missed this question, restudy Frame 9[1] before going on to Frame 10[1] on page 17.

Frame 10[1] continued

FIGURE 1.3
Summary of transactions

BOND COMPANY
Summary of Transactions
Month of July 1975

		Assets				= *Liabilities*		+ *Stockholders' Equity*	
Transaction	*Explanation*	*Cash* +	*Accounts Receivable* +	*Delivery Equipment* +	*Office Equipment*	*Accounts Payable* +	*Notes Payable*	*Capital Stock* +	*Retained Earnings*
	Beginning balances	$ 0	$ 0	$ 0	$ 0	$ 0	$ 0	$ 0	$ 0
(1)	Issued stock for cash	+30,000						+30,000	
(2)	Borrowed money on note	+ 6,000					+6,000		
(3)	Purchased equipment for cash	−21,500		+20,000	+1,500				
(4)	Purchased equipment on account				+1,000	+1,000			
(5)	Service revenue for cash	+ 3,800							+3,800 (Service revenue)
(6)	Service revenue on account		+900						+ 900 (Service revenue)
(7)	Collection on account	+ 200	−200						
(8)	Paid wages	− 1,600							−1,600 (Wages expense)
(9)	Paid rent	− 300							− 300 (Rent expense)
(10)	Paid utilities bill	− 100							− 100 (Utilities expense)
(11)	Bill for gas and oil used					+ 400			− 400 (Gas and oil expense)
(12)	Bill for July advertising					+ 200			− 200 (Advertising expense)
(13)	Payment on note and interest	− 3,030					−3,000		− 30 (Interest expense)
	Ending balances	$13,470 +	$700 +	$20,000 +	$2,500	= $1,600 +	$3,000 +	$30,000 +	$2,070
		$36,670				= $4,600		+ $32,070	

Indicate whether each of the following statements relating to the summary of transactions in Figure 1.3 is true or false.

_______ 1. The total assets of the company at the end of the month amounted to $36,670.

_______ 2. Of the total stockholders' equity, $30,000 was made up of contributed or invested capital and the remainder resulted from the retention of assets brought into the business by the earning process.

_______ 3. Of the expenses incurred in July, $600 have not been paid.

_______ 4. Of the revenues earned in July, $900 have not been collected in cash.

Now check your responses in Answer Frame 10[1] on page 20.

Frame 11[1]

THE STATEMENT OF RETAINED EARNINGS

The financial reporting of a business corporation may include the presentation of a statement summarizing the changes in stockholders' equity if numerous changes have occurred in the items comprising stockholders' equity. More typically, only a statement of retained earnings is presented because changes in other stockholders' equity items are relatively few in number. The purpose of the statement of retained earnings is to explain the changes in retained earnings that occurred between two statements of financial position dates. Usually, these changes consist of the addition of net earnings (or the deduction of net loss) and the deduction of dividends. Dividends are the means by which a corporation rewards its stockholders for providing it with capital. The effects of a cash dividend transaction (and most dividends involve the payment of cash to stockholders) is to reduce cash and retained earnings by the amount of cash paid out. In effect, earnings are no longer retained but have been passed on to the stockholders. And this, of course, is one of the primary reasons why stockholders organize corporations or invest in the stock of corporations.

The statement of retained earnings for the Bond Company for the month of July, 1975, would be quite simple. Since the company was organized on July 1, there would be no beginning balance of retained earnings. Net earnings would be added in the amount of $2,070, and since no dividends were paid, this would also be the ending balance.

To provide a more effective illustration, assume that the Bond Company's net earnings for August were $1,500 (revenues of $5,600 and expenses of $4,100) and that it declared and paid dividends of $1,000. Its statement of retained earnings for August is shown in Figure 1.4.

FIGURE 1.4
A statement of retained earnings

BOND COMPANY
Statement of Retained Earnings
For the Month Ended August 31, 1975

Retained earnings, July 31	$2,070
Add: Net earnings for August	1,500
	$3,570
Less: Dividends	1,000
Retained Earnings, August 31, 1975	$2,570

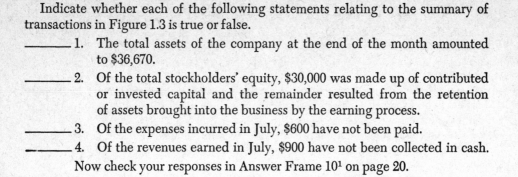

Answer frame 10[1]

1. True. If the dollar amounts of the four classes of assets are summed, they will amount to $36,670.
2. True. Invested capital is $30,000, and capital from retention of earnings amounted to $2,070.
3. True. Of the five expenses shown in retained earnings, a tracing of the balancing effect shows that all involved cash except the gas and oil expense of $400 and the utilities expense of $200.
4. False. Of the revenues earned in July, $900 were originally "on account." But $200 of this amount has been collected (see transaction 7) leaving but $700 of July's revenues uncollected.

If you missed any of the above, study Frame 10[1] again carefully in the light of the above explanations before proceeding to Frame 11[1] on page 19.

Frame 11[1] continued

Indicate whether each of the following statements is true or false.

_______ 1. Because dividends and expenses both reduce retained earnings, they are of the same basic nature.

_______ 2. Dividends usually consist of a cash distribution to stockholders.

_______ 3. Dividends should be deducted from revenues in calculating net earnings.

_______ 4. Generally, in order to pay dividends, a corporation should have retained earnings.

Check your responses in Answer Frame 11[1] on page 22.

Frame 12[1]

SOME BASIC CONCEPTS

The accountant in seeking to provide useful information on economic activity relies upon some basic assumptions, concepts, and principles. Those covered explicitly or implicitly thus far are summarized below.

Entity. The information gathered in an accounting information system relates to a specific business unit or entity. This entity is deemed to have an existence separate and apart from its owners, creditors, employees, or other interested parties.

Transaction. Those events or happenings that affect the assets, liabilities, owners' equity, revenues, and expenses of an entity are called transactions and are recorded in the accounting system. For the most part, transactions consist of exchanges.

Duality. Every transaction has a two-sided or dual effect upon each of the parties engaging in it. Consequently, if information is to be complete, both sides or both effects of every transaction must be included in the accounting system.

Money measurement. Economic activity is recorded and reported in terms of a common unit of measurement—the dollar. If not expressed in a common unit of measurement, accounting reports would be much less useful, if not unintelligible. Changes in the value of the dollar are usually ignored.

Cost. Most of the numbers entered in an accounting system are the bargained prices of exchange transactions. The result is that most assets (excluding cash and receivables) are recorded and reported at their cost of acquisition. Changes in the value of assets (with certain exceptions) are usually ignored. This practice is usually defended on the grounds of objectivity and the absence of evidence that the acquiring firm would have been willing to pay more.

Periodicity. To be useful, information must be (among other things) timely and current. To provide such information, the accountant assumes that he can subdivide the life of an entity into periods and report upon its activities for these periods. The requirement of periodic reporting will require the use of estimates, thus making every accounting report somewhat tentative in nature.

Continuity. Unless strong evidence exists to the contrary, the accountant assumes that the entity will continue operations into the indefinite future. Consequently, assets that will be used up or consumed in future operations need not be reported at their current liquidation values.

Accrual basis. Because the accountant seeks to record economic activity as it occurs, he records changes in assets, liabilities, stockholders' equity, revenues, and expenses as they occur, rather than waiting until such changes involve the receipt or payment of cash.

Indicate whether each of the following statements is true or false.

______ 1. All events or happenings that affect an entity are recorded in its accounting system.

______ 2. Assets are usually reported at their acquisition cost even though they may have a substantially higher current market value.

______ 3. Even though the value of the dollar may change as general price levels change, the accountant uses the dollar as if it was a constant unit of measure.

______ 4. Because of his basic assumption that assets equal equities, the accountant is forced to assume that every transaction has two sides.

Check your responses in Answer Frame 12[1] on page 22.

SUMMARY

Accounting is a systematic or organized means of gathering and reporting information on economic activity. The information provided is used by many external and internal parties, together with other information for a wide range of decisions.

An accountant may be employed in public, private, or governmental accounting and may be a specialist in one of many fields of expertise such as auditing, budgeting, systems development, taxation, or financial reporting.

Internally, accounting information is used by various levels of management personnel. External users include actual and potential stockholders and creditors and their professional advisers, employees and their unions, customers, suppliers, governmental agencies, and the public at large.

The basic end products of the financial accounting process are the statement of financial position, the earnings statement, and the statement of retained earnings.

All transactions can be analyzed and their effects upon assets and equities determined. Liabilities are a form of equity; revenues and expenses are subdivisions of the owner's equity, retained earnings. Thus, the basic elements of accounting are assets, liabilities, owners' equity, revenues, and expenses.

Fundamental to accounting are the assumptions, concepts, or principles of entity, transaction, duality, money measurement, cost basis of valuation, periodicity, continuity, and accrual basis.

You have completed the programmed portion of Chapter 1. As the first part of your review, read the Glossary which follows to study the definitions of the new terms introduced in this chapter. Then go on to the Student Review Quiz for a self-administered test of your comprehension of the material in the chapter.

Answer frame 11[1]

1. False. Although both reduce retained earnings (directly or indirectly), dividends and expenses are not of the same nature. Expenses are costs incurred to generate revenues in the expectation that revenues will exceed expenses—that is, that net earnings will result. Dividends are distributions of these net earnings, not costs incurred to generate revenues.
2. True. The common type of dividend usually involves a cash distribution to stockholders.
3. False. As explained in answer 1 above, dividends are distributions of net earnings, not expenses, and so should not be deducted from revenues in the determination of net earnings.
4. True. While covered only implicitly, the distribution of dividends usually requires the prior existence of retained earnings.

If you missed any of the above, you should read Frame 11[1] again before going on to Frame 12[1] on page 20.

Answer frame 12[1]

1. False. Many events or happenings occur that affect the well-being of a business. Some of these, such as a strike by the employees of a major competitor, are not recorded in an entity's accounting system simply because their effects cannot be measured. Unless the happening or event has a relatively direct effect upon the assets and equities of an entity, its effects will not be entered in the entity's accounting system.
2. True. Most assets are recorded and reported at their acquisition cost as reflected in the exchange transactions in which they were acquired.
3. True. No direct reflection of the changing value of the dollar is recognized in accounting systems employed in current practice.
4. True. The notion that a transaction has a dual nature, or two sides to it, is directly related to the basic assumption that assets equal equities.

If you answered incorrectly, you should read Frame 12[1] again before continuing with the Summary on page 21.

GLOSSARY

Accounting–a systematic process of measuring and reporting to various users relevant financial information for decision making regarding the economic activity of an organization. *Financial accounting* relates to the process of supplying financial information to parties external to the reporting entity. *Managerial accounting* relates to the process of supplying financial information for internal management use. As a field of employment, accounting is usually divided into *public accounting,* where accounting and related services are offered to the general public for a fee; *private* (or *industrial*) *accounting,* where the accountant performs services for one business employer; and *governmental accounting,* where the accountant is employed by and renders services for a governmental agency.

Accounting equation–basically, Assets = Equities; in slightly expanded form for a corporation, Assets = Liabilities + Stockholders' Equity.

Accounts payable–amounts owed to creditors for items or services purchased from them.

Accounts receivable–amounts owed to a concern by its customers.

Accrual basis–as contrasted to cash basis accounting, a manner of accounting whereby the effects of transactions and other economic activities are recorded in the accounting system as they occur rather than as they involve cash receipts or payments.

American Institute of Certified Public Accountants–a professional organization of certified public accountants, most of whom are in public accounting practice.

Annual report–a pamphlet or document of varying length containing financial and other information about a company to its stockholders and distributed annually to them.

Assets–roughly equatable to things of value or economic resources; things possessing service potential or utility to their owner that can be expressed in money terms.

Auditing–that branch of the accounting profession that is concerned with checking, reviewing, testing, and verifying the accounting work of others, generally with the objective of expressing a formal opinion on the fairness of the resulting information.

Auditor's opinion or report–the formal written statement by a public accountant (usually a CPA) attesting to the fairness of the information contained in a set of financial statements.

Capital stock–the title given to an equity account showing the investment in a business corporation by its stockholders.

Certified public accountant–an accountant who has been awarded a certificate and granted the right to refer to himself as a certified public accountant as a result of having passed a special examination and having met other requirements regarding such things as experience and education. In some states, the CPA certificate is a license to practice as a CPA; in others, an additional license must be obtained.

Continuity (going concern)–the assumption by the accountant that unless specific evidence to the contrary exists, a business firm will continue to operate into the indefinite future.

Corporation–an intangible creation of the law having many of the rights of individuals; a form of organization adopted by many businesses; a business that is owned by many stockholders and frequently directed by hired managers.

Cost–the sacrifice made or the resources given up to acquire some desired thing; the basis of measurement (valuation) of most of the assets of a business.

Dividends–the means by which stockholders share in the earnings of a corporation.

Duality–the assumption by the accountant that every transaction has a dual or two-sided effect upon the parties engaging in it.

Earnings statement–a formal array or summary of the revenues and expenses of an organization for a specified period of time.

Entity–a unit that is deemed to have an existence separate and apart from its owners, creditors, employees, and other interested parties and for which an accounting is undertaken.

Equities–broadly speaking, all claims to or interests in assets.

Expenses–the sacrifice made, usually measured in terms of the cost of the assets surrendered or consumed, to generate revenues.

Liabilities–debts or obligations that usually possess a known or determinable amount, maturity date, and party to whom payment is to be made.

Money measurement–expression of a property of an object in terms of a number of units of a standard monetary medium, such as the dollar.

Net earnings–the amount by which the revenues of a period exceed the expenses of the same period.

Net loss–the amount by which the expenses of a period exceed the revenues of the same period.

Notes payable–a written promise to pay another party a definite sum of money at a certain or determinable date, usually with interest at a specified rate.

Periodicity–the assumption that the life of an entity can be divided into periods of time and that useful information can be provided as to the activities of the entity for those periods.

Retained earnings–accumulated net earnings less dividends distributed to stockholders.

Revenues–the flow of goods or services from an enterprise to its customers, usually measured by the flow of assets received.

Statement of financial position–a formal statement or array of the assets, liabilities, and owners' equity of an entity as of a specific date; often called a balance sheet.

Statement of retained earnings–a formal statement showing the items causing changes in retained earnings during a stated period of time.

Transaction–a recordable happening or event (usually an exchange) that affects the assets, liabilities, owners' equity, revenues, or expenses of an entity.

STUDENT REVIEW QUIZ

For each of the following questions, choose the one best answer unless specifically directed otherwise.

1. If a company has stockholders' equity of $8,900, this means that–
   a. A total of $8,900 of cash was received for capital stock issued.
   b. The business has total assets of $8,900.
   c. Net earnings for the year were $8,900.
   d. Revenues less expenses equals $8,900.
   e. Total business assets less total liabilities equal $8,900.
2. Company Z has assets of $35,000, no liabilities, and stockholders' equity of $35,000. It buys delivery equipment on credit for $4,000. What effect would this transaction have on these amounts of assets and stockholders' equity.
   a. Both assets and stockholders' equity would decrease by $4,000.
   b. Assets would stay the same and stockholders' equity would increase by $4,000.
   c. Both assets and liabilities would increase by $4,000.
   d. Stockholders' equity would decrease by $4,000 and liabilities would increase by $4,000.
   e. Both assets and stockholders' equity would increase by $4,000.
3. Revenue is best defined as–
   a. The flow of products or services provided to customers.
   b. Cash received from customers.
   c. The difference between the selling price of a product or service and the cost of providing such product or service.
   d. A decrease in stockholders' equity.
   e. The same as net earnings.
4. The Acme Furniture Company recorded on the last day of the month the $400 of advertising that appeared in the local paper during the month. This advertising was contracted for on an annual basis, with payment required for each month's advertising by the 10th of the following month. Which statement describes the effects of this activity?
   a. Both assets and liabilities increased by $400.
   b. Liabilities increased by $400 and stockholders' equity decreased by $400.
   c. Liabilities decreased and stockholders' equity increased by $400.
   d. Liabilities decreased and assets increased by $400.
   e. None of the above.
5. Company J collected $800 of its $1,000 of accounts receivable. How are the elements in the basic accounting equation affected?
   a. Total assets are decreased but liabilities and stockholders' equity remain the same.
   b. Cash increased $800 and stockholders' equity also increased $800 because revenue was received.
   c. There is no change in total assets, liabilities, and stockholders' equity.
   d. Accounts receivable and stockholders' equity are both decreased $800.
   e. There is no change in any of the items reported in the statement of financial position.
6. Which of the following statements is *incorrect*?
   a. The earnings statement summarizes revenue and expense transactions for a period of operation between two statements of financial position dates.
   b. The heading of an earnings statement should clearly indicate the period of operation which the statement covers.
   c. The earnings statement shows as a final item the net earnings or net loss for the period.
   d. An earnings statement shows how much of the net earnings or net loss was de-

rived from operations and how much from other sources.

e. The earnings statement shows the changes in assets and liabilities that occurred during the period of operations covered by the statement.

7. Given two statements of financial position of the A Company dated December 31, 1975, and December 31, 1976, the retained earnings on the statement dated December 31, 1976—
   a. Shows the amount of 1976 net earnings less dividends declared and paid.
   b. Includes the net earnings or net loss for 1976.
   c. Is equal to the net earnings for 1976.
   d. Shows the change in total assets for 1976.
   e. Does none of the above.
8. Which of the following appear in more than one of the following three statements: the statement of financial position, the earnings statement, and the statement of retained earnings?
   a. Cash.
   b. Net earnings.
   c. Notes payable.
   d. Retained earnings
   e. Only (*b*)and (*d*).
9. With which of the following is accounting *not* likely to be concerned?
   a. Long-range financial planning.
   b. Cost studies of managerial effectiveness.
   c. Executive recruitment.
   d. Design of management information systems.
   e. Income tax planning.
10. Which of the following is generally the sole province of the CPA?
    a. Preparation of income tax returns.
    b. Providing management advisory services.
    c. Attesting to the fairness of published financial information.
    d. Auditing.
    e. Preparation of budgets.
11. The concept of an operating cycle is useful in classifying items for financial reporting as—
    a. Expenses.
    b. Revenues.
    c. Property, plant, and equipment.
    d. Current assets.
    e. Stockholders' equity.
12. Assets are—
    a. Things of value owned.
    b. Economic resources owned.
    c. Desired because of the future benefits they are expected to yield.
    d. Generally recorded and reported at cost.
    e. All of the above.
13. As contrasted with financial accounting information, managerial accounting information is—
    a. Accumulated only if it is believed to be worth more than it costs.
    b. Forward-looking rather than historical in nature.
    c. Used internally rather than released to outsiders.
    d. Likely to be related to a part rather than the whole of an entity.
    e. All of the above.
14. Financial accounting information is likely to be used for all of the following types of decisions except—
    a. Deciding whether to add a new product line.
    b. Deciding whether dividends should be increased.
    c. Deciding whether a potential customer should be allowed to purchase goods on a credit basis.
    d. Appraising the ability of an entity to pay its debts when they become due.
    e. Determining whether the net earnings last year were satisfactory.

Now compare your answers with the correct answers and explanations given on page 203.

chapter 2

ACCUMULATING ACCOUNTING INFORMATION

LEARNING OBJECTIVES

This chapter deals with the basic steps undertaken to accumulate accounting information. The learning objectives include an understanding of:

1. The account as the basic means of classifying and storing information in the accounting system.
2. The technical accounting terms of debit and credit and how the effects of business transactions must first be expressed in these terms before they can be entered into the accounting system.
3. How and why debits increase assets and expenses and decrease liabilities, stockholders' equity, and revenues; and how and why credits increase liabilities, stockholders' equity, and revenues and decrease assets and expenses.
4. Two formats of accounts and how the balances are determined in each type.
5. The use of a trial balance as a partial means of testing the accuracy of the operation of the accounting system.

Frame 1[2]

THE MEANS OF CLASSIFYING AND SUMMARIZING BASIC ACCOUNTING DATA

In discussing the effects of business transactions in Chapter 1, changes were discussed in terms of increases or decreases. In this chapter, more conventional accounting methods of classifying and summarizing the results of these business transactions are used.

The account. The account is a basic part of the plan to gather data and is used to classify and summarize the data found in business transactions according to some common characteristic. An account will be established whenever the data to be recorded in it are believed to constitute useful information to some party having a valid interest in the activities of the business. Thus, an account will be established in which all transactions involving the receipt or payment of cash are recorded because the amount of cash owned by a business at any moment in time is apt to be useful information to some interested party.

An account may take a variety of forms as will be discussed later. But it should be constructed so as to readily accept money measurements representing increases or decreases in the item for which it was established. Also, the difference between the recorded increases and decreases, the balance of the account, should be readily determinable. For the present, it shall be assumed that there is one account established for every item appearing in the statement of financial position or in the earnings statement.

The way an account functions is illustrated first through use of a "T-account." The "T-account" is used for teaching purposes only and derives its name from the fact that it resembles a capital letter "T." The name of the account is centered over the vertical line, and one side of the account is for increases in the item named, the other for decreases. A T-account is shown below:

A SIMPLE T-ACCOUNT
Name of Account

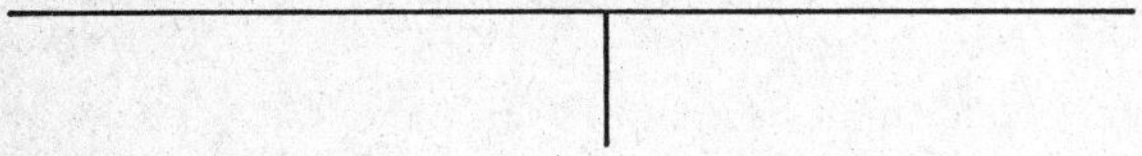

Equality of groups of accounts in double-entry accounting. In Chapter 1 it was indicated that at all times the assets of a business must be equal to the sum of its liabilities plus the interests of its owners. For a corporation, this equality is stated as Assets = Liabilities + Stockholders' Equity or, using symbols, A = L + SE. This equation provides two groups of accounts with equal totals. The total of all asset accounts always equals the total of all of the liabilities and stockholders' equity accounts.

Indicate whether each of the following statements is true or false by writing "T" or "F" in the space provided.

______ 1. The basic data entered into accounts are derived primarily from business transactions.

______ 2. The total of all liability accounts equals the total of all asset accounts less the total of all stockholders' equity accounts.

______ 3. Decreases and increases in an item may be shown on the same side of an account.

______ 4. There will generally be at least one account in the accounting system for every item shown in the financial statements.

Check your responses in Answer Frame 1^2 on page 28.

Frame 2^2

To secure the net amount—called the balance—of each account, all increases must be entered on one side and all decreases must be entered on the opposite side of the account. If every account was increased on the left side and decreased on the right side, the initial recording of a business transaction would be quite simple and all accounts would have positive arithmetic balances on the left side. But at the end of the period there would be no automatic check on the arithmetic accuracy of the accounts. The only possible check would consist of a complete duplication of the record keeping and a comparison of the results. Such a duplicate procedure may be acceptable for some phases of record keeping, but a more satisfactory overall procedure is one that contains an *automatic* arithmetic check.

To obtain such a check, accounts are divided into two groups, assets and equities, in keeping with the basic equation in accounting. By convention and by typical arrangement of items in the statement of financial position, increases in the asset group of accounts are entered on the left side of the account, decreases on the right side. In the equities group of accounts, since they usually appear on the right side of the statement of financial position, increases are recorded on the right side of the account and decreases on the left. The balance of any account is the *difference* between the total of the items on the left side of the account and the items entered on the right side. For the assets group of accounts, each account will normally have a left-side balance since positive amounts are entered on the left side and because assets cannot normally be

Answer frame 1²

1. True. In fact, some describe accounting as a system of accounting for business transactions.
2. True. If $A = L + SE$, then $L = A - SE$ by the laws of mathematics.
3. False. If both increases and decreases are entered on the same side of the account, there would be no simple and easy way to determine the balance of an account. Consider, for example, the task of determining the amount of cash on hand if both increases and decreases in cash are entered on the left side of the account. Only if the decreases were shown as negative items would the balance be readily available. But if decreases were entered negatively on the positive side of an account, there would be no need for the other side.
4. True. Although in published statements considerable adding together of similar items is commonplace, there will usually be at least one account for each item or group of items shown in the financial statements.

If you answered incorrectly, review Frame 1² before continuing in Frame 2² on page 27.

Frame 2² continued

reduced to a negative or minus quantity. For the equities group of accounts, each account will normally have a right-side balance since positive amounts are entered on the right side and equities cannot normally be reduced to minus or negative quantities. Then, if the dual effects of every transaction are recorded in the accounts properly, it follows that the total of the accounts with left-side balances will always equal the total of the accounts with right-side balances, that is, Assets = Equities. This constant equality of left-side balances with right-side balances constitutes a valuable automatic arithmetic check on the accuracy of the accounts. A periodic check of the total of the left-side balances against the total of the right-side balances is of great assistance in uncovering errors. This system of recording is called *double-entry accounting*, and it provides an effective framework for the classification, measurement, and control of financial data.

Indicate whether each of the following statements is true or false.

______ 1. Accounts normally having left-side balances often are reduced to a negative balance and, therefore, have a balance on the right side of the account.

______ 2. The double-entry system of accounting contains an automatic arithmetic check upon the amounts entered into it.

______ 3. The balance of any account is the total of the items on the left and the right sides of that account.

______ 4. It is purely conventional, rather than being required by some natural law, that increases in assets are entered on the left side of an account while increases in equities are entered on the right side.

Now check your responses in Answer Frame 2² on page 30.

Frame 3²

Asset and equity accounts and the statement of financial position. By convention, and for consistency between the accounts and the financial statements, asset accounts are shown on the left of the statement of financial position and increases in asset accounts are recorded on the left side of the asset accounts. Liability and stockholders' equity accounts are shown on the right side of the statement of financial position and are increased by entries on the right side of the equity accounts. The general framework of an accounting system can be kept in mind readily from these rules, plus knowledge of the fact that decreases are always recorded on the opposite side from increases.

A brief illustration may help to reinforce and clarify this recording technique. Assume that as transaction (A) the original owners invest $50,000 cash in the Otto Service Company, receiving shares of capital stock as evidence of their ownership. Further transactions of the Otto Service Company are (B) furniture and fixtures that cost $15,000 were purchased for $10,000 cash and a promise to pay the balance within 30 days; (C) a note was given by the company to the First National Bank when it borrowed $20,000; (D) services were rendered for customers who agreed to pay the company $25,000 later; (E) expenses for the month in the amount of $6,000 were paid in cash. These five transactions are recorded in the T-accounts given below, with the capital letters in the accounts tying the parts of each transaction together and keying them to the descriptions of the transactions given above.

Cash

(A) 50,000	(B) 10,000
(C) 20,000	(E) 6,000

Accounts Payable

	(B) 5,000

Capital Stock

	(A) 50,000

Accounts Receivable

(D) 25,000	

Notes Payable

	(C) 20,000

Retained Earnings

(E) 6,000	(D) 25,000

Furniture and Fixtures

(B) 15,000	

The analysis and recording procedure accorded each of the five transactions is:

(A) The asset, cash, increased $50,000—enter $50,000 on left side of Cash account; the owners' equity, capital stock, increased $50,000—enter $50,000 on right side of Capital Stock account.

(B) The asset, furniture and fixtures, increased $15,000—enter $15,000 on left side of the Furniture and Fixtures account; the asset, cash, decreased $10,000—enter $10,000 on right side of Cash account; the liability, accounts payable, increased $5,000—enter $5,000 on right side of Accounts Payable account.

(C) The asset, cash, increased $20,000—enter $20,000 on left side of Cash account; the liability, notes payable, increased $20,000 —enter $20,000 on right side of Notes Payable account.

(D) The asset, accounts receivable, increased by $25,000—enter $25,000 on left side of Accounts Receivable account; the owners' equity account, retained earnings, increased by $25,000—enter $25,000 on right side of Retained Earnings account.

(E) The owners' equity, retained earnings, decreased by $6,000—enter $6,000 on left side of Retained Earnings account; the asset, cash, decreased by $6,000—enter $6,000 on right side of Cash account.

Note in the above recording process how transactions are recorded in a manner such that the accounts representing items that commonly appear on the left side of the statement of financial position will have left-side balances and the accounts representing items that appear on the right side of the statement of financial position will have right-side balances. This means that increases in assets must be recorded on the left side of the account and increases in equities must be recorded on the right side of the account, with decreases in each type of account recorded as the opposite of an increase.

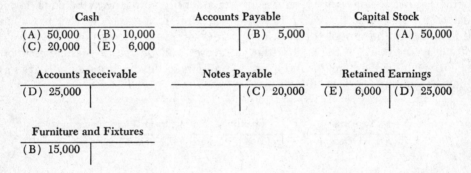

Answer frame 2^2

1. False. Just the reverse is true. Accounts having left-side balances are seldom reduced to negative balances nor do accounts having right-side balances often have negative balances. It is difficult to conceive of negative amounts of assets, liabilities, or owners' equity (although possible with the latter).
2. True. This is one of the most important reasons for engaging in double-entry accounting.
3. False. It is the difference between the two sides, not the total of both sides.
4. True. The system could be reversed and function equally as well.

Restudy Frame 2^2 if you missed any of the above before proceeding to Frame 3^2 on page 28.

Frame 3^2 continued

If this recording procedure is followed for each transaction, the left-side entry (entries) will be equal to the right-side entry (entries). From this it follows that the sum of the left-side balances will always be equal to the sum of the right-side balances. This is the fundamental basis of double-entry accounting, as derived from the basic assumption in accounting that the assets of an entity must always be equal to the equities or claims to assets. The way in which the two sides of every account are used to record increases and decreases in statement of financial position accounts can be summarized as follows:

Assets		=	**Liabilities**		+	**Stockholders' Equity**	
Increase	Decrease		Decrease	Increase		Decrease	Increase
+	−		−	+		−	+

Tracing the balances in the asset accounts given above for the Otto Service Company to its statement of financial position (Figure 2.1), we see that the three accounts on the left above are reported as assets (Cash, Accounts Receivable, and Furniture and Fixtures), that the two accounts in the middle are reported as liabilities (Accounts Payable and Notes Payable), and that the two accounts on the right above are reported as stockholders' equity (Capital Stock and Retained Earnings). Note how, in the Cash account and the Retained Earnings account, the entries in the accounts are "netted-out" to arrive at the balances reported in the statement of financial position.

FIGURE 2.1

OTTO SERVICE COMPANY
Statement of Financial Position
January 31, 1975

Assets			*Liabilities and Stockholders' Equity*		
Current Assets			Current Liabilities		
Cash	$54,000		Accounts payable	$ 5,000	
Accounts receivable	25,000	$79,000	Notes payable	20,000	
			Total Liabilities		$25,000
Property, Plant, and Equipment			Stockholders' Equity		
Furniture and fixtures		15,000	Capital stock	$50,000	
			Retained earnings	19,000	
			Total Stockholders' Equity		69,000
Total Assets		$94,000	Total Liabilities and Stockholders' Equity		$94,000

Indicate whether each of the following statements is true or false.

_______ 1. Assets are increased by entries on the left side of the account.

_______ 2. Liabilities are decreased by entries on the left side of the account.

_______ 3. The recording of a transaction involving the earning of revenue requires an entry on the right side of a stockholders' (owners') equity account.

_______ 4. The recording of increases and decreases is the same for liability and owners' equity accounts.

Now check your responses in Answer Frame 3^2 on page 32.

Frame 4^2

Revenue and expense accounts. All business transactions could be recorded by using only asset, liability, and stockholders' equity accounts. But since so many transactions affect retained earnings (because they involve expenses or revenues) recording them in a single Retained Earnings account would cause this account to contain a large number of unclassified items and consequently less useful information. The account for even a small business would cover many pages; and the analysis of the items in the account made necessary to prepare an earnings statement would be quite time-consuming and, perhaps, costly. For these reasons, the Retained Earnings account is usually subdivided into special temporary accounts in which are recorded all elements of expense and revenue.

Revenue, since it is a source of assets as are liabilities and stockholders' equity, is entered in accounts in the same manner as liabilities and stockholders' equity. That is, revenue accounts are increased by entries on the right side and decreased by entries on the left side. Because revenue is a source of assets from customers for services rendered and because it tends to increase stockholders' equity, revenue accounts may then be looked upon as periodic positive stockholders' equity accounts. A revenue account with an appropriate title is set up for each different type of revenue recorded during an accounting period. At the end of the period, the revenue accounts are totaled and their balances are transferred to the Retained Earnings account, often through a special summarizing account as discussed in Chapter 3. Typical revenue accounts reported in the earnings statement are those established for rent earned, interest earned, fees earned for services rendered, and sales of products.

Indicate whether each of the following statements is true or false.

_______ 1. The preparation of the earnings statement is made considerably easier through the use of separate accounts for each of the various types of expenses and revenues rather than entering such items directly in the Retained Earnings account.

_______ 2. The main revenue account for a firm engaged primarily in the sale of men's clothing would probably be called Sales.

_______ 3. Liabilities, stockholders' equity, and revenue are all sources of assets.

_______ 4. Revenue accounts, even though considered subdivisions of the statement of financial position account called Retained Earnings, are reported in the earnings statement.

Now check your answers in Answer Frame 4^2 on page 32.

Answer frame 3^2

1. True. By convention, increases in assets are recorded on the left side of the account.
2. True. Since liabilities are recorded in a manner just the opposite of assets, decreases must be recorded on the left side of the account.
3. True. As discussed in Chapter 1, the recording of the revenue generated results in an increase in stockholders' equity. If stockholders' equity is to be increased, an entry must be placed on the right side of the account.
4. True. Liabilities and owners' equity are both subdivisions of the broader classification, equities, and are therefore increased and decreased in the same way.

If you missed any of the above, study Frame 3^2 again before continuing in Frame 4^2 on page 31.

Answer frame 4^2

1. True. This is the basic reason for employing expense and revenue accounts.
2. True. The product of such a firm would indeed be its sales of merchandise to customers.
3. True. These are the major sources of asset inflows into a business.
4. True. Revenue is a flow concept and is reported in the earnings statement. But the residual effect of the revenue flow ends up in retained earnings, which is reported in the statement of financial position.

If you answered any of the above incorrectly, study Frame 4^2 again before continuing in Frame 5^2 below.

Frame 5^2

While revenue accounts are sources of assets and are increased by entries on the right side, expense accounts, being the opposite of revenue accounts, are uses of assets and are increased by entries on the left side. And expense results from the use or consumption of assets in the generation of revenue. Assets are defined as economic resources. As the resources (assets) are used or consumed in the operations of the business, they become expenses. Accounts must be kept for both assets and expenses. Simply stated, an expense account shows the cost of a used, consumed, or expired asset, that is, the measured benefit consumed. More precisely, an expense account contains the cost of that portion of an asset that has been used in generating the current period's revenue.

We have already seen that expenses tend to prevent stockholders' equity from increasing by the full amount of the revenue earned. We have also viewed expenses as items to be entered as decreases in retained earnings. But once again in order to prevent the left side of the Retained Earnings account from being cluttered with an unintelligible mass of data, expense accounts (as temporary accounts established for the left side of the Retained Earnings account) are used to bring order and classification to this mass of data. Since expenses tend to reduce retained earnings and are entered on the left side of the Retained Earnings account, it follows that accounts used to accumulate temporarily *reductions* in retained earnings should also be increased by entries on the left side. Increases and decreases in expense accounts thus follow the general rule for assets and normally have balances on the left side. At the end of the accounting period, the expense accounts are disposed of (after being reported in the earnings statement) by transfer to a special clearing account (discussed in Chapter 3) and then by transfer to the Retained Earnings account.

Indicate whether each of the following statements is true or false.

_______ 1. The cost of unexpired assets is reported as the measure of the assets in the statement of financial position.

_______ 2. The cost of the assets that expired during a period in the generation of the period's revenue is reported in the earnings statement.

_______ 3. Increases in expenses are entered on the left side of appropriate expense accounts.

_______ 4. Because assets differ sharply from expenses—assets being unexpired while expenses are expired benefits—it is only natural that the manner of increasing and decreasing an asset account should differ sharply from the manner of increasing and decreasing an expense account.

Turn to Answer Frame 5^2 on page 34 to check your response.

Frame 6^2

Since both the revenue and expense accounts of a business are ultimately transferred to the Retained Earnings account, this account will increase by a net excess of revenue over expense or decrease by a net excess of expense over revenue. A net excess of revenue is called net earnings; it increases retained earnings. A net excess of expense is called a net loss; it decreases retained earnings.

The number of expense accounts maintained by a business will vary according to its size and the nature of its activities. But even a relatively small business will have expense accounts for salaries, advertising, utilities, rent, insurance, taxes, pensions, contributions, and so on.

The accounts of the Otto Service Company, see Frame 3^2, are reproduced below as they would appear using expense and revenue accounts rather than retained earnings to record expense and revenue transactions.

Cash	
(A) 50,000	(B) 10,000
(C) 20,000	(E) 6,000

Accounts Payable	
	(B) 5,000

Retained Earnings	

Accounts Receivable	
(D) 25,000	

Notes Payable	
	(C) 20,000

Service Revenue	
	(D) 25,000

Furniture and Fixtures	
(B) 15,000	

Capital Stock	
	(A) 50,000

Expenses	
(E) 6,000	

The analyses for transactions (A), (B), and (C) do not change by the addition of expense and revenue accounts. Transaction (D) is now analyzed as follows: the asset, accounts receivable, increased by $25,000—enter $25,000 on the left side of the Accounts Receivable account; the revenue account, Service Revenue, increased by $25,000 (through rendition of services to customers)—enter $25,000 on the right side of the Service Revenue account. Transaction (E) is now analyzed as follows: The costs incurred in generating revenue for the period amounted to $6,000—enter $6,000 on the left side of the account entitled Expenses; the asset, cash, decreased by $6,000 of costs paid—enter $6,000 on the right side of the Cash account.

A summary of the effects that transactions will have upon the five different kinds of accounts is presented in the following equation:

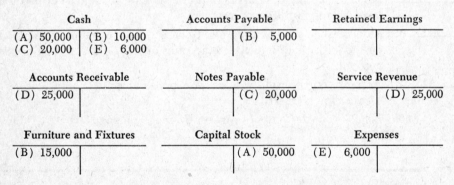

Answer frame 5²

1. True. This is the typical basis of valuation of assets.
2. True. Expenses are usually measured by the cost of the asset that expired and became an expense.
3. True. Expense accounts are increased by entries on the left side.
4. False. We wish to handle expense accounts in such a manner that they will have the same effect on the Retained Earnings account as if they had been entered directly in that account. Since expenses reduce retained earnings, and reductions in retained earnings are entered on the left side of the account, it follows that increases in expenses (reductions in retained earnings) should be entered on the left side of the account.

If you missed any of the above, restudy Frame 5² before proceeding to Frame 6² on page 33.

Frame 6² continued

Assets		=	Liabilities		+ Stockholders' Equity	
Increase +	Decrease −		Decrease −	Increase +	Decrease −	Increase +

Expenses		Revenue	
Inc. +	Dec. −	Dec. −	Inc. +

In the actual accounting for an entity, all business transactions are recorded in terms of their effects upon these five basic accounting elements.

Indicate whether each of the following statements is true or false.

______ 1. A net excess of revenues over expenses increases stockholders' equity.

______ 2. Expenses could be classified properly into accounts entitled rent, taxes, salaries, utilities, and repairs.

______ 3. A decrease in stockholders' equity is recorded by entering an amount on the left side of an expense account or the right side of a revenue account.

______ 4. An entry on the right side of an expense account would tend to increase owners' equity.

Now check your responses in Answer Frame 6² on page 36.

Frame 7²

The expanded accounting equation. With the addition of expense and revenue accounts, the basic accounting equation of Assets = Liabilities + Stockholders' Equity can be expanded or restated as follows:

A	=	L	+	SE	+	R	−	E
+ | −		− | +		− | +		− | +		+ | −

The stockholders' equity item included in this equation includes the Retained Earnings account *before* the current period's revenues and expenses have been transferred into it.

By simple algebraic transfer, the equation may be restated more usefully as:

A	+	E	=	L	+	SE	+	R
+ | −		+ | −		− | +		− | +		− | +

Since assets and expenses are both positive items on the left side of the equation, logic would suggest that increases in both types of accounts would be entered on the left side of the account. If so, then decreases would have to be entered on the right side. Since liabilities, stockholders' equity, and revenue are all positive items on the right of the equation, it is logical that increases in these accounts be entered on the right side of the account.

The logic of the equality in the above equation may be stated in yet another manner. A business can operate satisfactorily only by securing resources, initially in money form (cash or checks), which may be called funds or financial resources, and using them to good advantage. Business funds or financial resources are obtained from owners' investment, by borrowing from creditors, and from revenue transactions. These funds, and only these funds, are used (or applied) to acquire other forms of assets besides cash, to pay expenses, or to decrease liabilities or the stockholders' investment. Thus, the net funds received must always be equal to the net funds applied or used. And, in this sense, this is what the above equation shows.

Indicate whether each of the following statements is true or false.

_______ 1. $A - R = SE + L - E$.

_______ 2. An entry on the right side of a liability account would show an increase in funds or financial resources.

_______ 3. An entry on the left side of an equipment account would show a use or application of funds or financial resources.

_______ 4. The payment of a dividend would be an example of a use of funds.

Now check your responses in Answer Frame 7[2] on page 36.

Frame 8[2]

The account—an example. As already noted, the number of accounts and the titles thereto will vary according to the nature and size of the business for which they are established. But all accounts will fall into two major groups: (1) the statement of financial position accounts—asset, liability, and owners' (stockholders') equity accounts; and(2) the earnings statement accounts —expense and revenue accounts. The list of the names of the accounts in an accounting system is called the *chart of accounts*. The accounts in an accounting system are often also identified by account number. Collectively, the accounts in an accounting system are known as the *ledger;* that is, the ledger contains all of the accounts—whether there is one or more pages per account. Accounts are sometimes referred to as ledger accounts. The accounts are usually arranged in a ledger in the order of assets, liabilities, stockholders' equity, revenue, and expense accounts to facilitate easy finding of a particular account and statement preparation.

There are several rather standardized forms of the account, which is a means of summarizing money measurements of economic activity. The divided, or two-section, form of account is shown below. The two sides of the account are identical; one side for increases, the other for decreases. Each side contains space for the following information:

Date: The date that the transaction recorded took place.

Explanation: A brief descriptive explanation of the transaction.

Folio: The source from which information regarding the transaction was obtained, as will be explained later.

Amount: The money measurement, in dollars and cents, of the effect of the transaction.

Answer frame 6^2

1. True. If revenues exceed expenses, assets flowing into the firm from customers for services rendered or goods delivered exceed assets consumed in serving customers. The equity in this increase in assets rests in the stockholders and in retained earnings since the growth in assets was earned rather than resulting from stockholder capital investment.
2. True. These, as well as other accounts, might be established by a firm in order to classify its expenses.
3. False. One half of the statement is true—a decrease in stockholders' equity can be recorded by entering an entry on the left side of an expense account. But an entry on the right side of a revenue account will increase stockholders' equity, not decrease it.
4. True. Such an entry would decrease an expense, and since expenses are in effect negative stockholder equity accounts, the entry would increase stockholders' equity.

If you answered incorrectly, study Frame 6^2 again before continuing in Frame 7^2 on page 34.

Answer frame 7^2

1. True. The equation constitutes a true statement and follows logically from the rules of algebra. But, as we shall see, it does not have much use in this form.
2. True. This is so even though the funds received are used immediately to pay another liability. It is a receipt of funds from one source and the use of funds in another.
3. True. One way in which financial resources or funds can be used is to acquire productive assets to be used in operations.
4. True. One common use of the funds available to a business is to pay dividends to stockholders.

If you answered incorrectly, restudy Frame 7^2 and then continue in Frame 8^2 on page 35.

Frame 8^2 continued

LEDGER ACCOUNT
Name of Account

Date	Explanation	Folio	Amount	Date	Explanation	Folio	Amount

In an accounting system, the same form of account is usually established for each individual element of the five basic elements of accounting—assets, liabilities, owners' equity, expenses, and revenues. The type of analysis engaged in to determine which accounts are affected and in what direction by transactions has already been illustrated.

Debit and credit defined. In accounting, special terminology is used to refer to and to describe the two sides of an account rather than saying left side or right side. The terms used are *debit* and *credit.* Although these terms had a special meaning in their Latin origin, this has long disappeared. Today, debit means simply the left side of an account; a *debit entry* means an entry on the left side of an account; and *debit balance* means that the items on the left side, or debit side, of an account exceed those on the opposite side. *To debit* means to place an entry on the left side of an account.

Similarly, the word *credit* refers to the right side of *any* account. Thus, *credit side* means right side; a *credit entry* means an entry on the right side of an account; and *credit balance* means that the items on the right side, or credit side, of an account exceed those of the opposite side. *To credit* means to record an entry on the right side of an account.

An account is *in balance, or closed,* when the sum of the debits equals the sum of the credits in it. An account is *open* when it has a balance.

Fill in the blanks in the following statements.

1. The right side of an account is the ______________ (debit or credit) side.
2. A ______________ (debit or credit) balance is said to exist when the sum of the entries on the right side of an account exceed those of the left side.
3. When the sum of the debits equals the sum of the credits in an account, the account is said to be ______________.
4. Accounts may be identified by account ______________ as well as by account title.
5. The list of the accounts in an accounting system is called the ______________ ______________.
6. Collectively, all of the accounts in an accounting system are referred to as the ______________.

Now check your responses in Answer Frame 8[2] on page 38.

Frame 9[2]

Since assets and expenses are increased by entries on the debit (left) side, it follows that they will normally have debit balances. Similarly, since liabilities, owners' equity, and revenues are increased by entries on the credit (right) side, it follows that they will normally have credit balances.

All business transactions are analyzed and their effects stated in terms of debit and credit. Thus, a particular transaction may be analyzed as a debit to the asset, cash, and a credit to the liability, notes payable, to indicate its effect upon the five basic elements of accounting (only two of which are affected by this particular transaction). This means that knowledge of whether a given element is increased or decreased by a debit or a credit is quite imperative. For example, when an asset is debited, depending upon the transaction, there may be any of five credits:

1. Another asset account may be decreased, that is, credited.
2. A liability account may be increased, that is, credited.
3. A stockholders' equity account may be increased, that is, credited.
4. A revenue account may be increased, that is, credited.
5. An expense account may be decreased, that is, credited.

Note that when an asset account is debited, some other account must be credited, regardless of whether the credit in that account increases or decreases it. This double-entry form of recording keeps the accounts with debit balances always in agreement in total with the accounts with credit balances. The possible opposite entries for a debit or a credit to any type of account can be similarly analyzed.

The rules of debit and credit may be presented in an account form as follows:

Debits	Credits
1. Increase assets.	1. Decrease assets.
2. Decrease liabilities.	2. Increase liabilities.
3. Decreases stockholders' equity.	3. Increase stockholders' equity.
4. Decrease revenues.	4. Increase revenues.
5. Increase expenses.	5. Decrease expenses.

Answer frame 8^2

The words to be inserted in the blank spaces are:

1. credit.
2. credit.
3. in balance (or closed).
4. number.
5. chart of accounts.
6. ledger.

If you missed any of the above, restudy Frame 8^2 before proceeding to Frame 9^2 on page 37.

Frame 9^2 continued

The effect of entering a debit or a credit in an account can also be illustrated as follows for one account for each of the five basic elements of accounting:

An Asset Account

Debit for increases	Credit for decreases
+	−

A Liability Account

Debit for decreases	Credit for increases
−	+

An Expense Account

Debit for increases	Credit for decreases
+	−

A Stockholders' Equity Account

Debit for decreases	Credit for increases
−	+

A Revenue Account

Debit for decreases	Credit for increases
−	+

An alternative graphic presentation would be as follows:

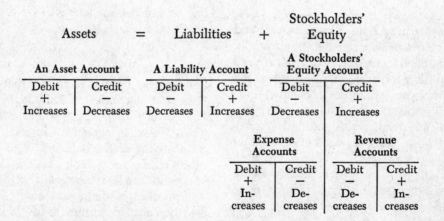

Assets = Liabilities + Stockholders' Equity

An Asset Account

Debit	Credit
+	−
Increases	Decreases

A Liability Account

Debit	Credit
−	+
Decreases	Increases

A Stockholders' Equity Account

Debit	Credit
−	+
Decreases	Increases

Expense Accounts

Debit	Credit
+	−
Increases	Decreases

Revenue Accounts

Debit	Credit
−	+
Decreases	Increases

In summary, the system of double-entry accounting, whether expressed as Assets = Equities, Assets = Liabilities + Stockholders' Equity, or Assets + Expenses = Liabilities + Stockholders' Equity + Revenues, provides a means of verifying the arithmetic accuracy of recording business transactions. Since transactions are analyzed and recorded in terms of debits and credits to accounts, the operation of the verification provided by double-entry accounting is expressed in the rule that every transaction is recorded by *equal* debits and credits. That is, in the analysis of every transaction, the debits must equal the credits.

Fill in the blanks in the spaces below.

1. Debits increase ______________ and ______________ and decrease ______________, ______________, and ______________.
2. Credits increase ______________, ______________ and ______________ and decrease ______________ and ______________.

Now check your responses in Answer Frame 9² on page 40.

Frame 10²

AN EXTENDED ILLUSTRATION

The following transactions are those of a company called the Hillard Delivery Service for the month of March, 1975. The letters in parentheses identifying the statements of fact—(*a*), (*b*), etc.—do not appear in actual practice. They are inserted here to aid tracing from the description of the transaction to the ledger which will be prepared from the entries made below.

The procedure to be followed is: Before recording an entry in the accounts—

1. Analyze the transaction to determine whether the accounts affected are asset, liability, stockholders' equity, revenue, or expense accounts.
2. Determine the names of the accounts affected by the transactions.
3. Determine the amounts of the individual increases or decreases.

Then apply the rules of double-entry by recording the debit and credit entries in the proper accounts.

Fill in the blank spaces with the required words.

a. *March 1, 1975:* The Hillard Delivery Service is organized and received $50,000 of cash in exchange for capital stock issued to its owners.
The asset account, Cash, is increased; Capital Stock is the stockholders' equity account increased.
Debit Cash, $50,000. Credit Capital Stock, $50,000.

b. *March 4, 1975:* The company borrows $10,000 from the bank on its note.
The asset account, Cash, is increased. The liability account, Notes Payable, is increased.
Debit Cash, $10,000. Credit Notes Payable, $10,000.

c. *March 6, 1975:* The company spent cash of $12,000 for delivery trucks and $1,900 for office equipment.
The asset account, Equipment, increased, and the asset account, Office Equipment, increased. The asset account, Cash, decreased.
Debit ______________, $12,000. Credit ______________, $12,000.
Debit ______________, $1,900. Credit ______________, $1,900.

d. *March 8, 1975:* Office equipment costing $600 is purchased on open account. The asset, Office Equipment, increased and the liability account, Accounts Payable, increased.
Debit ______________, $600. Credit ______________, $600.

e. *March 10, 1975:* Cash of $2,000 is received from customers for delivery services performed for them.

Answer frame 9²

The words to be inserted in the blank spaces are:

1. assets; expenses; liabilities; stockholders' equity; revenues.
2. liabilities; stockholders' equity; revenues; assets; expenses.

If you do not have the effects of entering debits and credits in the five basic types of accounts rather firmly in mind by now, it would be wise for you to take some time and study Frame 9² again very carefully before continuing on in Frame 10² on page 39.

Frame 10² continued

The ____________ account is increased. The ____________ account is increased.

Debit ____________, $2,000. Credit ____________, $2,000.

f. *March 11, 1975:* Delivery services priced at $800 are performed for customers who promise to pay later.

The asset account, ____________, is increased. The ____________ account is increased.

Debit ____________, $800. Credit ____________, $800.

g. *March 14, 1975:* Rent of $500 for the month of March is paid by the company.

The ____________ account is increased. The ____________ account is decreased.

Debit ____________, $500. Credit ____________, $500.

h. *March 15, 1975:* The company received services from its employees which were used in operating the business in the first half of March and for which it has agreed to pay $700 on the 19th.

The expense account, Wages, increased and the liability account, Wages Payable, increased.

Debit ____________, $700. Credit ____________, $700.

i. *March 16, 1975:* The company pays $4,000 on its note to the bank.

The liability account, ____________, is decreased. The asset account, ____________, is decreased.

Debit ____________, $4,000. Credit ____________, $4,000.

j. *March 17, 1975:* Of the $800 of accounts receivable due from customers, $600 is collected.

The asset account, ____________, is increased. The asset account, ____________, is decreased.

Debit ____________, $600. Credit ____________, $600.

k. *March 19, 1975:* The wages payable in (*h*) are paid, $700.

The liability account, ____________, is decreased. The asset account, ____________, is decreased.

Debit ____________, $700. Credit ____________, $700.

l. *March 21, 1975:* Cash received for the week's delivery services is $1,100.

The asset account, ____________, is increased. The revenue account, ____________, is increased.

Debit ____________, $1,100. Credit ____________, $1,100.

m. *March 24, 1975:* The gas and oil used during the month was purchased on account, $350.

The expense account, ______________________, increased. The liability account, ______________________, increased.

Debit ______________________, $350. Credit ______________________, $350.

n. *March 24, 1975:* Hillard purchased another delivery truck costing $2,100 by paying $700 cash and by giving a note for the $1,400 balance.

The asset account, ______________________, is increased $2,100. The asset account, ______________, is decreased $700. The liability account, ______________________, is increased by $1,400.

Debit ______________________, $2,100. Credit Cash, $700. Credit ______________________, $1,400.

o. *March 31, 1975:* Newspaper advertising for the month of March costing $200 is paid in cash.

The expense account, ______________________, is increased. The asset account, ______________________, is decreased.

Debit ______________________, $200. Credit ______________________, $200.

p. *March 31, 1975:* Wages for the last half of March are paid in cash, $700.

The expense account, ______________________, is increased. The asset account, ______________, is decreased.

Debit ______________________, $700. Credit ______________________, $700.

Now check your responses in Answer Frame 10[2] on page 42.

Frame 11[2]

Following is the ledger as it would look after the entries you have made are entered in the accounts. The small letters in the fourth column of each side of the account correspond to the letters before the descriptions of each transaction given in Frame 10[2]. For example, referring to Frame 10[2], you should see that the first transaction, lettered (*a*), called for a debit to Cash of $50,000 and a credit to Capital Stock of $50,000. In the ledger below, notice that the first debit to Cash contains the small letter (*a*) in the fourth column. Now using the answers you have given in Frame 10[2], trace each of the transaction entries to the appropriate account.

Cash — *Account No. 1*

1975					1975				
Mar.	1	Capital stock	*a*	50,000	Mar.	6	Delivery equipment	*c*–1	12,000
	4	Notes payable	*b*	10,000		6	Office equipment	*c*–2	1,900
	10	Delivery sales	*e*	2,000		14	Rent expense	*g*	500
	17	Accounts receivable	*j*	600		16	Notes payable	*i*	4,000
	21	Delivery sales	*l*	1,100		19	Wages payable	*k*	700
						28	Delivery equipment	*n*	700
						31	Advertising	*o*	200
						31	Wages expense	*p*	700

Accounts Receivable — *Account No. 2*

1975					1975				
Mar.	11	Delivery sales	*f*	800	Mar.	17	Cash	*j*	600

Answer frame 10^2

The correct answers for the blank spaces in the questions asked in Frame 10^2 are the italicized words below:

c. Debit *Delivery Equipment.* Credit *Cash.*
Debit *Office Equipment.* Credit *Cash.*
d. Debit *Office Equipment.* Credit *Accounts Payable.*
e. *Cash, Delivery Sales* (or Delivery Revenue).
Debit *Cash.* Credit *Delivery Sales.*
f. *Accounts Receivable; Delivery Sales.*
Debit *Accounts Receivable.* Credit *Delivery Sales.*
g. *Rent Expense; Cash.*
Debit *Rent Expense.* Credit *Cash.*
h. Debit *Wages Expense.* Credit *Wages Payable.*
i. *Notes Payable; Cash.*
Debit *Notes Payable.* Credit *Cash.*
j. *Cash; Accounts Receivable.*
Debit *Cash.* Credit *Accounts Receivable.*
k. *Wages Payable; Cash.*
Debit *Wages Payable.* Credit *Cash.*
l. *Cash; Delivery Sales.*
Debit *Cash.* Credit *Delivery Sales.*
m. *Gas and Oil Expense; Accounts Payable.*
Debit *Gas and Oil Expense.* Credit *Accounts Payable.*
n. *Delivery Equipment; Cash; Notes Payable.*
Debit *Delivery Equipment.* Credit *Notes Payable.*
o. *Advertising Expense; Cash.*
Debit *Advertising Expense.* Credit *Cash.*
p. *Wages Expense; Cash.*
Debit *Wages Expense.* Credit *Cash.*

If you missed any of the above, make sure that you understand why your answer was wrong and the above answers are correct, and then continue in Frame 11^2 on page 41.

Frame 11^2 continued

Delivery Equipment — *Account No. 3*

1975									
Mar.	6	Cash	*c*–1	12,000					
	28	Cash and notes payable	*n*	2,100					

Office Equipment — *Account No. 4*

1975									
Mar.	6	Cash	*c*–2	1,900					
	8	Accounts payable	*d*	600					

Accounts Payable — *Account No. 5*

					1975				
					Mar.	8	Office equipment	*d*	600
						24	Gas and oil expense	*m*	350

Notes Payable — *Account No. 6*

1975 Mar.	16	Cash	*i*	4,000	1975 Mar.	4	Cash	*b*	10,000
						28	Delivery equipment	*n*	1,400

Wages Payable — *Account No. 7*

1975 Mar.	19	Cash	*k*	700	1975 Mar.	15	Wages expense	*h*	700

Capital Stock — *Account No. 8*

					1975 Mar.	1	Cash	*a*	50,000

Indicate whether each of the following statements is true or false.

_____ 1. Proper analysis of a transaction must be undertaken before any attempt is made to record or enter its affects in the accounts.

_____ 2. The Notes Payable account in the above ledger has a debit balance of $4,000.

_____ 3. The debits and credits in each entry do not have to be equal, although the totals for all entries must be equal.

_____ 4. Each entry must have one debit and one credit.

Now check your responses in Answer Frame 11[2] on page 44.

Frame 12[2]

Computing the account balance. To compute the balance of an account, the debit side and the credit side is each separately totaled, in small pencil figures, and the smaller figure is subtracted from the larger. The resultant figure is either the debit or credit balance of the account.

The Cash account of the Hillard Delivery Service is reproduced below. Because the sum of the debits exceeds the sum of the credits, the balance is written on the debit side—in small penciled in figures.

Cash — *Account No. 1*

1975 Mar.	1	Capital stock	a	50,000	1975 Mar.	6	Delivery equipment	*c*–1	12,000
	4	Notes payable	*b*	10,000		6	Office equipment	*c*–2	1,900
	10	Delivery sales	e	2,000		14	Rent	*g*	500
	17	Accounts receivable	*j*	600		16	Notes payable	*i*	4,000
	21	Delivery sales	*l*	1,100		19	Wages payable	*k*	700
				63,700		28	Delivery equipment	*n*	700
		63,700				31	Advertising	*o*	200
		20,700				31	Wages expense	*p*	700
		43,000							*20,700*

Below is a different form of ledger account in which a continuous or perpetual account balance is maintained. This is the form of ledger account most commonly used in machine-based accounting systems. It eliminates the necessity of periodically adding the debit and credit entries and determining the balance. This format is used throughout this text, beginning in Chapter 3. The illustration is also the Cash account of the Hillard Delivery Service.

Answer frame 11²

1. True. Without proper analysis it is highly unlikely that the accounts will contain information that reflects the activities, resources, and obligations of an entity.
2. False. There is a $4,000 entry on the debit side of the account, but the balance of the account is $7,400, credit, as will be explained further below.
3. False. The debits and credits in each entry must be equal, as well as in total for all entries.
4. False. An entry can have a number of debits or a number of credits (more than one) or both. It must have a minimum of one of each.

Restudy Frame 11² if you answered incorrectly and then continue in Frame 12² on page 43.

Frame 12² continued

Cash — Account No. 1

Date		Explanation	Folio	Debit	Credit	Balance
1975						
Mar.	1	Capital stock		50,000 00		50,000 00
	4	Notes payable		10,000 00		60,000 00
	6	Delivery equipment			12,000 00	48,000 00
	6	Office equipment			1,900 00	46,100 00
	10	Delivery sales		2,000 00		48,100 00
	14	Rent			500 00	47,600 00
	16	Notes payable			4,000 00	43,600 00
	17	Accounts receivable		600 00		44,200 00
	19	Wages payable			700 00	43,500 00
	21	Delivery sales		1,100 00		44,600 00
	28	Delivery equipment			700 00	43,900 00
	31	Advertising			200 00	43,700 00
	31	Wages expense			700 00	43,000 00

THE TRIAL BALANCE OF LEDGER ACCOUNTS

If transactions are correctly entered in the accounts, the ledger will balance. That is, there will be overall equality of debits and credits recorded. A trial balance is thus a means of testing the mathematical accuracy of the ledger at a specific date.

A trial balance is a list of the names and dollar balances of all of the ledger accounts. In preparing a trial balance, the name of each account is listed at the left of a sheet of paper, together with the number of the account. Debit *balances* are listed in one column; credit balances are listed in a column to the right of the debit balances. The illustration below shows the heading and arrangement of a trial balance. From the trial balance, the statement of financial position and the earnings statement may be prepared.

HILLARD DELIVERY SERVICE
Trial Balance, March 31, 1975

Account No.		Debits	Credits
1	Cash	$43,000	
2	Accounts receivable	200	
3	Delivery equipment	14,100	
4	Office equipment	2,500	
5	Accounts payable		$ 950
6	Notes payable		7,400
8	Capital stock		50,000
9	Delivery sales		3,900
10	Rent expense	500	
11	Gas and oil expense	350	
12	Advertising expense	200	
13	Wages expense	1,400	
		$62,250	$62,250

Indicate whether each of the following statements is true or false.

_______ 1. The trial balance contains exactly the same accounts as the statement of financial position.

_______ 2. The trial balance must always balance or there is an error.

_______ 3. Account balances must be determined before a trial balance can be prepared.

_______ 4. In a trial balance, the accounts are usually listed in the order in which they appear in the ledger.

Now check your responses in Answer Frame 12² on page 46.

Frame 13²

Date at which trial balance is taken. A trial balance may be taken daily, weekly, monthly, quarterly, or annually or at the end of any period of time that one is desired. Normally, a trial balance is prepared prior to the preparation of financial statements. But, if statements are not prepared monthly, it may be wise to prepare a monthly trial balance if for no other reason than to identify errors within relatively short periods of time.

If the accounting period is one year in length, and if a trial balance is taken each month, the trial balances subsequent to the first are cumulative in nature. The trial balance at the end of the first month contains account balances for assets, liabilities, stockholders' equity, revenues, and expenses based on transactions for one month only; the trial balance at the end of the second month contains account balances summarizing transactions in the five elements of accounting for two months; and so on.

Uses of the trial balance. The trial balance serves the following purposes:

1. It shows whether equality of debit and credit account balances has been maintained in the ledger.
2. It localizes errors within an identified time period and thus facilitates finding the errors enabling prompt correction.
3. It is a convenient listing of account balances to be used in financial statement preparation.

Indicate whether each of the following statements is true or false.

_______ 1. The trial balance is most useful in locating errors in the selection of proper account titles.

_______ 2. If the total of the accounts with debit balances does not equal the total of the accounts with credit balances, this means that there were net earnings or a net loss for the period covered.

_______ 3. The trial balance contains much useful information to external parties and is regularly published by companies and distributed to outsiders.

_______ 4. A trial balance can be taken covering any period of time less than a year in length.

Now check your responses in Answer Frame 13² on page 46.

SUMMARY

This chapter introduces the basic means by which business transactions are analyzed for their effects, and these effects are classified and summarized in a permanent record from which financial statements can be prepared.

The effects of business transactions upon the assets, liabilities, stockholders' equity, revenues, and expenses of an entity are entered into a system of accounts. The balance of any account is the difference between the items entered on the left side (the debit side) and the items entered on the right side (the credit side). Every time a transaction is recorded, the left (debit) side of one account is affected and the right (credit)

Answer frame 12²

1. False. The trial balance also contains earnings statement accounts.
2. True. If a trial balance doesn't balance, an error of some kind has been made. More will be said about this in Chapter 3.
3. True. Since a trial balance is a listing of ledger account *balances,* it follows that account balances must be determined first.
4. True. They are usually listed in this manner because they are arranged in the ledger in this order. When taken from the ledger in the order they appear, the chance of omitting an account is lessened.

If you answered incorrectly, restudy Frame 12² before proceeding to Frame 13² on page 45.

Answer frame 13²

1. False. A trial balance will not reveal whether an error was made in selecting an account title. A trial balance will still balance even though an amount of advertising expense, say, was debited to salaries expense.
2. False. A trial balance says nothing about profitability. And it reveals only that an error has been made when the total of the debit balances does not equal the total of the credit balances.
3. False. A trial balance, in a sense, contains raw data which must be recast into useful financial information. It is an internal working paper prepared by the accountant for his personal use, not for publication.
4. True. A person can sit down on any given day of the year and prepare a list of the accounts in a ledger and their balances. Trial balances usually do not cover a period of more than one year because (as we shall see in Chapter 3) the balances in the expense and revenue accounts are removed at the end of every annual accounting period.

If you answer incorrectly, restudy Frame 13² before proceeding to the Summary on page 45.

SUMMARY continued

side of another account is affected. As a result the total of the accounts with debit balances must equal the total of the accounts with credit balances. Thus, the debit side of any account is the left side; the credit side of any account is the right side. Asset and expense accounts are increased by debits and consequently usually have debit balances; liability, stockholders' equity, and revenue accounts are increased by credits and consequently normally have credit balances. This is reflected in the expanded accounting equation of Assets + Expenses = Liabilities + Stockholders' Equity + Revenues. Items on the left side of the equation can be looked upon as representing the way funds brought into the entity have been used, while items on the right side of the equation can be looked upon as the sources of the funds flowing into an entity.

The list of the names of the individual accounts that summarize the accounting information for a particular company is called a chart of accounts. The entire collection of ledger accounts in an accounting system is called the ledger.

A trial balance is a list at any given time of all of the accounts in the ledger with their debit or credit balances. The trial balance shows whether equality of debits and credits has been maintained in the ledger; it localizes errors within an identified period of time; and it provides a convenient listing of the account balances to be used in statement preparation.

Now study the terms in the Glossary and then go to the Student Review Quiz for a self-administered test of your comprehension of the material in the chapter.

GLOSSARY

Account–a means used to classify and summarize money measurements of business activity.

Chart of accounts–the complete listing of all of the accounts in a ledger; comparable to a table of contents.

Credit–the right side of any account; to place an entry on the right side of an account.

Credit balance–the amount by which the total of the credits to an account exceed the total of the debits to the account.

Debit–the left side of any account; to place an entry on the left side of an account.

Debit balance–the amount by which the total of the debits to an account exceed the total of the credits to the account.

Debit entry–an entry on the left side of an account; debits increase assets and expenses, and decrease liabilities, stockholders' equity, and revenues.

Credit entry–an entry on the right side of any account; credits increase liabilities, stockholders' equity, and revenues, and decrease assets and expenses.

Ledger–the complete collection of accounts in an accounting system.

Rule of double-entry–every transaction is recorded by an entry which has equal debits and credits.

Trial balance–a list of the debit balances and credit balances of all ledger accounts as of a given moment in time; account names and account numbers are usually shown on the left with the debit balances in one column and the credit balances in a second column on the right.

STUDENT REVIEW QUIZ

For each of the following questions select the one best answer.

1. The entering of debits into accounts has which of the following effects upon assets (A), liabilities (L), stockholders' equity (SE), revenues (R), and expenses (E)?
   a. Increases (A) and decreases (L), (SE), (R), and (E).
   b. Increases (A) and (E) and decreases (L), (SE), and (R).
   c. Increases (A) and (SE) and decreases (L), (R), and (E).
   d. Decreases (A) and (E) and increases (L), (SE), and (R).
   e. Decreases (A) and (R) and increases (E), (L), and (SE).
2. Expense accounts–
   a. Eventually decrease the balance in Retained Earnings.
   b. Usually have debit balances.
   c. Show the costs associated with producing revenue in an accounting period.
   d. Usually show the costs of expired assets.
   e. All of the above.
3. Steno Services, Inc. issued $10,000 of capital stock for cash. What entry should be made?
   a. Debit Cash, $10,000; credit Capital Stock, $10,000.
   b. Debit Cash, $10,000; credit Retained Earnings, $10,000.
   c. Debit Capital Stock, $10,000; credit Cash, $10,000.
   d. Debit Cash, $10,000; credit Stockholders' Equity, $10,000.
   e. Debit Assets, $10,000; credit Stockholders' Equity, $10,000.
4. Steno Services, Inc. performed services for customers during a month for which it billed its customers $1,400. What entry should be made?
   a. Debit Cash, $1,400; credit Service Revenue, $1,400.
   b. Debit Accounts Receivable, $1,400; credit Service Revenue, $1,400.
   c. Debit Notes Receivable, $1,400; credit Service Revenue, $14,000.
   d. Debit Service Revenue, $1,400; credit Accounts Receivable, $1,400.
   e. Debit Assets, $1,400; credit Revenue, $1,400.
5. Steno Services, Inc. received a bill for newspaper advertising for the past week of $25. The bill will be paid next week. What entry is required?
   a. Debit Advertising Expense, $25; credit Accounts Payable, $25.
   b. Debit Accounts Receivable, $25; credit Advertising Revenue, $25.

c. Debit Cash, $25; credit Advertising Revenue, $25.
d. Debit Accounts Payable, $25; credit Cash, $25.
e. Debit Advertising Expense, $25; credit Cash, $25.

6. Received $825 from customers for services rendered and billed to them several weeks ago ("on account" in business terminology). What entry is required?
   a. Debit Cash, $825; credit Accounts Payable, $825.
   b. Debit Assets, $825; credit Assets, $825.
   c. Debit Cash, $825; credit Accounts Receivable, $825.
   d. Debit Accounts Receivable, $825; credit Cash, $825.
   e. Debit Accounts Payable, $825; credit Cash, $825.

7. Steno Services, Inc. purchased an electric calculator for $400 and a new typist chair for $120, on account from Office Equipment Company. What entry is required?
   a. Debit Office Machines, $400; credit Accounts Payable, $400.
   b. Debit Office Machines, $520; credit Notes Payable, $520.
   c. Debit Office Machines, $400, and Office Furniture and Fixtures, $120; credit Cash, $520.
   d. Debit Office Machines, $400, and Office Furniture and Fixtures, $120; credit Accounts Payable, $520.
   e. Debit Assets, $520; credit Liabilities, $520.

8. Steno Services, Inc. performed a rush manuscript typing job for Stu Stowell and received immediate cash payment upon delivery of $18. What entry is required?
   a. Debit Assets, $18; credit Revenues, $18.
   b. Debit Cash, $18; credit Service Revenue, $18.
   c. Debit Cash, $18; credit Accounts Receivable, $18.
   d. Debit Accounts Receivable, $18; credit Service Revenue, $18.
   e. Debit Cash, $18; credit Office Supplies, $18.

9. Steno Services, Inc. paid the weekly salary of its one typist of $275. What entry is required?
   a. Debit Salary Expense, $275; credit Salaries Payable, $275.
   b. Debit Accounts Payable, $275; credit Cash, $275.
   c. Debit Salary Expense, $275; credit, Accounts Payable, $275.
   d. Debit Salaries Payable, $275; credit Cash, $275.
   e. Debit Salary Expense, $275; credit Cash, $275.

10. Which of the following statements regarding a trial balance is *incorrect?*
   a. A trial balance is a test of the equality of debits and credits in the ledger.
   b. A trial balance is a list of all of the open accounts in the ledger with their balances as of a given date.
   c. A trial balance proves that no error of any kind has been made in the accounting for the activities of a period.
   d. A trial balance helps to identify the period in which an error has been made.
   e. A trial balance provides a convenient list of the accounts that can be used in preparing the financial statements.

11. A ledger is defined as__
   a. A collection of transactions.
   b. A collection of all of the statement of financial position accounts.
   c. A collection of all of the earnings statement accounts.
   d. A listing of all of the accounts in a ledger and their balances.
   e. None of the above.

12. The published financial statements of an entity include all of the following except—
   a. The statement of financial position.
   b. The earnings statement.
   c. The statement of retained earnings.
   d. The trial balance.
   e. Both (*c*) and (*d*) are not published.

Now compare your answers with the correct answers and explanations given on page 204.

chapter 3

INTRODUCTION TO THE ACCOUNTING SYSTEM

LEARNING OBJECTIVES

Study of the material in this chapter is designed to enable the reader to—

1. Prepare journal entries to record the effects of business transactions and post the entries from the journal to the ledger.
2. Cross-index the journal page number and the account number in the posting process.
3. Prepare a trial balance from the ledger accounts.
4. Locate trial balance errors in an efficient manner.
5. Prepare a six-column work sheet.
6. Prepare closing journal entries to empty the expense and revenue accounts at the end of the accounting period.
7. Prepare a post-closing trial balance.
8. Learn the steps in the accounting cycle.

Frame 1[3]

JOURNAL ENTRIES AND POSTING

The general journal. Every business transaction affects at least two ledger accounts. Each ledger account shows the increases and decreases in the item for which the account is established. The effect on an entire business transaction, therefore, does not appear in any *one* account. For example, the Cash account contains only information with respect to increases and decreases in cash, as shown by debits and credits to the account. It does not necessarily show the source of the cash (the account credited) or the purpose for which cash was disbursed (the account debited), although it may do so in the explanation column. The Accounts Payable account contains only information with respect to the amounts owed and amounts paid to creditors—not the items purchased.

A complete statement of transactions analyzed in terms of debit and credit is needed. Hence journals have been developed. A *journal* is a chronological record of business transactions showing the changes to be recorded as a result of each transaction. Each transaction is initially recorded in a *journal;* for this reason, a *journal* is called a record or book of *original entry*. It is the place in which the first formal record of a business transaction is entered in terms of related debits and credits.

Each business transaction is entered in a journal in chronological order, analyzed in terms of its debit and credit elements, and completely segregated from every other transaction. Each entry states the names of the accounts to be debited and credited, the dollar amount of each debit and credit, and any necessary explanation of the transaction. A journal is thus a chronological history of a business.

This chapter deals with the simplest type of journal—the *general journal.* As shown in Figure 3.1, there are columns for—

1. The date.
2. The name of the account to be debited; the name of the account to be credited, shown on the following line and indented to the right.
3. The Ledger Folio (L.F.) column; this will be explained in the section, "cross-indexing."
4. The debit column, in which the money amount of the debit is placed on the same line as the name of the account debited.
5. The credit column, in which the money amount of the credit is placed on the same line as the name of the account credited.

A blank line should appear between transactions for purposes of easy identification of the complete journal entry for each transaction.

Journalizing is the act of entering a transaction in a journal. All transactions are entered in a journal before being entered in any other formal accounting record. Information for a journal entry originates from such source material as invoices, cash register tapes, timecards, and checks issued.

FIGURE 3.1

GENERAL JOURNAL *Page 1*

Date		*Accounts and Explanation*	*L.F.*	*Debit*	*Credit*
1975					
Jan.	1	Cash	100	5,000	
		Capital Stock ...	300		5,000
		Capital stock issued for cash.			
	5	Office Equipment	110	1,200	
		Accounts Payable	201		1,200
		Equipment purchased for the office on account.			

Indicate whether each of the following statements is true or false by writing "T" or "F" in the space provided.

______ 1. The account to be credited is the first account to be named in a journal entry.

______ 2. Each entry in the journal gives the names of the accounts debited and credited, their dollar amounts, and an explanation of the transaction.

______ 3. A journal is a chronological record of business transactions and is called a record of original entry.

______ 4. A transaction can only involve two accounts.

Now turn to Answer Frame 1[3] on page 52 to check your answers.

Frame 2[3]

Posting. After a transaction has been entered in a journal, it is transferred to the proper accounts in the ledger. The transfer of entries *from* the journal *to* the ledger is known as *posting.*

A debit in a journal is posted to the left side, as a debit, of the named account in the ledger. A credit in a journal is posted to the right side, as a credit, of the named account in the ledger. For example, a debit to Cash in the journal is posted to the debit side of the Cash account in the ledger; a credit to Revenue from Fees in the journal is posted to the credit side of the Revenue from Fees account in the ledger.

Postings to the ledger accounts may be made:

1. At the time the transaction is journalized; or
2. At the end of or during the day, week, or month; or
3. As each journal page is filled.

When postings are made, each transaction debit and credit may be posted in chronological order, or all the debits may be posted, followed by the posting of all the credits. Accounts with individual customers and creditors should receive their postings daily so that the account balances will show the amounts currently receivable or payable.

Is each of the following statements true or false?

_____ 1. Postings to the ledger may be made at almost any time before financial statements are prepared.

_____ 2. A credit in a journal is posted to the right side of the account named.

_____ 3. The act of entering a transaction in a journal is called posting.

_____ 4. All the debits may be posted before any of the credits are posted.

Now turn to Answer Frame 2^3 on page 52 to check your answers.

Frame 3^3

CROSS-INDEXING

The number of the ledger account *to* which the posting was made is placed in the Ledger Folio (L.F.) column of the journal. The number of the journal page *from* which the entry was posted is placed in the Folio column of the ledger account. Posting in the system described in this chapter is always *from the journal to the ledger account. Cross-indexing* is the placing of the account number in the journal and the placing of the journal page number in the account, as shown in Figure 3.2.

FIGURE 3.2

GENERAL JOURNAL — *Page 1*

Date		*Accounts and Explanation*	*L.F.*	*Debit*	*Credit*
1975					
May	1	Cash	100	10,000	
		Capital Stock	300		10,000
		Cash invested in the business.			
	2	Rent Expense	401	500	
		Cash	100		500
		Rent for May 1975.			
	3	Equipment	110	2,200	
		Accounts Payable	201		2,200
		Table and chairs, Apex Company.			

GENERAL LEDGER

Cash — *Account No. 100*

Date		*Explanation*	*Folio*	*Debit*	*Credit*	*Balance*
1975						
May	1		J 1	10,000		10,000
	2		J 1		500	9,500

Equipment — *Account No. 110*

Date		*Explanation*	*Folio*	*Debit*	*Credit*	*Balance*
1975						
May	3		J 1	2,200		2,200

Answer frame 1[3]

1. False. The first account named in a journal entry is the account to be debited. This practice is traditional in accounting.
2. True. This is exactly what each entry does.
3. True. It is a record of original entry and is in chronological order.
4. False. As will be illustrated later, there may be more than one debit or one credit or both in an entry. The only requirement is that the total of the debits equals the total of the credits for any journal entry.

If you missed any of the above, reread Frame 1[3] before beginning Frame 2[3] on page 50.

Answer frame 2[3]

1. True. Postings may be made when the transaction is journalized, when a journal page is filled, or at the end of the day, week, or month. While it may be more efficient to stay current in the posting effort, it *may* be done at any time before financial statements are prepared without interfering with the accuracy of the results.
2. True. Credits are posted to the right side of an account. Debits are posted to the left side. If you do not understand this, it may be worth your while to go back and rework Chapter 2. Apparently you have missed one of the major points of that chapter.
3. False. The act of entering a transaction in a journal is called journalizing–not posting.
4. True. It is possible to post in any sequence you wish so long as all items for a period are posted in that period.

If you missed any of the above, restudy Frame 2[3] before beginning Frame 3[3] on page 51.

Frame 3[3] continued

Figure 3.2 (continued)

Accounts Payable — *Account No. 201*

Date		Explanation	Folio	Debit	Credit	Balance
1975						
May	3	Apex Company	J 1		2,200	2,200

Capital Stock — *Account No. 300*

Date		Explanation	Folio	Debit	Credit	Balance
1975						
May	1		J 1		10,000	10,000

Rent Expense — *Account No. 401*

Date		Explanation	Folio	Debit	Credit	Balance
1975						
May	2		J 1	500		500

Cross-indexing aids the tracing of any recorded transaction, either from the journal to the ledger or from the ledger to the journal. Cross-reference numbers usually are not placed in the L.F. column of the journal *until the entry is posted;* thereafter, the cross-reference numbers indicate that the entry has been posted.

By tracing the entries in the journal to the entries in the ledger, the reader will understand the posting and cross-indexing process. The ledger accounts need not contain explanations of all the entries since they can be obtained from the journal. In spite of this, some accountants favor placing explanations in the ledger accounts. No harm results, and the practice may be helpful, particularly if the transaction is one of a nonroutine nature.

When a necessary explanation is placed in the journal, it should be complete enough to describe fully the transaction, informative enough to prove or disprove the entry's accuracy and validity, and, at the same time, be concise and pointed. If a journal is self-explanatory, the explanation may be omitted.

Indicate whether each of the following statements is true or false by writing "T" or "F" in the space provided.

_______ 1. Cross-indexing is the placing of the journal page number in the journal and the placing of the account number in the account.

_______ 2. Neither the ledger accounts nor the journal need contain specific explanations of all the entries.

_______ 3. As described in this chapter, posting is usually, although not always, from the journal to the ledger account.

_______ 4. The general ledger accounts in Figure 3.2 do not contain explanations.

Now turn to Answer Frame 3[3] on page 54 to check your answers.

Frame 4[3]

The advantages of using a journal are listed below.

1. It sets forth the transactions of each day.
2. It records the transactions in chronological order.
3. It shows the analysis of each transaction in terms of debit and credit.
4. It supplies an explanation of each transaction when an explanation is necessary.
5. It serves as a source for future reference to accounting transactions.
6. It removes lengthy explanations from the accounts.
7. It makes possible posting to the ledger at convenient times.
8. It assists in maintaining the ledger in balance.
9. It is an aid in the tracing of errors.
10. It promotes the division of labor.

Indicate whether each of the following is true or false concerning a journal.

_______ 1. It allows several persons to work with the accounting records at the same time.

_______ 2. It provides a place for lengthy explanations.

_______ 3. It is an aid in locating errors.

_______ 4. It lists transactions in the order of their importance.

Now check your answers by turning to Answer Frame 4[3] on page 54.

Frame 5[3]

The analysis of a business transaction often shows that more than two accounts are directly affected. In such cases the journal entry involves more than one debit or more than one credit or both. A journal entry with more than one debit or credit or both is a compound journal entry. An entry with one debit and one credit is a simple journal entry. Illustrations of compound journal entries follow:

1. R. D. Hillard purchases $8,000 of machinery from the Huxley Company, paying $2,000

Answer frame 3^3

1. False. Cross-indexing is the placing of the *account number* in the journal and the placing of the *journal page number* in the account.
2. True. Since explanations of the account entries can be obtained from the journal, they need not be repeated in the ledger accounts. In the journal, if an entry is self-explanatory, the explanation may be omitted.
3. False. Posting as described in this chapter is *always* (rather than usually) from the journal to the ledger account. While this response may be somewhat on the "tricky" side, it emphasizes the need for great care in reading—especially in accounting.
4. True. But no harm would have resulted from including explanations, especially for nonroutine type entries.

If you missed any of the above, reread Frame 3^3 before starting Frame 4^3 on page 53.

Answer frame 4^3

1. True. Because it promotes the division of labor, it allows several persons to work with the records at the same time.
2. True. It does provide a place for lengthy explanations. In this way it removes them from the accounts.
3. True. It *is* an aid in locating errors.
4. False. It records the transactions in chronological order, which means in the order in which they occur through time.

If you missed any of the above, restudy Frame 4^3 before starting Frame 5^3 on page 53.

Frame 5^3 continued

cash with the balance due on open account. The journal entry for Hillard is as follows:

Machinery	8,000	
Cash		2,000
Accounts Payable, Huxley Company		6,000
Machinery purchased from Huxley Company, Invoice No. 42.		

2. James Thomas owes $5,000 on a note payable. He pays the note, together with interest of $150. The journal entry on Thomas' book would be:

Notes Payable	5,000	
Interest Expense	150	
Cash		5,150
Paid note and interest.		

Three men, A, B, and C, form a corporation. A invests $20,000 in cash, B invests a building worth $30,000 and $5,000 in cash, and C invests machinery worth $16,000. In return, the corporation issues capital stock to A, B, and C. Provide the journal entry to record these investments of assets in the corporation.

______________________ .... ____
______________________ .... ____
______________________ .... ____
______________________ .... ____

To record the investment of assets in the corporation. A invested $20,000 cash, B invested $5,000 cash and a building worth $30,000, and C invested machinery worth $16,000.

Now turn to Answer Frame 5^3 on page 56 to check your response.

Frame 6[3]

ILLUSTRATIVE GENERAL JOURNAL AND LEDGER

The general journal and general ledger shown in this section for the Gokey Company illustrate journalizing, posting, cross-indexing, and the taking of a trial balance. Assume that the statement of financial position of the company at December 31, 1975, is as shown below:

GOKEY COMPANY
Statement of Financial Position
December 31, 1975

Assets			*Liabilities and Stockholders' Equity*		
Current Assets			Current Liabilities		
Cash		$10,000	Accounts payable		$ 2,000
Accounts receivable		4,500	Stockholders' Equity		
Total Current Assets		$14,500	Capital stock	$15,000	
Property, Plant, and Equipment			Retained earnings	3,500	
Office furniture		6,000	Total Stockholders' Equity		18,500
Total Assets		$20,500	Total Liabilities and Stockholders' Equity		$20,500

The statement of financial position reflects ledger account balances as of the close of business on December 31, 1975. These balances are the same, of course, at the opening of business on January 1, 1976.

In a corporation the stockholders' equity is expressed in at least two accounts: Capital Stock, which represents the amount of capital stock issued to the owners; Retained Earnings, which represents the increase in stockholders' equity brought about by retaining past net earnings in the business. Note that all items in the statement of financial position are the initial balances in the illustrated ledger accounts.

During the month of January, 1976, the following transactions were completed by the Gokey Company:

Jan. 2 Paid office rent for the month of January, $400.
3 Purchased additional office furniture for cash, $1,500.
4 Received an invoice for $200 from Art Advertising Agency for services rendered in planning January's advertising.
4 Collected $3,000 of the accounts receivable.
6 Paid the accounts payable of $2,000 open at December 31, 1975.
6 Fees earned but not received for the week were $3,200.
8 Paid the advertising bill entered January 4.
9 Paid an invoice for $120 for office supplies received and used.
10 Collected $1,500, the balance of the accounts receivable open at December 31, 1975.
13 Fees earned but not received for the week were $1,100.
15 Paid administrative salaries for the first half of the month, $2,100.
16 Paid sundry general administrative expenses, $150.
17 Collected all fees earned for the week ended January 6.
20 Fees earned but not collected for the week were $1,400.
23 Received an invoice from the *New York News* for advertising for the first half of January, $300.
27 Fees earned but not collected were $1,600.
30 Paid invoice for $80 for additional office supplies received and used this month.
31 Paid administrative salaries for the last half of the month, $2,100.
31 Paid sundry general administrative expenses, $250.
31 Collected all fees earned for the week ended January 13.

Answer frame 5[3]

The correct answer is:

Cash	25,000	
Building	30,000	
Machinery	16,000	
Capital Stock		71,000

If you answered incorrectly, restudy Frame 5[3] before beginning Frame 6[3] on page 55.

Frame 6[3] continued

From the information above, insert the missing items in the transactions journalized below. It will help you to look at the account titles being used in the general ledger which appears on pages 59 and 60.

GENERAL JOURNAL — *Page 1*

Date		Account	Ref.	Debit	Credit
1976					
Jan.	2	Office Rent Expense	21	400	
		Cash	1		400
		Rent for January 1976.			
	3	Office Furniture	3	1,500	
		Cash	1		1,500
		Purchased additional furniture.			
	4	Advertising Expense	22	200	
		Accounts Payable	4		200
		Advertising on account.			
	4	Cash	1	3,000	
		Accounts Receivable	2		3,000
		Collection of accounts receivable.			
	6	____________	—	2,000	
		____________	—		2,000
		Paid the open balance of December 31, 1975.			
	6	____________	—	3,200	
		____________	—		3,200
		Fees for the week ended January 6.			
	8	____________	—	200	
		____________	—		200
		Invoice of January 4.			
	9	____________	—	120	
		____________	—		120
		Supplies purchased and used.			
	10	____________	—	1,500	
		____________	—		1,500
		Balances of December 31, 1975, collected.			
	13	____________	—	1,100	
		____________	—		1,100
		Fees for the week ended January 13.			
	15	____________	—	2,100	
		____________	—		2,100
		Salary expense for one-half month.			

Page 2

1976					
Jan.	16	______________	—	150	
		______________	—		150
		Paid sundry administrative expenses.			
	17	______________	—	3,200	
		______________	—		3,200
		Receivables collected.			
	20	______________	—	1,400	
		______________	—		1,400
		Fees for the week ended January 20.			
	23	______________	—	300	
		______________	—		300
		Advertising, on account.			
	27	______________	—	1,600	
		______________	—		1,600
		Fees for the week ended January 27.			
	30	______________	—	80	
		______________	—		80
		Supplies purchased and used.			
	31	______________	—	2,100	
		______________	—		2,100
		Salaries for the last half of January.			
	31	______________	—	250	
		______________	—		250
		Paid sundry administrative expenses.			
	31	______________	—	1,100	
		______________	—		1,100
		Receivables collected.			

Now check your responses with the correct ones in Answer Frame 6[3] on page 58.

Answer frame 6³

Following are responses for the general journal:

			Account No.
1976			
Jan.	6	*Accounts Payable*	*4*
		Cash	*1*
	6	*Accounts Receivable*	*2*
		Fees Earned	*11*
	8	*Accounts Payable*	*4*
		Cash	*1*
	9	*Office Supplies Expense*	*24*
		Cash	*1*
	10	*Cash*	*1*
		Accounts Receivable	*2*
	13	*Accounts Receivable*	*2*
		Fees Earned	*11*
	15	*Administrative Salaries*	*23*
		Cash	*1*
	16	*General Administrative Expense*	*25*
		Cash	*1*
	17	*Cash*	*1*
		Accounts Receivable	*2*
	20	*Accounts Receivable*	*2*
		Fees Earned	*11*
	23	*Advertising Expense*	*22*
		Accounts Payable	*4*
	27	*Accounts Receivable*	*2*
		Fees Earned	*11*
	30	*Office Supplies Expense*	*24*
		Cash	*1*
	31	*Administrative Salaries*	*23*
		Cash	*1*
	31	*General Administrative Expense*	*25*
		Cash	*1*
	31	*Cash*	*1*
		Accounts Receivable	*2*

If you missed any of the above, review Frame 6³ before beginning Frame 7³ on page 59.

Frame 7[3]

Provide the missing items in the following ledger by referring to the general journal in Frame 6[3]:

GENERAL LEDGER

Cash — *Account No. 1*

Date		Explanation	Folio	Debit	Credit	Balance
1976						
Jan.	1	Balance				10,000
	2		J 1		400	9,600
	3		J 1		1,500	8,100
	4		J 1	3,000		11,100
	6		J 1		2,000	9,100
	8		J 1		200	8,900
	9		J 1		120	8,780
	10		J 1	1,500		10,280
	15		J 1		2,100	8,180
	16		J 1		150	8,030
	17		J 1	3,200		11,230
	30		J 2		80	11,150
	31		—		2,100	9,050
	31		J 2		250	8,800
	31		J 2	1,100		9,900

Accounts Receivable — *Account No. 2*

Date		Explanation	Folio	Debit	Credit	Balance
1976						
Jan.	1	Balance				4,500
	4		J 1		3,000	1,500
	6		J 1	3,200		4,700
	10		J 1		1,500	3,200
	13		J 1	1,100		4,300
	17		J 1		3,200	1,100
	20		J 2	1,400		2,500
	27		J 2	1,600		4,100
	31		J 2		1,100	3,000

Office Furniture — *Account No. 3*

Date		Explanation	Folio	Debit	Credit	Balance
1976						
Jan.	1	Balance				6,000
	—		J 1	1,500		7,500

Accounts Payable — *Account No. 4*

Date		Explanation	Folio	Debit	Credit	Balance
1976						
Jan.	1	Balance				2,000
	4		J 1		200	2,200
	6		J 1	2,000		200
	8		J 1	200		–0–
	23		J 2		300	300

Capital Stock — *Account No. 5*

Date		Explanation	Folio	Debit	Credit	Balance
1976						
Jan.	1	Balance				15,000

GENERAL LEDGER (continued)

Retained Earnings — *Account No. 6*

Date		Explanation	Folio	Debit	Credit	Balance
1976						
Jan.	1	Balance				3,500

Fees Earned — *Account No. 11*

Date		Explanation	Folio	Debit	Credit	Balance
1976						
Jan.	6		J 1		3,200	3,200
	13		J 1		1,100	4,300
	20		J 2		1,400	5,700
	27		J 2		———	———

Office Rent Expense — *Account No. 21*

Date		Explanation	Folio	Debit	Credit	Balance
1976						
Jan.	2		J 1	400		400

Advertising Expense — *Account No. 22*

Date		Explanation	Folio	Debit	Credit	Balance
1976						
Jan.	4		J 1	200		200
	23		J 2	300		500

Administrative Salaries — *Account No. 23*

Date		Explanation	Folio	Debit	Credit	Balance
1976						
Jan.	15		J 1	2,100		2,100
	31		J 2	2,100		4,200

Office Supplies Expense — *Account No. 24*

Date		Explanation	Folio	Debit	Credit	Balance
1976						
Jan.	9		J 1	120		120
	30		J 2	80		200

General Administrative Expense — *Account No. 25*

Date		Explanation	Folio	Debit	Credit	Balance
1976						
Jan.	16		J 1	150		150
	31		J 2	250		400

Now refer to Answer Frame 7[3] on page 62 to check your responses.

Frame 8[3]

Provide the missing items in the following trial balance by referring to the general ledger in Frame 7[3]:

GOKEY COMPANY
Trial Balance
January 31, 1976

Account No.	*Account Name*	*Debits*	*Credits*
1	Cash	$ 9,900	
2	Accounts receivable	———	
3	Office furniture	7,500	
4	____________		$____
5	Capital stock		15,000
6	Retained earnings		3,500
—	Fees earned		———
21	Office rent expense	400	
22	Advertising expense	500	
23	Administrative salaries	4,200	
24	Office supplies expense	200	
25	General administrative expense	400	
		$____	$26,100

Now refer to Answer Frame 8[3] on page 62 to check your responses.

Frame 9[3]

Summary of the procedures for preparing a trial balance. Following is a summary of the procedures to be used in the preparation of a trial balance.

Provide the appropriate missing words.

1. Be certain that all ____________ have been made correctly to the accounts and that the balance in each account has been correctly determined.
2. List the account ____________ and ____________ on a sheet of two-column paper. Follow the order in which the accounts appear in the ____________, as shown in the trial balance of the Gokey Company in Frame 8[3].
3. List the debit balances of the accounts on the left in the ____________ money column.
4. List the ____________ balances of the accounts on the right in the credit money column.
5. Add the columns to obtain the trial ____________.

Now turn to Answer Frame 9[3] on page 62 to check your answers.

Frame 10[3]

Trial balance errors. A trial balance may balance even though errors have been made. A balanced trial balance simply proves that total debits equal total credits. If the trial balance does not balance, an error exists. Errors may be classified as: (*a*) errors of omission and (*b*)

Answer frame 7^3

The correct responses for the general ledger are: The missing folio number in the Cash account on January 31, 1976 is J2. The missing date in the Office Furniture account is January 3, 1976. The missing credit in the Fees Earned account is $1,600, and the missing balance is $7,300.

Be sure you understand where the missing data came from before starting Frame 8^3 on page 61.

Answer frame 8^3

When completed, the trial balance would appear as follows (the italicized items were the requested answers):

GOKEY COMPANY
Trial Balance
January 31, 1976

Account No.	*Account Name*	*Debits*	*Credits*
1	Cash	$ 9,900	
2	Accounts receivable	*3,000*	
3	Office furniture	7,500	
4	*Accounts payable*		*$ 300*
5	Capital stock		15,000
6	Retained earnings		3,500
11	Fees earned		*7,300*
21	Office rent expense	400	
22	Advertising expense	500	
23	Administrative salaries	4,200	
24	Office supplies expense	200	
25	General administrative expense	400	
		$26,100	$26,100

Be sure you understand where the missing data come from before beginning Frame 9^3 on page 61.

Answer frame 9^3

The missing words are as follows:

1. postings.
2. numbers; names; ledger.
3. debit.
4. credit.
5. balance totals.

Be sure you understand the correct answer before going on to Frame 10^3 on page 61.

Frame 10^3 continued

errors of commission. Either or both types may exist when a trial balance is either in balance or out of balance.

If a transaction is not journalized and posted, the trial balance will be in balance and will not indicate this error of omission. If an Advertising Expense account debit is erroneously posted as a debit to the Rent Expense account, the trial balance will be in balance and will not indicate this error of commission.

Certain other errors of omission and commission that throw a trial balance out of balance are:

1. Errors in addition or subtraction.
2. Mistakes in posting debits as credits and credits as debits.
3. Transposition of numbers, for example, entering 17 as 71, or 724 as 742.
4. Transplacement of numbers—a slide—for example, entering $100 as $10 or $1,000; a slide occurs by moving the digits, or any one of them, to the right or left.
5. Omission of a debit or a credit.

Indicate whether each of the following statements is true or false.

______ 1. An example of an error of omission would be failing to journalize a transaction.

______ 2. A transposition error is entering $100 as $1,000.

______ 3. A trial balance may balance even though errors have been made.

______ 4. If the trial balance does not balance, you know an error has been made.

______ 5. An example of an error of omission would be posting a credit to the wrong account.

Now turn to Answer Frame 10[3] on page 64 to check your answers.

Frame 11[3]

Locating errors. If a trial balance does not balance, the errors may be in the journal, the ledger, the trial balance, or in any combination of the three. The following steps should be taken in an attempt to locate errors that cause the trial balance to be out of balance.

1. If there is an error of 1, 10, 100, etc., the mistake may be one of addition or of subtraction, or it may be the result of incorrectly copying a number in the journal, the ledger, or the trial balance.
2. If the difference between the debit and the credit totals of the trial balance is divisible by 2—
   a. A posting equal to one half of the difference may have been made to the wrong side of an account.
   b. The balance of an account equal to one half the difference may have been entered on the wrong side of the trial balance.
3. If the difference is divisible by 9, the error may be due to a transposition or to a slide of one place.
4. If the difference is divisible by 99, a slide of two places may have occurred.

If the error still cannot be located, the accountant must:

1. Re-add the trial balance.
2. Compare the trial balance figures with the account balances, and review to ascertain that the account balances are in the appropriate money columns.
3. Verify the balance of each ledger account.
4. Verify postings to the ledger.
5. Verify journal entries.
6. Review the transactions.

Answer frame 10³

1. True. Leaving something out is an error of omission.
2. False. Entering $100 as $1,000 is a *transplacement* of numbers or a *slide*. A transposition error is when two digits are interchanged. An example is writing 54 instead of 45.
3. True. There could still be errors of omission or commission.
4. True. Some errors caused the inequality of totals in the trial balance.
5. False. This is an example of an error of commission rather than omission. The accountant journalized and posted the transaction but used the wrong account when posting.

If you missed any of the above, restudy Frame 10³ before starting Frame 11³ on page 63.

Frame 11³ continued

Is each of the following true or false?

______ 1. If the difference between totals is divisible by 9 or 99, a "slide" may have taken place.

______ 2. A mistake in only one digit can mean an error in copying a number in the journal, ledger, or trial balance.

______ 3. If after dividing by 2, 9, and 99 the error still cannot be located, it is advisable to start at the beginning of the accounting work for the month and rework everything up through the trial balance.

______ 4. If the difference is divisible by 2, a posting equal to one half of the difference may have been made to the wrong side of an account.

______ 5. A transposition error may be present if the difference is divisible by 9.

Now turn to Answer Frame 11³ on page 66 to check your answers.

Frame 12³

THE CLOSING PROCESS

The work sheet. The work sheet may be used to classify the accounts in a trial balance in such a way that they can be conveniently reported in an earnings statement and a statement of financial position. The six-column work sheet shown below in Figure 3.3 is one of the simplest types of work sheets. Chapter 7 will give more detailed examples. The first two money columns are used for the trial balance, the next two are used for earnings statement items, and the last two are used for statement of financial position items.

All debits in the Trial Balance debit column are extended to either the debit Earnings Statement column *or* the debit Statement of Financial Position column, depending on whether the debits are expenses or assets. All credits in the Trial Balance credit column are carried into the credit Earnings Statement column if they are revenue items *or* into the credit Statement of Financial Position column if they are either liabilities or stockholders' equity items.

When there are net earnings for the period, the total of the credits carried to the Earnings Statement credit column exceeds the total of the debits carried to the Earnings Statement debit column by the amount of the net earnings. The excess is determined by comparing the subtotals of the columns. The net earnings, as computed, are entered into the debit Earnings Statement column to balance the Earnings Statement columns. They are also transferred to the credit Statement of Financial Position column, because stockholders' equity at the end of a period includes net earnings—and, of course, stockholders' equity is increased by a credit.

When there is a net loss for the period, the total debits exceed the total credits that are carried to the Earnings Statement columns. The excess is the net loss. The net loss is entered as a balancing figure in the credit Earnings Statement column. It is also transferred to the debit Statement of Financial Position column because stockholders' equity is reduced by a net loss—and, of course, stockholders' equity is reduced by a debit.

The data for Figure 3.3 are from Frames 7[3] and 8[3] of this chapter continuing the example involving the Gokey Company.

The financial statements prepared from the work sheet are shown on page 66. It may be noted that the retained earnings item of $5,100 in the statement of financial position at January 31, 1976, is the sum of the retained earnings of $3,500 at January 1, 1976, and the net earnings of $1,600 for January. These two items appear separately on the work sheet. They are added together and presented in the statement of financial position.

To this point, the sequence of accounting actions and the resulting financial statements may be summarized as follows:

Business documents are analyzed to determine the effect the transaction data will have on the accounts. From this analysis, entries describing what has happened are recorded in the journal—a process referred to as journalizing. The entries are then posted to the ledger accounts. At the end of the accounting period, a trial balance is prepared as the first step in preparing the work sheet. From the work sheet, financial statements are prepared, and (as discussed below) closing entries are journalized and posted.

The above may be summarized more briefly as follows: Business Documents→Journal Entries→Posted to Ledger Accounts→Trial Balance→Work Sheet→Financial Statements. (A separate trial balance is prepared only when the work sheet is not prepared.)

FIGURE 3.3

GOKEY COMPANY
Work Sheet for the Month Ended January 31, 1976

Account No.	*Account Name*	*Trial Balance*		*Earnings Statement*		*Statement of Financial Position*	
		Dr.	*Cr.*	*Dr.*	*Cr.*	*Dr.*	*Cr.*
1	Cash	9,900				9,900	
2	Accounts receivable	3,000				3,000	
3	Office furniture	7,500				7,500	
4	Accounts payable		300				300
5	Capital stock		15,000				15,000
6	Retained earnings		3,500				3,500
11	Fees earned		7,300		7,300		
21	Office rent expense	400		400			
22	Advertising expense	500		500			
23	Administrative salaries	4,200		4,200			
24	Office supplies expense	200		200			
25	General administrative expense	400		400			
		26,100	26,100	5,700	7,300	20,400	18,800
	Net earnings for January			1,600			1,600
				7,300	7,300	20,400	20,400

Answer frame 11[3]

1. True. This does not indicate that a slide of either one or two places may have occurred.
2. True. Possibly a number such as $100 was copied as $180.
3. False. You would *not* start at the *beginning* of the accounting work for the month and rework everything up through the end. If you did, you would probably be disgusted after spending 10 hours rechecking everything only to find that the error was a mistake in adding one of the columns of the trial balance. For this reason, it is advisable to start by summing the trial balance again and working *backwards* to locate the error.
4. True. A $50 debit may have been posted as a $50 credit, thus causing the credit total to be $100 greater than the debit total.
5. True. A figure of $118 may have been posted $181, thus causing a difference of $63.

If you missed any of the above, restudy Frame 11[3] before starting Frame 12[3] on page 64.

Frame 12[3] continued

Provide the missing response below by referring to the work sheet in Figure 3.3.

GOKEY COMPANY
Statement of Financial Position
January 31, 1976

Assets			*Liabilities and Stockholders' Equity*		
Current Assets			Current Liabilities		
Cash	$____		Accounts payable		$____
Accounts receivable	3,000		Stockholders' Equity		
Total Current Assets		$12,900	Capital stock	$15,000	
Property, Plant, and Equipment			__________	5,100	
Office furniture			Total Stockholders' Equity		20,100
Total Assets		$20,400	Total Liabilities and Stockholders' Equity		$20,400

GOKEY COMPANY
Earnings Statement
For the Month Ended January 31, 1976

Fees earned			$7,300
Deduct: Operating expenses			
Selling expenses			
Advertising		$____	
Administrative expenses			
Office rent	$400		
Administrative salaries	____		
__________	200		
General administrative expense	400		
Total Administrative Expenses		5,200	
Total Operating Expenses			5,700
Net Earnings, to Retained Earnings			$1,600

Now check your responses by referring to Answer Frame 12[3] on page 68.

Frame 13[3]

Closing entries. Expense and revenue account balances are used in an earnings statement to explain in detail the increase or decrease in stockholders' equity resulting from net earnings or a net loss incurred during a period of time. After the earnings statement is prepared, the expense and revenue accounts for the period —a month or a year—have served their purpose, and these accounts are brought to a zero balance in order to be ready to receive the entries for the next period.

The balance of each expense and revenue account should be transferred by journal entry to an account that will summarize the expenses and revenues for the period. The account to which each expense and revenue account balance is transferred—*or closed*—at the end of the period is the Expense and Revenue Summary account.

For instance, to transfer or close the Fees Earned account the following entry would be made:

GENERAL JOURNAL

Date		Accounts and Explanation	L.F.	Debit	Credit
1976					
Jan.	31	Fees Earned	11	7,300	
		Expense and Revenue Summary	30		7,300
		To close the revenue account.			

The Fees Earned account has a $7,300 credit balance before this entry is posted. After the above entry is posted, the Fees Earned account would have a zero balance (meaning it is closed) and the Expense and Revenue Summary account has a credit balance of $7,300. By making the above entry, the $7,300 has been "transferred" from the Fees Earned account to the Expense and Revenue Summary account.

As shown above, to close revenue accounts (bring them to a zero balance) it is necessary to debit them and to credit the Expense and Revenue Summary. The procedure is just the opposite for expense accounts. To close expense accounts, the Expense and Revenue Summary account is debited and the expense accounts are credited.

The Expense and Revenue Summary account is a *clearing* account. Revenue account balances for the period will appear as credits, and expense account balances for the period will appear as debits in the Expense and Revenue Summary account. The balance of the Expense and Revenue Summary account will show the net earnings or loss for the period, and that balance is immediately closed to the Retained Earnings account. In this manner the accounts will be *closed* for the period.

The Expense and Revenue Summary account is not used for the entry of current transactions during the accounting period. It is used only at the end of the period when expenses and revenues are brought together in one place to show in the ledger the periodic net earnings or net loss. After closing, each expense and revenue account is ready to receive the transactions of the next accounting period.

To illustrate closing, the closing entries (including the one made above) for the expense and revenue accounts of the Gokey Company, at January 31, 1976, are presented below. In this method, accounts with credit balances are closed in one entry and accounts with debit balances are closed in another entry. A more cumbersome method is to close *each* expense account and *each* revenue account, individually, to the Expense and Revenue Summary account.

Answer frame 12[3]

The correct responses for the statement of financial position and earnings statement are (the italicized items are the answers sought):

GOKEY COMPANY
Statement of Financial Position
January 31, 1976

Assets			*Liabilities and Stockholders' Equity*		
Current Assets			Current Liabilities		
Cash	*$9,900*		Accounts payable		$ *300*
Accounts receivable	3,000		Stockholders' Equity		
Total Current Assets		$12,900	Capital stock	$15,000	
Plant, Property, and Equipment			*Retained earnings*	5,100	
Office furniture		*7,500*	Total Stockholders' Equity		20,100
Total Assets		$20,400	Total Liabilities and Stockholders' Equity		$20,400

GOKEY COMPANY
Earnings Statement
For the Month Ended January 31, 1976

Fees earned			$7,300
Deduct: Operating expenses			
Selling expenses			
Advertising		$ *500*	
Administrative expenses			
Office rent	$ 400		
Administrative salaries	*4,200*		
Office supplies expense	200		
General administrative expense	400		
Total Administrative Expenses		5,200	
Total Operating Expenses			5,700
Net Earnings, to Retained Earnings			$1,600

Be sure sure you understand where the missing data came from before beginning Frame 13[3] on page 67.

Frame 13[3] continued

Provide the missing responses by referring to the Earnings Statement columns of the work sheet in Figure 3.3 on page 65.

GENERAL JOURNAL — *Page 3*

Date		*Accounts and Explanation*	*L.F.*	*Debit*	*Credit*
1976					
Jan.	31	Fees Earned	11	7,300	
		Expense and Revenue Summary	30		7,300
		To close the revenue account.			
	31	Expense and Revenue Summary	30	5,700	
		Office Rent Expense	21		400
		Administrative Salaries	23		———
		Advertising Expense	—		500
		Office Supplies Expense	24		200
		____________________	25		———
		To close the expense accounts.			
	31	Expense and Revenue Summary	30	1,600	
		Retained Earnings	6		1,600
		Expense and Revenue Summary account closed to Retained Earnings.			

Now refer to Answer Frame 13[3] on page 70 to check your responses.

Frame 14[3]

After posting the entries journalized above, the Expense and Revenue Summary account will appear as follows:

Expense and Revenue Summary — *Account No. 30*

Date		*Explanation*	*Folio*	*Debit*	*Credit*	*Balance*
1976						
Jan.	31		J 3		7,300	7,300
	31		J 3	5,700		1,600
	31		J 3	1,600		–0–

The balance of the account before closing ($1,600) is calculated in the usual manner, and the net earnings are closed to the Retained Earnings account.

Data for the closing entries may be taken directly from the Earnings Statement columns of the work sheet.

POST-CLOSING TRIAL BALANCE

After the expense and revenue accounts have been closed, it is desirable to test the accuracy of the ledger with respect to the equality of debits and credits. A *post-closing* trial balance of the open accounts proves this equality. A post-closing trial balance of the accounts of the Gokey Company at January 31, 1976, is shown below. Sometimes, a post-closing trial balance is simply an adding machine tape of the debit account balances and the credit account balances taken from the ledger.

Answer frame 13[3]

The correct responses for the general journal are:

Expense and Revenue Summary	30	5,700	
Office Rent Expense	21		400
Administrative Salaries	23		*4,200*
Advertising Expense	22		500
Office Supplies Expense	24		200
General Administrative Expense	25		*400*
To close the expense accounts.			

Be sure you understand where the missing data came from before beginning Frame 14[3] on page 69.

Frame 14[3] continued

Complete the post-closing trial balance given below by referring to the ledger accounts in Frame 7[3]. Remember that all expense and revenue accounts would have zero balances after they have been closed. Also, remember that the balance in the Expense and Revenue Summary account would have been closed to Retained Earnings before the post-closing trial balance is prepared.

GOKEY COMPANY
Post-closing Trial Balance
January 31, 1976

	Debits	*Credits*
Cash	$ 9,900	
________	____	
________	____	
________		$ ____
________		____
________		
	$20,400	$20,400

Now refer to Answer Frame 14[3] on page 72 to check your responses.

Frame 15[3]

FORWARDING OF ACCOUNT BALANCE

When an account page is filled with entries, the account is carried forward to a new page by carrying the balance forward as shown below:

Cash — *Account No. 100 Page 1*

Date		*Explanation*	*Folio*	*Debit*	*Credit*	*Balance*
1975						
Mar.	2		J 1	50,000		50,000
	4		J 1		20,000	30,000
	5		J 1		500	29,500
	8		J 2	2,000		31,500
	9		J 2		7,500	24,000
	14		J 3		4,000	20,000

Cash — *Account No. 100 Page 2*

Date		*Explanation*	*Folio*	*Debit*	*Credit*	*Balance*
1975						
Mar.	14	Balance carried forward from page 1				20,000

A series of questions concerning the closing process is now given to test your understanding of it.

Indicate whether each of the following statements is true or false.

_______ 1. The account to which each expense and revenue account is closed (or transferred) at the end of the period is the Expense and Revenue Summary account.

_______ 2. After closing, all expense and revenue accounts have zero balances.

_______ 3. Closing entries for expenses and revenues cannot be made by looking only at the completed work sheet.

_______ 4. The Expense and Revenue Summary account is used for the entry of current transactions during the accounting period.

Now turn to Answer Frame 15[3] on page 72 to check your answers.

Frame 16[3]

To further test your understanding of the material covered, indicate whether each of the following statements is true or false.

_______ 1. The post-closing trial balance does not contain a listing of exactly the same accounts as the regular trial balance.

_______ 2. The totals of the post-closing trial balance columns will usually be larger than those of the trial balance.

_______ 3. Each of the two trial balances is dated for an accounting period rather than as of a particular date.

_______ 4. The amounts shown for each of the accounts will be the same in each of the two trial balances.

Now turn to Answer Frame 16[3] on page 72 to check your answers.

Answer frame 14^3

The correct responses for the post-closing trial balance are:

GOKEY COMPANY
Post-closing Trial Balance
January 31, 1976

	Debits	*Credits*
Cash	$ 9,900	
Accounts receivable	*3,000*	
Office furniture	*$ 7,500*	
Accounts payable		*$ 300*
Capital stock		*$15,000*
Retained earnings		*$ 5,100*
	$20,400	$20,400

Be sure you understand where the missing data came from before beginning Frame 15^3 on page 70.

Answer frame 15^3

1. True. If you missed this you may be well advised to go back and restudy Frame 13^3. An understanding of that material is essential to an understanding of the accounting process.
2. True. One of the main purposes of closing is to empty the expense and revenue accounts so as to prepare them to receive and hold amounts during the next accounting period.
3. False. Closing entries *can* be made by looking only at the completed work sheet. This is one of the main purposes for preparing the work sheet.
4. False. The Expense and Revenue Summary account is used only when closing the books. It is not used during the accounting period for current transactions.

If you missed any of the above, reread Frames 13^3 through 15^3 before beginning Frame 16^3 on page 71.

Answer frame 16^3

1. True. If you answered correctly you have realized that in the closing process all of the expense and revenue accounts have been reduced to zero balances and would, therefore, not be listed on the post-closing trial balance.
2. False. The totals of the trial balance will be larger because all of the expense and revenue accounts will be included. These accounts are closed before the post-closing trial balance is prepared. Only the net amount of earnings is closed to retained earnings.
3. False. The trial balances (both the regular and post-closing) are dated as of a particular date. For instance, they would be dated "January 31, 1976," rather than "For the Month of January, 1976."
4. False. The regular trial balance (it could be called pre-closing trial balance) shows the amounts *before* closing. Only if there were no revenues or expense would the statement be true. This is highly improbable.

If you missed any of the above, restudy Frames 13^3 through 15^3 before starting 17^3 on page 73.

Frame 17[3]

CLOSING PROCEDURE SUMMARIZED

The closing process described in this chapter is summarized below.

Provide the appropriate missing words.

1. As each expense and revenue account is closed to the ______________ ______________ account, it is left without a balance.
2. After closing, each expense and revenue account is in readiness to receive the transactions of the ______________ accounting period.
3. The Expense and Revenue Summary account's balancing figure shows the net ______________ or the net loss for the accounting period.
4. The Expense and Revenue Summary account is closed to the stockholders' equity account, ______________, as follows:
   a. If there are net earnings–

      Dr. ______________ xxx
         Cr. ______________ xxx

   b. If there is a net loss–

      Dr. Retained Earnings xxx
         Cr. Expense and Revenue Summary xxx

   c. At this point the Expense and Revenue Summary account has a ______________ balance.
5. In the process of closing, new information is not presented. The expense and revenue data in the ledger are merely rearranged and cleared through the ______________ account to the ______________ ______________ account.
6. Asset, liability, and stockholders' equity accounts are not ______________.

Now go to Answer Frame 17[3] on page 74 to check your responses.

Frame 18[3]

THE ACCOUNTING CYCLE SUMMARIZED

The entire accounting procedure of a business concern is known as the accounting cycle. As described in this chapter, the steps in the accounting cycle covered thus far are as given below.

Answer frame 17[3]

The statements are reproduced below with the missing words supplied.

1. As each expense and revenue account is closed to the *Expense and Revenue Summary* account, it is left without a balance.
2. After closing, each expense and revenue account is in readiness to receive the transactions of the *next* accounting period.
3. The Expense and Revenue Summary account's balancing figure shows the net *earnings* or the net loss for the accounting period.
4. The Expense and Revenue Summary account is closed to the stockholders' equity account, *Retained Earnings,* as follows:
   a. If there are net earnings—

Dr. *Expense and Revenue Summary*	xxx	
Cr. *Retained Earnings*		xxx

   b. If there is a net loss—

Dr. Retained Earnings	xxx	
Cr. Expense and Revenue Summary		xxx

   c. At this point the Expense and Revenue Summary account has a *zero* balance.
5. In the process of closing, new information is not presented. The expense and revenue data in the ledger are merely rearranged and cleared through the *Expense and Revenue Summary* account to the *Retained Earnings* account.
6. Asset, liability, and stockholders' equity accounts are not *closed.*

Be sure you understand why each of the above answers is correct before beginning Frame 18[3] on page 73.

Frame 18[3] continued

Provide the appropriate missing words.

1. Recognize business events that are called ______________________________.
2. ____________________ the business transactions on business documents or mechanisms (in terms of debits and credits).
3. ____________________ the transactions recorded on the documents or mechanisms.
4. ____________________ the transactions.
5. ____________________ the journal entries to the ledger accounts.
6. Take a ____________________ balance.
7. Complete the ____________________ sheet.
8. Prepare the ____________________ statement.
9. Prepare the ____________________ of financial position.
10. Journalize the ____________________ entries.
11. ____________________ the closing entries.
12. Take a ____________________ trial balance.

Now refer to Answer Frame 18[3] on page 76 to check your responses.

SUMMARY

A journal is a chronological record of business transactions analyzed in terms of debit and credit. It is a book of original entry since it is the place in which the first formal record of a transaction is made. Each entry made in the journal states the names of the accounts to be debited and credited, the dollar amount of each debit and credit, and any necessary explanation of the transaction.

After the entry has been entered in a journal it is transferred (or posted) to the proper accounts in the ledger. The ledger account numbers are referenced in the journal, and the journal page number is referenced beside each item entered into the ledger. This is called cross-indexing. The balances of the accounts are brought forward whenever a new ledger page for an account is started.

A trial balance is prepared periodically to prove the equality of debits and credits. Errors that prevent the trial balance from balancing include: errors in addition or subtraction, the posting of debits as credits and vice versa, transpositions, slides, and the failure to post a debit or credit. The procedure to follow in locating errors is described in Frame 11[3]. If after dividing the difference by 2, 9, and 99 the error still cannot be located, it is advisable to sum the amounts in the trial balance again and then work back through the accounting process to locate the error.

A work sheet may be used to classify the accounts in a trial balance in such a way that financial statements can be prepared more readily. In the six-column work sheet the first two colums are used for the trial balance, the next two for earnings statement items, and the last two for statement of financial position items.

After the balances in the expense and revenue accounts have been used to prepare the earnings statement, these accounts are brought to a zero balance. This is accomplished by preparing closing journal entries. All revenue accounts are debited with amounts necessary to bring them to a zero balance and the Expense and Revenue Summary account is credited for the total. All expense accounts are credited and the Expense and Revenue Summary account is debited for the total. The balance in the Expense and Revenue Summary account is then transferred to Retained Earnings. If there were net earnings for the period, the Expense and Revenue Summary account will have a credit balance before it is closed. The entry required to close the account would be a debit to the Expense and Revenue Summary account and a credit to Retained Earnings. If there were a net loss for the period, the debit and credit would be reversed.

After the closing entries have been journalized and posted, a post-closing trial balance of the accounts which are still open (assets, liabilities, and stockholders' equity accounts) may be prepared.

The accounting cycle is made up of the steps listed below.

1. Recognize business transactions.
2. Record the business transactions on business documents or mechanisms.
3. Analyze the transactions recorded on the documents or mechanisms.
4. Journalize the transactions.
5. Post the journal entries to the ledger accounts.
6. Take a trial balance.
7. Complete the work sheet.
8. Prepare the earnings statement.
9. Prepare the statement of financial position.
10. Journalize the closing entries.
11. Post the closing entries.
12. Take a post-closing trial balance.

Now continue by studying the terms in the Glossary below. Then work the Student Review Quiz for a self-administered test of your comprehension of the material in the chapter.

GLOSSARY

Closing–the act of transferring the balances in the expense and revenue accounts to the Expense and Revenue Summary account and then to the Retained Earnings account.

Compound journal entry–a journal entry with more than one debit and/or credit.

Cross-indexing–is the placing in the journal of the number of the ledger account to which an entry was posted and the placing in the ledger account

Answer frame 18[3]

The following set of statements describes the accounting cycle covered thus far and provides the missing words asked for:

1. Recognize business events that are called *transactions*.
2. *Record* the business transactions on business documents or mechanisms.
3. *Analyze* the transactions recorded on the documents or mechanisms.
4. *Journalize* the transactions.
5. *Post* the journal entries to the ledger accounts.
6. Take a *trial* balance.
7. Prepare a *work* sheet.
8. Prepare the *earnings* statement.
9. Prepare the *statement* of financial position.
10. Journalize the *closing* entries.
11. *Post* the closing entries.
12. Take a *post-closing* trial balance.

Be sure you understand each of the above answers before continuing with the Summary on page 75.

GLOSSARY continued

of the page number of the journal on which an entry can be found.

Expense and Revenue Summary account–a clearing account used to summarize all revenue and expense account balances at the end of an accounting period.

Journal–a chronological record of business transactions showing the changes to be recorded as a result of each transaction.

Journalizing–the act of entering a transaction in a journal.

Post-closing trial balance–a trial balance taken after the expense and revenue accounts have been closed.

Posting–the transfer of entries from the journal to the ledger.

Transplacement–(also known as a slide) occurs by moving the digits, or any one of them, to the right or left.

Transposition error–when two digits are interchanged.

Work sheet–an informal accounting statement used to summarize the trial balance and information needed to prepare the financial statements and the closing entries.

STUDENT REVIEW QUIZ

1. Which of the following statements is *incorrect?*
   a. The general journal is a record of transactions in chronological sequence.
   b. Each general journal entry includes the date of the transaction, the title of the account debited, the title of the account credited, the amount of the debit, and the amount of the credit.
   c. The general journal is the source of postings to the ledger accounts.
   d. When making entries in the general journal, the accountant need not concern himself with equality of debits and credits.
2. Cross-indexing–
   a. Provides a link between the journal and the ledger accounts.
   b. Facilitates the finding of errors.
   c. Reduces the likelihood of double posting or forgetting to post an item.
   d. Accomplishes all of the above.
   e. Accomplishes only two of the above.
3. Which of the following types of errors will *not* be detected by taking a trial balance?
   a. Posting an amount to Salary Expense instead of to Supplies Expense.
   b. An error in addition of the debit side of the Cash account.
   c. Neglecting to post the credit portion of a journal entry.

d. Posting a debit item of $62 as a credit of $62.
e. None of the above.

4. If the total of the debit column of a trial balance is $900 larger than the total of the credit column—
a. A credit of $900 may have been posted as a debit of $900.
b. The error may be due to a transposition.
c. An account having a credit balance of $900 may be listed in the trial balance as having a debit balance of $900.
d. All of the above could have occurred.
e. None of the first three could have occurred.

5. Which of the following accounts will appear in a post-closing trial balance?
a. Rent Expense, $300.
b. Insurance Expense, $50.
c. Service Revenue, $4,800.
d. None of the above.
e. All of the first three items.

6. Which of the following accounts is closed by an entry which includes a debit to Expense and Revenue Summary?
a. Service Revenue.
b. Accounts Receivable.
c. Rent Expense.
d. Accrued Salaries Payable.
e. Retained Earnings.

7. Given that net earnings for the period are $700, the last closing entry would be:
a. Debit Retained Earnings, $700; credit Expense and Revenue Summary, $700.
b. Debit Service Revenue, $700; credit Expense and Revenue Summary, $700.
c. Debit Expense and Revenue Summary, $700; credit Retained Earnings, $700.
d. Debit Expense and Revenue Summary, $700; credit Capital Stock, $700.
e. Debit Retained Earnings, $700; credit Capital Stock, $700.

8. The Expense and Revenue Summary account—
a. Generally has a credit balance after all the accounts that should be closed have been closed.
b. Summarizes revenue, expense, and net earnings (or loss) for the accounting period.
c. Summarizes changes in assets, liabilities, and net earnings (or loss) for the accounting period.
d. Is used to close the Retained Earnings account.
e. None of the above is true.

9. After the accounts have been closed—
a. All of the accounts have zero balances.
b. The asset, liability, and stockholders' equity accounts have zero balances.
c. The revenue, expense, Expense and Revenue Summary, and Retained Earnings accounts have zero balances.
d. The revenue, expense, and Expense and Revenue Summary accounts have zero balances.
e. None of the above is true.

10. "Posting" is the act of—
a. Recording entries in the journal.
b. Transferring the balances in the ledger to the trial balance.
c. Entering amounts in the accounts in the ledger as indicated in the journal.
d. Tracing amounts from the journal to the ledger in an attempt to find errors.
e. Transferring amounts from the ledger to the journal so that balances may be determined for each account.

11. Which of the following statements is *incorrect?*
a. The journal shows all transactions chronologically while the ledger shows only those transactions affecting a given account in chronological sequence.
b. Every account title mentioned in the journal over a period of time also appears in the ledger, but accounts appearing in the ledger may not appear in the journal over a period of time.
c. The totals of all the debits and all the credits in the journal will equal the totals of the debit and credit balances in the ledger accounts if all entries have been posted.
d. The ledger represents a grouping of the amounts for the various accounts mentioned in the journal.

12. Which of the following steps in the accounting cycle are listed in logical order?
   a. Post the journal entries to the ledger accounts, prepare a work sheet, and then take a trial balance.
   b. Journalize the closing entries, post the closing entries, and then take a post-closing trial balance.
   c. Prepare the earnings statement, prepare the statement of financial position, and then prepare a work sheet.
   d. Post the closing entries, take a post-closing trial balance, and then journalize the closing entries.

Now compare your answers with the correct answers and explanations given on page 205.

chapter 4

ADJUSTING ENTRIES

LEARNING OBJECTIVES

Study of the material in this chapter is designed to achieve the following learning objectives:

1. An understanding of why adjusting entries are necessary.
2. A knowledge of the four types of adjusting entries, which are:
   a. Incurrence of an expense which results from the gradual use of a previously recorded asset
   b. Incurrence of an expense which is equaled by the gradual increase in an unrecorded liability.
   c. Earning of revenue for which collection had been previously received and recorded in a liability account for unearned revenue.
   d. Earning of revenue which is equaled by the gradual increase in an unrecorded asset.
3. An ability to prepare adjusting entries for each of the categories given in (2).
4. An understanding of when adjusting entries are made.

Frame 1[4]

THE NEED FOR ADJUSTING ENTRIES

The net earnings or net loss of a business cannot be known exactly until the business is terminated. The managers and owners of a business, however, cannot wait indefinitely to find out the results of operations. They must know whether to continue the business or not. They must know whether the scale of operations should be expanded or contracted. They must also have financial statements for raising additional capital, for reporting to owners, creditors, and governmental authorities, and for other purposes.

Whenever financial statements are to be prepared, the accountant must determine that each account has its proper balance. The date at which financial statements are regularly prepared by a firm is called the "end of the accounting period." For most firms, this occurs at least once a year, although monthly statements are quite common. Regardless of when the "end of period" occurs, it is called the "cutoff."

The "cutoff" requires entires to adjust the balances of the accounts to their proper amounts. There are various reasons why accounts will not be at their proper balances at the "cutoff." For instance, suppose that whenever supplies are purchased, the accountant debits the Supplies Inventory account. At the end of the accounting period it is discovered that part of these supplies have been used. In order to adjust the accounts to their proper balances, it is necessary to debit an expense account, Supplies Expense, and credit the asset account, Supplies Inventory, for the used portion. If this is not done, expenses for the current period (in the earnings statement) will be understated and assets (in the statement of financial position) will be overstated.

In the example just given, suppose that whenever supplies are purchased the accountant debits the expense account, Supplies Expense, rather than the asset account, Supplies Inventory (either method of recording the purchase of supplies is correct). At the end of the accounting period it is discovered that some of the supplies were unused. It is then necessary to adjust the balances in the accounts by debiting the Supplies Inventory account and crediting the Supplies Expense account for the amount unused.

Entries necessary to adjust the accounts to their proper balances are explained in this chapter. The circumstances requiring adjusting entries are classified for convenience into two groups. One group consists of the entries required subsequent to the occurrence of transactions which are recorded on the books before the end of the period. These require entries to transfer data from asset and liability accounts to expense and revenue accounts. The second group consists of the entries to give initial recording to activity which has not been recorded on the books prior to the end of the period. These require entries to reflect the revenue and expense transactions on the books. Since each of the two groups affects both revenue and expense items, there are four types of entries for previously unrecorded economic activity. Entries of these types are often called *adjusting entries*. They are described as follows:

1. *Expense recorded as expiration of recorded asset*, or the incurrence of an expense which results from the *gradual use* of a previously recorded asset.
2. *The equal growth of an expense and a liability*, or the incurrence of an expense which is equaled by the gradual increase in an unrecorded liability.
3. *Earning of revenue collected for in advance*, the earning of revenue for which collection previously has been received and recorded in a liability account for unearned revenue.
4. *The equal growth of an asset and revenue*, or the earning of revenue which is equaled by the *gradual increase* in an unrecorded asset.

Indicate whether each of the following is true or false by writing "T" or "F" in the space provided.

______ 1. The entries made at the end of the accounting period for previously unrecorded economic activity are called adjusting entries.

______ 2. Adjusting entries are necessary in order to improve the accuracy of the financial statements.

______ 3. The net earnings or net loss of a business cannot be accurately known until the business is ended.

______ 4. The need for timely information on the financial affairs of a firm means that adjusting entries become necessary.

Now turn to Answer Frame 1[4] on page 82 to check your responses.

Frame 2[4]

EXPENSE RECORDED AS AN EXPIRATION OF A RECORDED ASSET

Unexpired insurance. Unexpired insurance is an example of a recorded asset that expires and becomes an expense with the passage of time. To illustrate, the advance payment of the premium on a one-year insurance policy that runs from August 1, 1975 to July 31, 1976, creates an asset called unexpired, or prepaid, insurance on August 1, 1975, because benefits—insurance protection—will be secured in the future. The journal entry to record the payment appears as follows:

1975				
Aug.	1	Unexpired Insurance	3,600	
		Cash		3,600
		To record prepayment of one year's premium.		

At December 31, part of the coverage provided by the insurance policy has been received; thus, an entry is made (assuming a calendar year accounting period) to record the expense applicable to the months of August, September, October, November, and December, 1975. Since 5 of the 12 months of coverage provided by the policy have passed, 5/12 of the premium is now an expense and thus 5/12 of the annual premium is charged to expense on December 31.

The journal entry and the accounts after posting appear as follows:

1975			
Dec. 31	Insurance Expense	1,500	
	Unexpired Insurance		1,500
	To record expense for five months, August 1 to December 31, 1975.		

Unexpired Insurance Account No. 104

Date		Explanation	Folio	Debit	Credit	Balance
1975						
Aug.	1	Cash paid	J 7*	3,600		3,600
Dec.	31	Adjustment	J 12		1,500	2,100

* Note: In this and all future illustrations, the folio references are assumed.

Insurance Expense Account No. 408

Date		Explanation	Folio	Debit	Credit	Balance
1975						
Dec.	31	Adjustment	J 12	1,500		1,500

The Insurance Expense account, just as any other expense account, is closed to the Expense and Revenue Summary account as part of the closing entries. The portion of such a closing entry applicable to the Insurance Expense account is shown to complete the illustration of the flow through the accounts.

1975			
Dec. 31	Expense and Revenue Summary .	1,500	
	Insurance Expense		1,500
	To close.		

Expense and Revenue Summary Account No. 500

Date		Explanation	Folio	Debit	Credit	Balance
1975						
Dec.	31	Insurance	J 12	1,500		1,500

After this sequence of entries and posting, the balance of $2,100 in the Unexpired Insurance account represents the cost of the insurance coverage which remains to be received during 1976. The balance in the Unexpired Insurance account appears in the statement of financial position as an asset. The $1,500 entry in the Insurance Expense account appears as an operating expense in the earnings statement for the period.

If the above policy had been dated June 1, 1975, and was for one year of coverage, the dollar amount of the entry at December 31, 1975, would have been __________________________________.

Now turn to Answer Frame 2[4] on page 82 to check your answer.

Frame 3[4]

Prepaid rent. Prepaid rent is another example of the incurrence of an expense which results from the gradual use or expiration of a previously recorded asset. The prepayment is debited to the Prepaid Rent account, an asset account, at the date it is paid. Because the benefits resulting from the expenditure are yet to be received, the expenditure creates an asset. Services from facilities being rented are received on a continuing basis, and thus the expense is incurred each successive day or month the item rented is used. The amount of expense that is incurred by the end of the accounting period is transferred to the Rent Expense account by an adjusting journal entry.

It is usually easy to compute the amount of rent allotted to each month because the rental contract generally indicates the length of time involved and the amount of rent per unit of time.

Answer frame 1[4]

1. True. These entries are called adjusting entries.
2. True. This is the primary purpose of making adjusting entries.
3. True. Until the business is terminated the exact net earnings or loss cannot be known.
4. True. The accounts must be brought to their correct balances before timely and accurate financial statements can be prepared.

If you missed any of the above, reread Frame 1[4] before beginning Frame 2[4] on page 80.

Answer frame 2[4]

The dollar amount of the entry would have been 7/12 × $3,600 = $2,100. This is the portion of the asset which has expired and has become an expense because the benefits have been received.

Be sure you understand this answer before you begin Frame 3[4] on page 81.

Frame 3[4] continued

Assume that on September 1, 1975, a year's rent of $600 was paid in advance for the rent year beginning on that date; the entry made at that time was:

1975			
Sept. 1	Prepaid Rent	600	
	Cash		600
	To record the payment of rent for one year.		

The entry required at December 31, 1975, to record the expiration of the asset as an expense would be which one of the following? Place a check beside the correct entry.

______ 1.	Rent Expense	200	
	Prepaid Rent		200
______ 2.	Prepaid Rent	400	
	Rent Expense		400
______ 3.	Rent Expense	400	
	Prepaid Rent		400
______ 4.	Rent Expense	200	
	Cash		200

Now turn to Answer Frame 3[4] on page 84 to check your answer.

Frame 4[4]

Depreciation of assets. The ownership and use of a building is also an example of the incurrence of an expense which results from the gradual use of a previously recorded asset. The overall period of time involved in the use of a building is less definite than in the case of an insurance policy or a rental agreement. In the case of an insurance policy or a rental agreement, the time period involved can be definitely stated in advance. In the case of a building owned, the life of the building must be *estimated* in advance. Nevertheless, the pattern of incurring an expense by the expiration of an asset is basically the same. The cost of the building (less salvage) is divided by the estimated months or years in the life of the building to find the amount of the building cost to be charged as an expense to each time period. This process is called *depreciation accounting,* and the cost allocated to each time period is called *depreciation expense.* The method illustrated is known as the straight-line method.

It is important to realize at this point that *depreciation expense* records the portion of the cost of certain assets that becomes expense with the passage of time. To illustrate, if a building costs $120,000, has an estimated salvage value of $20,000, and is expected to have a useful life of 20 years, $100,000 ÷ 20, or $5,000, is the amount of depreciation expense each year.

The three factors involved in the computation of depreciation are:

1. The cost of the asset.
2. The estimated useful life of the asset.
3. The estimated salvage value of the asset.

Expressed in equation form, the computation of straight-line depreciation is as follows:

$$\text{Annual Depreciation} = \frac{\text{Cost} - \text{Salvage}}{\text{Number of Years Estimated Life}}$$

The annual *rate* of depreciation is an expression of the percentage relationship of annual depreciation to the cost of the asset.

If the rate is known from prior years' experience and the cost of the asset is given, the annual depreciation equals the rate times the cost of the asset.

If a building has a cost of $100,000 with an estimated scrap value of $25,000 and is expected to have a useful life of 25 years, the amount of depreciation expense per year will be ____________________; and the rate of depreciation is __________ percent.

Now turn to Answer Frame 4[4] on page 84 to check your answer.

Frame 5[4]

Accounting for depreciation illustrated. The accounts involved in depreciation accounting and the effect of depreciation accounting on the statements are illustrated as follows:

Assume that a trial balance at December 31, 1975, includes an account with one delivery truck that cost $4,200. The truck was purchased on January 1, 1975. It is expected to have a useful life of five years; scrap value is estimated at $200. Therefore, the depreciation expense for one year equals ($4,200 minus $200) divided by 5, or $800. This is the amount of depreciation expense allocable to the production of revenue for the year 1975.

Depreciation for 1975 is recorded by the following entry:

1975			
Dec. 31	Depreciation Expense, Delivery Equipment	800	
	Allowance for Depreciation of Delivery Equipment		800
	To record the depreciation expense for the year.		

The ledger accounts will appear as follows:

Delivery Equipment Account No. 130

Date		Explanation	Folio	Debit	Credit	Balance
1975 Jan.	1	One truck	J 8	4,200		4,200

Allowance for Depreciation of Delivery Equipment Account No. 131

Date		Explanation	Folio	Debit	Credit	Balance
1975 Dec.	31	Adjustment	J 14		800	800

Depreciation Expense, Delivery Equipment Account No. 418

Date		Explanation	Folio	Debit	Credit	Balance
1975 Dec.	31	Adjustment	J 14	800		800

At December 31, 1975, after the adjustment, $3,200 of the cost of the truck remains to be converted into expense while the truck is used during future years.

Answer frame 3[4]

Answer No. 1 is correct. If you chose this response you are well along the way to an understanding of adjusting entries.

If you answered incorrectly, be sure you understand why this answer is correct before beginning Frame 4[4] on page 82.

Answer frame 4[4]

The correct answers are as follows:
The amount of depreciation is:

$$\frac{\$100,000 - \$25,000}{25} = \$3,000.$$

The depreciation rate is 3 percent $\left(\frac{\$3,000}{\$100,000}\right)$.

If you answered incorrectly, restudy Frame 4[4] before beginning Frame 5[4] on page 83.

Frame 5[4] continued

The allowance for depreciation account. The allowance for depreciation (also called accumulated depreciation) account is an example of a contra account and is merely a special subdivision of the credit side of the related plant asset account. The debit balance in the related asset account minus the credit balance in the allowance for depreciation contra account equals the cost of that portion of the asset that has not yet expired through usage and the passage of time.

It is desirable, largely because of the tentative nature of the amount of depreciation recorded, to maintain the depreciable assets in the accounts at original cost figures and to credit the periodic depreciation to an allowance for depreciation account. The allowance account increases in size at the end of each accounting period by the portion of the total cost of the asset charged to expense during the period, until it finally reaches an amount equal to the cost of the asset (less estimated scrap). When this stage is reached, the asset is fully depreciated. No more depreciation should be recorded for that asset.

Allowance for depreciation in the statement of financial position. In the statement of financial position at December 31, 1975, the asset accounts include the following:

Delivery equipment	$4,200	
Less: Allowance for depreciation of delivery equipment	800	$3,400

The portion of the cost of the asset not yet charged to expense at the end of one year is $3,400. If the estimated $200 scrap value is accurate, only $3,200 will be charged to expense during succeeding periods. At the end of the second year, the statement of financial position accounts will appear as follows:

Delivery Equipment Account No. 130

Date		Explanation	Folio	Debit	Credit	Balance
1975 Jan.	1	One truck	J 8	4,200		4,200

Allowance for Depreciation of Delivery Equipment Account No. 131

Date		Explanation	Folio	Debit	Credit	Balance
1975 Dec.	31	Adjustment	J 14		800	800
1976 Dec.	31	Adjustment	J 32		800	1,600

In the statement of financial position at December 31, 1976, the asset accounts will include the following:

Delivery equipment	$4,200	
Less: Allowance for depreciation of delivery equipment	1,600	$2,600

The portion of the cost of the asset not yet transferred to expense at the end of the two years is $2,600.

At the end of the fifth year, the entries in the allowance account will have accumulated to the amount of $4,000, the original cost less scrap value. At this point, the total cost of the asset less scrap value has been charged to expense in the previous accounting periods. Generally, assuming that the five-year life estimate was correct and the asset is sold for $200, it is necessary to remove the asset from the accounts by the following entry:

Cash	200	
Allowance for Depreciation of Delivery Equipment	4,000	
Delivery Equipment		4,200

It must be realized that an allowance (for depreciation) account is but a subdivision of the credit side of an asset account. The allowance account is used to record that portion of the cost of the asset that has been debited to Depreciation Expense. Instead of crediting the asset account directly, an allowance account is credited. The allowance account must always be considered along with its related asset account.

Assume that a delivery truck costing $3,800, and having an estimated scrap value of $200, is purchased on the first day of a firm's accounting year and is expected to have a useful life of six years. The entry to record depreciation expense at the end of the first year is which of the following? Place a check by the correct answer.

______ 1.	Depreciation Expense	600.00	
	Delivery Equipment		600.00
______ 2.	Depreciation Expense	633.33	
	Allowance for Depreciation of Delivery Equipment		633.33
______ 3.	Depreciation Expense	600.00	
	Allowance for Depreciation of Delivery Equipment		600.00
______ 4.	Delivery Equipment	600.00	
	Depreciation Expense		600.00

Now turn to Answer Frame 5[4] on page 86 to check your response.

Frame 6[4]

At the end of the sixth year, the accounts would have balances as shown in the partial statement of financial position below:

Delivery equipment	$3,800	
Less: Allowance for depreciation of delivery equipment	3,600	$200

The entry required, assuming the asset is now sold for its scrap value, would be:

______________ .... ____
______________ .... ____
______________ ....   ____

Now refer to Answer Frame 6[4] on page 86 to check your response.

Frame 7[4]

The depreciation expense accounts. Depreciation expense is an operating expense in the same sense that rent expense is an operating expense. Accordingly, it is closed to the Expense and Revenue Summary account when the accounts are closed at the end of an accounting

Answer frame 5^4

Answer No. 3 is correct. If this was your choice you have realized that a special "allowance" account is credited rather than the asset account itself. You have also correctly calculated the amount of depreciation expense. If you answered incorrectly, restudy Frame 5^4 before beginning Frame 6^4 on page 85.

Answer frame 6^4

The correct response is:

Cash	200	
Allowance for Depreciation of Delivery Equipment	3,600	
Delivery Equipment		3,800

If you answered incorrectly, restudy Frame 5^4 and 6^4 before beginning Frame 7^4 on page 85.

Frame 7^4 continued

period. The title of each depreciation expense account should identify the type of asset being used. This helps classify depreciation expense into the selling and administrative expense groups on the earnings statement.

Depreciation expense accounts to be shown as selling expenses include:

Depreciation Expense, Store Building.
Depreciation Expense, Delivery Equipment.

Depreciation expense accounts to be shown as administrative expenses include:

Depreciation Expense, Office Building.
Depreciation Expense, Office Equipment.

Indicate whether each of the following statements is true or false.

_____ 1. Depreciation expense accounts for an office building and office equipment are administrative expenses.

_____ 2. The balances in the allowance for depreciation accounts are closed to the Expense and Revenue Summary account at the end of the accounting period.

_____ 3. Depreciation expense accounts for a store building and delivery equipment are classified as selling expenses.

_____ 4. The type of asset being used should be identified in the title of each depreciation expense account.

Now turn to Answer Frame 7^4 on page 88 to check your answers.

Frame 8^4

Supplies used. Other items that follow the general pattern of being recorded first in asset accounts and then being recorded as expenses when they are consumed or expire include office supplies and uncollectible accounts receivable. In these cases the pattern is less clearly discernible, yet it is there. Office supplies are generally acquired in relatively large quantities and are stored until used. They may be recorded as assets when purchased. The expense is incurred when the supplies are used. When a small quantity is drawn from the storeroom for use, the cost of the amount used may be so small in relation to the total that it is inadvisable to make an entry at that time for such a small amount. But at the end of an accounting period the cost of the aggregate amount of supplies used during the period should be transferred from the Office Supplies Inventory asset account to the Office Supplies Used expense account.

To illustrate, assume that office supplies that cost $700 were purchased throughout the year 1975. The Office Supplies Inventory account was debited each time. At December 31, 1975, an inventory of the storeroom showed that $200 of supplies were on hand. The difference between $700 and $200, or $500, is the amount of the asset that has expired and must be charged to expense.

The adjusting entry is as follows:

Office Supplies Used	500	
Office Supplies Inventory		500
To record the cost of the office supplies used.		

The ledger accounts are as follows:

Office Supplies Inventory *Account No. 116*

Date		Explanation	Folio	Debit	Credit	Balance
1975						
Various dates		Acquired	Various	700		700
Dec.	31	Adjustment	J 14		500	200

Office Supplies Used *Account No. 427*

Date		Explanation	Folio	Debit	Credit	Balance
1975						
Dec.	31	Adjustment	J 14	500		500

The Office Supplies Used account will be closed to the Expense and Revenue Summary account at the end of the accounting period.

If the December 31, 1976, inventory showed that $120 more of the original $700 supplies were used, what would be the entry to record the expiration of the asset? (Furnish account titles and amounts.)

________________ .... ____

________________ .... ____

Now go to Answer Frame 8[4] on page 88 and check your response.

Frame 9[4]

The ledger accounts on December 31, 1976, before closing would appear as follows:

Office Supplies Inventory *Account No. 116*

Date		Explanation	Folio	Debit	Credit	Balance
1975						
Various dates		Acquired	Various	700		700
Dec.	31	Adjustment	J 14		500	200
1976						
Dec.	31	Adjustment	J 32		120	80

Office Supplies Used *Account No. 427*

Date		Explanation	Folio	Debit	Credit	Balance
1975						
Dec.	31	Adjustment	J 14	500		500
	31	To close	J 15		500	-0-
1976						
Dec.	31	Adjustment	J 32	120		120

Of course, if the Office Supplies Used account is debited when supplies are purchased and some of them remain unused at the end of the accounting period, it is necessary to make the following adjusting entry for the cost of the unused supplies:

Office Supplies Inventory	xx	
Office Supplies Used		xx

This entry reduces the expense to its proper amount and establishes the unused supplies as an asset at the statement of financial position date.

Bad debts expense. Accounts receivable result from sales on credit terms that permit the customers to pay some time after the sale is made. It is not unusual for some of the accounts receivable to prove to be uncollectible. Receivables that are collected result in the decrease of the

Answer frame 7⁴

1. True. They are administrative expenses.
2. False. It is not the *allowance* for depreciation (also called accumulated depreciation) accounts which are closed to the Expense and Revenue Summary. These accounts represent the credit side of the asset account and are therefore "open" accounts after the closing process. The depreciation expense accounts, on the other hand, *are* closed to the Expense and Revenue Summary.
3. True. They are classified as selling expenses.
4. True. This is helpful when preparing financial statements.

If you missed any of the above, restudy Frame 7[4] before starting Frame 8[4] on page 86.

Answer frame 8[4]

The correct response is:

Office Supplies Used	120	
Office Supplies Inventory		120

If you answered incorrectly, restudy Frame 8[4] before starting Frame 9[4] on page 87.

Frame 9[4] continued

asset, accounts receivable, and in the increase of the asset, cash. All expenses related to a sale should be debited to the period in which the sale is made in order to match revenues and expenses. Bad debts expense is incurred when the eventually uncollectible sale is made. The amount of receivables *estimated* to be uncollectible results in a decrease in the asset, accounts receivable, and in the increase of the expense called bad debts expense. It is important at this point to recognize that this is another example of a previously recorded asset expiring and becoming an expense. The amount estimated to be uncollectible measures the portion of the assets arising from a period's sales which are worthless and must be recognized as a cost of doing business on a credit basis.

The *estimate* of the receivables from the year's sales that will not be collected is made at the end of an accounting period so that the expense arising from bad debts will appear in the same period in which the sales are made. Since the accounts which will prove to be uncollectible cannot be specifically identified as being those of certain customers, it is necessary to credit the estimated amount to an Allowance for Doubtful Accounts account. The Allowance for Doubtful Accounts account is a contra account and can be considered as a special subdivision of the credit side of the Accounts Receivable account. The credit balance in the Allowance for Doubtful Accounts account is deducted from total receivables in the statement of financial position. Bad debts expense is shown among the operating expenses in the earnings statement (although it can also be argued that it should be deducted from sales in arriving at net sales). The expense of worthless receivables is an ordinary and unavoidable occurrence when credit sales are made.

To illustrate one method of estimating the bad debts expense for a period, assume that at December 31, 1975, the unadjusted trial balance of a certain company includes the following: accounts receivable (all from 1975 sales), $25,000; sales for 1975, $400,000. Also assume that experience shows that 1 percent of the annual sales ($4,000) will ultimately be uncollectible. The estimated cash to be collected from the receivables is $21,000, not $25,000. The $4,000 estimate of uncollectible accounts is an expense of the year 1975. The entry to record the bad debts estimate is as follows:

Bad Debts Expense	4,000	
Allowance for Doubtful Accounts		4,000
To record estimated bad debts expense for the year as 1 percent of 1975 sales of $400,000.		

The ledger accounts after posting appear as follows:

Accounts Receivable — Account No. 102

Date		Explanation	Folio	Debit	Credit	Balance
1975						
Dec.	31	Balance				25,000

Allowance for Doubtful Accounts — Account No. 103

Date		Explanation	Folio	Debit	Credit	Balance
1975						
Dec.	31	Adjustment	J 15		4,000	4,000

Bad Debts Expense — Account No. 419

Date		Explanation	Folio	Debit	Credit	Balance
1975						
Dec.	31	Adjustment	J 15	4,000		4,000

The bad debts expense of $4,000 is closed to the Expense and Revenue Summary account at the accounting period and usually appears in the earnings statement as an operating expense. Unless responsibility for collecting the accounts receivable belongs to the sales department, bad debts expense is preferably shown among the administrative expenses.

Assume now that sales for 1976 are $300,000. Also assume that experience now shows that 2 percent of the annual sales will ultimately prove to be uncollectible. The entry to record the bad debts estimate would be:

__________________ .... _____

__________________ .... _____

Now go to Answer Frame 9[4] on page 90 to check your response.

Frame 10[4]

Since the uncollectible receivables amount is estimated, it is preferable to show the gross amount of accounts receivable in the statement of financial position, with the estimated allowance for doubtful accounts subtracted from it to arrive at the net amount of receivables. The manner of disclosure in the statement of financial position is as follows:

Accounts receivable	$25,000	
Less: Allowance for doubtful accounts	4,000	$21,000

At the end of the accounting period, when the account, Allowance for Doubtful Accounts, is increased, the amount debited to the Bad Debts Expense account and credited to the Allowance for Doubtful Accounts account is not an actual amount known to be uncollectible. Rather, it is an estimate of the amount that probably will become uncollectible some time in the future. The sales that gave rise to the uncollectible accounts receivable were made in the accounting period being closed and not in the future period in which the uncollectible accounts will actually be identified. Each accounting period is charged with the bad debts expense incurred as a result of sales made in the same period; this is an example of the application of the matching concept.

A company has *net* accounts receivable of $22,500 and an allowance for doubtful accounts of $4,000. Show how this information should be shown in the statement of financial position.

Now turn to Answer Frame 10[4] on page 90 to check your answer.

Answer frame 9^4

The correct response is:

Bad Debts Expense	6,000	
Allowance for Doubtful Accounts		6,000

If you answered incorrectly, reread Frame 9^4 before beginning Frame 10^4 on page 89.

Answer frame 10^4

The correct response is:

Accounts receivable	$26,500	
Less: Allowance for doubtful accounts	4,000	$22,500

If you did not indicate this response in your first try, you may not understand the difference between *gross* and *net* accounts receivable. The situation posed was that the amount of *net* (and not gross) accounts receivable was $22,500.

Be sure you understand this answer before beginning Frame 11^4 below.

Frame 11^4

Methods of estimating bad debts. Experience in a particular company is often the best guide in arriving at the method to be used in estimating the amount of the uncollectible receivables. An estimate may be secured by employing one of the following methods:

1. Taking a percentage of net sales (credit, or cash and credit) made during the period and making the entry debiting Bad Debts Expense and crediting the Allowance for Doubtful Accounts for this amount.
2. Taking a percentage of accounts receivable open at the end of a period and making the entry for an amount which will build the Allowance for Doubtful Accounts to its required balance. Alternatively, an "aging" schedule of accounts receivable can be prepared to determine the required balance in the allowance account.

Method 1 focuses attention on the required debit to Bad Debts Expense. In strict logic the percentage should be related to net credit sales only because credit sales, not cash sales, are the source of the uncollectible accounts receivable. But when the proportion of credit sales to cash sales remains relatively constant for successive periods, a percentage based on net combined cash and credit sales does not distort the estimate. While past experience is the chief guide, each year's estimate should give effect to known changing conditions. The same percentage of net sales should not be used blindly period after period. When the percentage is based on net combined cash and credit sales, it should be modified for known changes in the proportions of credit sales to total sales. The percentage should be modified also as a result of changing business factors or conditions which influence the collections. These include external factors such as the prosperity-recession cycle and internal factors such as the management's decision to pursue strict or lenient collection or credit-granting policies. This decision is based upon analyses of data in the accounts showing the expenses incurred in the collection function, as compared with the alternative expense of the bad debts themselves.

As an example of Method 1, assume the following at December 31, 1975: in the trial balance, an accounts receivable debit of $60,000, an allowance for doubtful accounts credit of $375, and sales of $500,000. It is estimated that the bad debts expense is 1 percent of net sales. The required entry is:

Bad Debts Expense	5,000	
Allowance for Doubtful Accounts		5,000
To record bad debts expense estimated at 1 percent of net sales.		

The Allowance for Doubtful Accounts account now has a credit balance of $5,375. This amount is deducted on the statement of financial position from the $60,000 of accounts receivable.

Either of the alternatives mentioned under *Method 2* focuses attention on the required credit balance in the Allowance for Doubtful Accounts account. Before adjustment, there may be a small credit balance in the Allowance for Doubtful Accounts account left over from the preceding adjustment. This happens when the receivables of prior periods are still carried as debits and include some balances that are probably uncollectible. In these cases the debit to Bad Debts Expense equals the difference between the required percentage of total receivables and the preadjustment credit balance in the Allowance for Doubtful Accounts account.

For example, assume that the December 31, 1975, trial balance shows an accounts receivable debit balance of $50,000 and that past experience shows that an allowance of 2 percent of the accounts receivable ($1,000) should exist. The allowance account before adjustment has a credit balance of $600. Thus, the amount of the necessary adjustment is $400. The required entry would be:

Bad Debts Expense	400	
Allowance for Doubtful Accounts		400
To increase allowance for uncollectibles.		

The Allowance for Doubtful Accounts account now has a credit balance of $1,000.

Using Method 2, determine the correct entry to record bad debts expense given the following:

	Existing Balances Dr.	Existing Balances Cr.
Accounts Receivable	150,000	
Allowance for Doubtful Accounts		400

It is estimated that the allowance should be 1 percent of the accounts receivable.

The required entry would be:

______________ .... ____

______________ .... ____

Now go to Answer Frame 11[4] on page 92 to check your response.

Frame 12[4]

Often the required balance in the Allowance for Doubtful Accounts account is not determined by merely taking a percentage of outstanding accounts receivable. Instead, an "aging" schedule for accounts receivable is prepared.

When an aging schedule is prepared, all accounts receivable are grouped according to due date (i.e., not yet due, 1 to 30 days past due, over 120 days past due). Based on past experience and analysis of the individual accounts, it may be estimated that 1 percent of the accounts not yet due will prove to be uncollectible, 5 percent of the ones 1 to 30 days past due may prove to be so, etc. The percentage for the group that is over 120 days past due may be very high, such as 50 to 60 percent.

This method results in a fairly accurate determination of the proper balance for the Allowance for Doubtful Accounts in the statement of financial position. But it may not result in the uncollectible accounts being charged against revenues in the accounting period in which the sales creating them were made.

Answer frame 11[4]

The correct response is:

Bad Debts Expense	1,100	
Allowance for Doubtful Accounts		1,100

Calculation:

One percent of accounts receivable of $150,000 =	$1,500
Present balance in the allowance account	400
Amount of adjustment needed to bring balance up to required level	$1,100

If you answered incorrectly, restudy Frame 11[4] before starting Frame 12[4] on page 91.

Frame 12[4] continued

Determine whether each of the following statements is true or false concerning the method based on a percentage of net sales made during the period (Method 1).

_____ 1. Under this method the only facts needed are the sales and the percent of sales estimated to become uncollectible.

_____ 2. The same percentage relationship between sales and bad debts expense should be used each year to ensure consistency and accuracy.

_____ 3. Method 1 focuses attention on the required credit balance in the Allowance for Doubtful Accounts account.

_____ 4. The existing balance in the Allowance for Doubtful Accounts account is ignored in the computation.

Now turn to Answer Frame 12[4] on page 94 to check your answers.

Frame 13[4]

Indicate whether each of the following statements is true or false concerning Method 2, which is based either on a percentage of accounts receivable open at the end of an accounting period or on an "aging" of accounts receivable.

_____ 1. It focuses attention on the required debit to the Bad Debts Expense account.

_____ 2. The amount of the entry equals the difference between the amount determined by applying the required percentage to total receivables and the preadjustment balance in the Allowance for Doubtful Accounts account.

_____ 3. The percentage or percentages used to compute the required balance in the allowance account may vary from period to period.

_____ 4. The amount of total sales for the period can be ignored under this method.

Now turn to Answer Frame 13[4] on page 94 to check your answers.

Frame 14[4]

Writing off uncollectible accounts. In April, 1976, an individual account receivable of $75, arising from a 1975 sale, is identified as being definitely uncollectible. The expense for this has been debited to operations for 1975 by an adjusting journal entry for the year 1975. In April, 1976, no additional expense is incurred. The entry to write off the uncollectible account in April is as follows:

Allowance for Doubtful Accounts	75	
Accounts Receivable, Moore Company		75
To write off an account receivable as uncollectible.		

The debit to the Allowance for Doubtful Accounts indicates that $75 of the total allowance has been used to eliminate a specific account receivable. If the Bad Debts Expense account were debited when the Moore Company account is written off, a double charge to expense would result because the estimated uncollectibles were charged to expense in 1975. The correct entry transfers the credit from the allowance account to the identified uncollectible account receivable. The net amount of receivables remains unchanged.

The Allowance for Doubtful Accounts account in the ledger is credited periodically when the adjusting entries are recorded: it is debited at irregular intervals when specific accounts receivable are identified as uncollectible. It may be that before the end-of-year adjustment is entered, some receivables from the current year's sales are identified as uncollectible and are charged to the allowance account. This chronology of entries explains the possibility of a debit balance in the Allowance for Doubtful Accounts account in an unadjusted trial balance. When the adjustments are recorded at shorter intervals, perhaps monthly, the allowance account usually has a credit balance. After adjustment, the Allowance for Doubtful Accounts account always has a credit balance.

Indicate whether each of the following statements is true or false concerning the above.

______ 1. The Allowance for Doubtful Accounts account is periodically credited when the adjusting entries are recorded.

______ 2. Before adjustments have been made and posted, the Allowance for Doubtful Accounts account may have either a debit or a credit balance.

______ 3. When an account becomes uncollectible in a subsequent year, a debit should be made to the Bad Debts Expense account to record the transaction.

______ 4. After adjusting entries have been made and posted, the Allowance for Doubtful Accounts account always has a credit balance.

Now turn to Answer Frame 14[4] on page 94 to check your answers.

Frame 15[4]

Occasionally a customer pays his account after it has been written off by a debit to the account, Allowance for Doubtful Accounts. In such a situation the entry writing off the account should be reversed because the original write-off was made in error. This entry restores the account receivable as an asset, and the entry to record collection shows that it finally has become collectible.

Answer frame 12[4]

1. True. If you know only these two things, you *can* make the computation under Method 1. It is true that other information is necessary to establish the percentage to use, but if the percentage itself is known, the computation can be made.
2. False. The same percentage relationship should *not* be used blindly each year. The actual relationship can change, and if it does, the percent used in the calculation should be varied.
3. False. A computation is made of the expense rather than of the balance which should exist in the Allowance for Doubtful Accounts account.
4. True. Attention *is* focused on the amount of bad debts expense rather than on the balance in the Allowance for Doubtful Accounts account.

If you missed any of the above, reread Frame 12[4] before starting Frame 13[4] on page 92.

Answer frame 13[4]

1. False. Attention is focused instead on the required credit balance in the Allowance for Doubtful Accounts account.
2. True. The existing balance in the Allowance for Doubtful Accounts account must be given consideration.
3. True. The chapter did not specifically make this statement, but logic dictates it is so.
4. True. Total sales need not be known in order to make the computation.

If you missed any of the above, restudy Frames 11[4], 12[4], and 13[4] before starting Frame 14[4] on page 93.

Answer frame 14[4]

1. True. The adjusting entry is:

Bad Debts Expense	xx	
Allowance for Doubtful Accounts		xx

2. True. Whether the account has a debit or credit balance depends on how much has been set up in the account in previous periods and how much has been written off as uncollectible.
3. False. The debit should be to the Allowance for Doubtful Accounts account. The expense was recorded when the adjusting entry was made establishing the allowance at the end of the previous year.
4. True. If the account had a debit balance you would have to *add* it to the accounts receivable balance. This would be incorrect as *net* accounts receivable should never be larger than gross accounts receivable.

If you missed any of the above, reread Frame 14[4] before starting Frame 15[4] on page 93.

Frame 15[4] continued

Furthermore, the collection of the account may reestablish the credit of the customer. To illustrate:

1975				
May	6	Allowance for Doubtful Accounts	50	
		Accounts Receivable, W. C. Cline		50
		To write off the account as uncollectible.		
Aug.	18	Cash	50	
		Accounts Receivable, W. C. Cline		50
		Collected in full from W. C. Cline.		
	18	Accounts Receivable, W. C. Cline	50	
		Allowance for Doubtful Accounts		50
		To reestablish the account written off as uncollectible on May 6, 1975.		

The customer's ledger account would appear as follows:

Accounts Receivable—W. C. Cline

Date		Explanation	Folio	Debit	Credit	Balance
1975						
Jan.	1	Balance		50		50
May	6	To write off as uncollectible			50	-0-
Aug.	18	To show collection of amount previously written off			50	50 Cr.
	18	To reestablish account written off previously		50		-0-

Assume the following facts: On June 12, 1975, the account of John C. Doe, in the amount of $150, appears uncollectible and is written off. On September 5, 1975, he calls and indicates he will pay his bill. That afternoon he brings $150 cash to the office in payment of his account. What are the entries required to record these transactions?

1975				
June	12	________________	____	
		________________		____
Sept.	5	________________	____	
		________________		____
Sept.	5	________________	____	
		________________		____

Now go to Answer Frame 15[4] on page 96 to check your responses.

Frame 16[4]

EQUAL GROWTH OF EXPENSE AND LIABILITY

Accrued salaries payable. Another type of activity requiring adjusting entries at the end of the accounting period embraces those which appear to be simultaneous and equal growths in expense and liabilities. These are commonly called accrued liabilities: an example is the accrued salaries payable to the employees of a company. The word "accrued" refers to assets and liabilities which exist at the end of the accounting period but have not been recorded in the normal course of business.

A complete understanding of the actual transaction involving the securing of services of employees is rendered difficult by the accounting shortcuts adopted for the sake of economy and convenience. The receipt of services from employees literally involves the purchase of an *asset* by the employer. An expense is an *expired* asset, and no rational person deliberately purchases expenses. Thus, the exchange consists of the receipt of an asset and the giving of a promise to pay. As soon as the service is rendered, an entry *could* be made as follows:

Employee Services Received (an asset)	xxx	
Salaries Payable		xxx

Answer frame 15[4]

The correct responses are:

1976				
June	12	Allowance for Doubtful Accounts	150	
		Accounts Receivable, John C. Doe		150
Sept.	5	Cash	150	
		Accounts Receivable, John C. Doe		150
	5	Accounts Receivable, John C. Doe	150	
		Allowance for Doubtful Accounts		150

If you answered incorrectly, restudy Frame 15[4] before starting Frame 16[4] on page 95.

Frame 16[4] continued

This entry is seldom made for a number of reasons. When should it be made? The liability to the employee literally grows minute by minute as the services are rendered. And, of course, the amount changes through time. Therefore, it is convenient to wait until some period of time has passed. If this is to be done, why not, as a matter of convenience, wait until the salaries are paid? This is frequently done.

If an entry recognizing the receipt of employee services is not made until payment is made, a further bit of short-cutting may be included. The asset received—employee services—may have expired by the time it is recorded; and, therefore, it may be recorded directly as an expense rather than as an asset with subsequent write-off to expense. Thus, the entry often made to record salaries is simply a debit to Salary Expense and a credit to Cash for the weekly, semimonthly, or monthly salaries paid. This entry makes it appear that a cash purchase of an expense has occurred. But it is for the sake of convenience and economy in the accounting routine rather than as a literal interpretation of the transaction that the entry appears as given.

If the receipt of employee services is recognized only when paid, an adjusting entry may be required at the end of an accounting period to record those services received for which payment has not been made. This will usually occur unless services are paid for daily or the end of a payroll period and payday for that period fall on the last day of the accounting period. If not, an entry will be required which will usually consist of a debit to Salaries Expense and a credit to Accrued Salaries Payable.

To illustrate, assume that a trial balance at the end of the first month of the year shows office salaries, $4,400. The salaries for each week, Monday through Saturday (the payroll period), are paid on Saturday (payday). This particular month, however, ends on Wednesday; therefore, salaries for Monday, Tuesday, and Wednesday (the last three days of the month) are not shown in the trial balance since the accounting routine calls for recording salaries when paid, and the salaries for the three days have not been paid. The company has received the services of its employees for the three days and must recognize its liability to them. Since the benefits to be received from the employment of the employees have been received, the cost of the benefits received can be charged to expense. Assume that the salaries for the last three days amount to $550. The adjusting entry required is:

Office Salaries Expense	550	
Accrued Office Salaries Payable		550
To record salaries for last three days of month.		

Office Salaries Expense *Account No. 422*

Date		Explanation	Folio	Debit	Credit	Balance
1975						
Jan.	6	1st week cash	J 3	1,100		1,100
	13	2d week cash	J 4	1,100		2,200
	20	3d week cash	J 4	1,100		3,300
	27	4th week cash	J 5	1,100		4,400
	31	Adjustment	J 5	550		4,950

Accrued Office Salaries Payable — Account No. 309

Date		Explanation	Folio	Debit	Credit	Balance
1975 Jan.	31	Adjustment	J 5		550	550

The adjusting journal entry brings the month's salary expense up to the correct amount of $4,950 for the earnings statement. The credit shows the correct liability of $550 for statement of financial position purposes. Other expense accruals are handled in a similar manner.

Accrued interest payable. Another example of a transaction which is viewed as the incurrence of an expense and the equal growth of a liability is the incurrence of interest expense on borrowed money. The interest payable increases day by day. At the end of an accounting period the accumulated, unpaid interest must be recorded to bring the expense and liability accounts up to date. The entry is a debit to Interest Expense and a credit to Accrued Interest Payable.

Assume that a company borrows $10,000 for a one-year period on October 1, 1975, at an interest rate of 6 percent. No payments of interest or principal are payable until September 30, 1976. The adjusting entry required at December 31, 1975, would be:

______________ .... ____

______________ .... ____

Now turn to Answer Frame 16[4] on page 98 to check your answer.

Frame 17[4]

EARNING REVENUE COLLECTED FOR IN ADVANCE

In some instances the usual procedure of the seller extending credit upon the sale of goods or the rendering of services is reversed. That is, the customer pays assets into the selling company prior to receipt of merchandise or services. Because these assets are advanced with the clear expectation that goods will subsequently be delivered or services rendered, they are commonly called *prepaid* (although actually received) *revenues, revenues received in advance,* or *unearned revenues.* Better terminology would be *advances by customers* as this would clearly indicate the liability nature of the account since, literally, that is what is involved. The seller has the obligation either to render the services, deliver the goods, or return the customers' money.

A revenue account cannot be credited upon receipt of the assets because revenue has not been earned. In the vast majority of cases the earning of the revenue consists of providing services through time. Thus, there is a gradual earning of the revenue which means that the recorded liability is being gradually reduced. Simply speaking, that which was recorded as a liability is changed into revenue through the earning process. The amount earned during an accounting period is recorded by an entry at the end of the period. This entry consists of a debit to the liability account and a credit to a revenue account.

Subscriptions received. It is customary practice for subscribers to magazines to pay for the entire number of magazines to be received in advance of actual receipt. These subscriptions can serve as an illustration of the earning of prepaid revenues. Assume that a company receives $2,400 in cash on June 1, 1975, as payment in full of a number of one-year subscriptions to the monthly news magazine it sells. The entry to record the cash receipt should show a debit to Cash and a credit to Subscriptions Received in Advance. Collection of this cash creates a liability on the part of the company either to deliver each magazine as contracted or to refund the subscription price. As each month's issue is delivered, 1/12 of the annual subscription price already collected is earned. By December 31, 1975, seven of the 12 issues are delivered and 7/12 of the liability has been satisfied. On

Answer frame 16[4]

The correct entry is:

Interest Expense	150	
Accrued Interest Payable		150

The calculation is as follows: \$10,000 × 0.06 = \$600; \$600 × 3/12 = \$150. The entry properly charges \$150 to interest expense for the year 1975 rather than charging the whole \$600 of interest expense to the 1976 accounting year.

If you answered incorrectly, reread Frame 16[4] before starting Frame 17[4] on page 97.

Frame 17[4] continued

December 31, 1975, the adjusting journal entry and the ledger accounts appear as follows:

Subscriptions Received in Advance	1,400	
Subscription Revenue		1,400
To record revenue for June 1 to December 31, 1975.		

Subscriptions Received in Advance — *Account No. 320*

Date		Explanation	Folio	Debit	Credit	Balance
1975						
June	1	Cash collected	J 7		2,400	2,400
Dec.	31	Adjustment	J 14	1,400		1,000

Subscription Revenue — *Account No. 507*

Date		Explanation	Folio	Debit	Credit	Balance
1975						
Dec.	31	Adjustment	J 14		1,400	1,400

The credit balance of \$1,000 in the Subscriptions Received in Advance account at December 31, 1975, represents the amount of assets advanced for which services will be provided and recorded as revenue in 1976. It is a liability on the statement of financial position at December 31, 1975. The \$1,400 balance in the Subscription Revenue account is shown on the earnings statement as earned during the year 1975.

Rental advances received by a lessor and ticket revenue advances received by public carriers or amusement companies also are examples of liabilities that are satisfied as service is performed for the person who paid in advance. Liabilities of this kind are often referred to as *deferred credits to revenue.* This is technical jargon which is largely unintelligible to the layman.

On August 1, 1975, a company receives \$5,000 in cash as payment for tickets for a series of 10 plays, one to be given each month starting in August, 1975. At the time the cash is received, what entry should be made?

1975
Aug. 1 ______________ .... ____
______________ .... ____

The adjusting entry required on December 31, 1975, would be:

1975
Dec. 31 ______________ .... ____
______________ .... ____

Now go to Answer Frame 17[4] on page 100 to check your responses.

Frame 18[4]

SIMULTANEOUS GROWTH OF ASSET AND REVENUE

Accrued interest receivable. In some instances, agreements are entered into from which there arises the right to collect an increasing amount of assets through time. Periodically, collection is effected. This growth in the right to collect is an asset which arises through the rendering of services to others. For example, the interest paid periodically on investments such as bonds and savings accounts is literally earned moment by moment through time as the funds invested are used by the borrower. Except in the rare instance of payment of the interest on the last day of the accounting period, the accounting records will not show the amount of interest revenue earned nor the total assets owned by the investor unless an adjusting entry is made. An entry at the end of the accounting period is needed which debits a receivable account (an asset) and credits a revenue account to record the asset owned and the interest earned.

For example, assume that a company invests some funds in an interest-paying security. The interest is paid twice a year on May 1 and November 1 in the amount of $900 on each date. If the investment were purchased on May 2, 1975, Interest Revenue would be credited with the $900 of cash received on November 1. At December 31, 1975, an additional two months' interest of the six months' interest to be received on May 1, 1976, has been earned. An entry must be made to show the amount of interest earned and the asset, the right to receive this interest, at December 31, 1975. The entry, which is said to be an entry to record the accrual of revenue, would read:

Accrued Interest Receivable	300	
Interest Revenue		300
To record two months' interest revenue.		

The ledger accounts would appear as follows:

Accrued Interest Receivable *Account No. 107*

Date		Explanation	Folio	Debit	Credit	Balance
1975						
Dec.	31	Adjustment	J 14	300		300

Interest Revenue *Account No. 506*

Date		Explanation	Folio	Debit	Credit	Balance
1975						
Nov.	1	Cash received	J 13		900	900
Dec.	31	Adjustment	J 14		300	1,200

The debit balance of $300 in the Accrued Interest Receivable account is an asset that appears in the statement of financial position. The $1,200 credit balance in the Interest Revenue account is the interest earned, whether received in cash or not, during the year. It appears in the earnings statement for the year 1975.

Determine whether each of the following statements is true or false concerning the above adjusting entry.

_____ 1. If no adjusting entry were made, the interest earned in November and December, 1975, would be recorded for the year 1976 when it was collected in May, 1976.

_____ 2. The debit balance in the Accrued Interest Receivable account represents the amount of interest which was earned, but not yet received, through December 31, 1975.

_____ 3. The entry was made so that the portion of interest which was earned in 1975 during November and December would be recorded as revenue in that year.

_____ 4. The credit balance (after adjustment) in the Interest Revenue account includes only amounts received in cash for interest during the year.

Now turn to Answer Frame 18[4] on page 100 to check your answers.

Answer frame 17[4]

The correct responses are:

1975				
Aug.	1	Cash	5,000	
		Admissions Received in Advance		5,000
		To record the receipt of payment for tickets.		
1975				
Dec.	31	Admissions Received in Advance	2,500	
		Revenue from Plays		2,500
		To record the earning of revenue.		

The above records the fact that of the $5,000 of assets received on August 1, 1975, $2,500 was in collection of revenue earned by year-end and is therefore transferred from a liability to a revenue account. Of the total of 10 plays to be given, 5 have already been given; thus, one half of the services to be rendered have now been provided.

If you missed either of the entries, restudy Frame 17[4] before starting Frame 18[4] on page 99.

Answer frame 18[4]

1. True. This is the main reason for making adjusting entries. Revenues and expenses of an accounting period must be matched in order to determine the proper net earnings for a particular period. If a revenue which was actually earned in 1975 was recorded as a revenue of the year 1976, the net earnings of each of the years would be misstated.
2. True. It represents an amount which has already been earned but has not yet been received. On May 1, 1976, however, the $300 earned in 1975 will be received along with another $600 which will be earned during January through April of 1976.
3. True. This was the main purpose of making the adjusting entry.
4. False. The credit balance in the Interest Revenue account is the total interest earned during the year, not the amount of cash received as interest payments. The cash received in a year may include payment for interest earned the previous year and does not include interest earned between the last interest-payment date and the end of the year.

If you missed any of the above, reread Frame 18[4] before starting Frame 19[4] below.

Frame 19[4]

WHEN ARE ADJUSTING ENTRIES MADE?

Adjustments are made at the end of the accounting period after the trial balance has been taken and before the closing entries are made and financial statements are prepared. The adjustments are entered in the journal and are posted to the ledger accounts in the same manner as other journal entries. The adjustments are also entered in the work sheet (see Chapter 7) because the amounts involved affect both the computation of net earnings for the period and the preparation of the statement of financial position.

SUMMARY OF ADJUSTING ENTRIES

The four types of adjusting entries are summarized below. Each type requires an entry at the end of an accounting period to record properly the expense that is incurred or the revenue that is earned for the period. Each adjustment affects both an earnings statement item and a statement of financial position item. The statement of financial position effect of each adjustment carries forward to the future. The earnings statement effect of the adjustment aids the proper determination of net earnings on the accrual basis for the current period.

Summary of adjusting entries

	Prior periods or current period	Current period	Future period
I. Expense incurred by gradual use of asset (prepaid expense).	Recorded in asset account.	Amount used is transferred from asset to expense.	Balance in asset account for future use.
II. Expense and liability increase continuously as incurred (accrued liability and increase in expense).		Amount used is added to expense and liability.	Liability is paid.
III. Revenue earned by gradual performance of service (revenue collected in advance).	Recorded in liability account.	Amount earned is transferred from liability to revenue.	Balance in liability account to be earned by future performance of service
IV. Revenue and asset increase continuously as earned (accrued receivable and increase in revenue).		Amount earned is added to asset and revenue.	Asset is converted to cash.

Indicate whether each of the following statements is true or false.

_______ 1. Adjustments are excluded from the work sheet.

_______ 2. Each adjustment shown above affects both an earnings statement item and a statement of financial position item.

_______ 3. Adjustments are made at the end of an accounting period before the trial balance has been taken.

_______ 4. The earnings statement effect of each adjustment carries forward to affect future earnings statements.

Now turn to Answer Frame 19[4] on page 102 to check your answers.

SUMMARY

Whenever financial statements are to be prepared, the accountant must determine that each account has its proper balance. This usually necessitates making adjusting entries. Four different types of adjusting entries are required to account properly for four different types of situations. These entries record:

1. Incurrence of an expense which results from the gradual use of a previously recorded asset.
2. Incurrence of an expense which is equaled by the gradual increase in an unrecorded liability.
3. Earning of revenue for which collection had previously been made and recorded in a liability account for unearned revenue.
4. Earning of revenue which is equaled by the gradual increase in an unrecorded asset.

An example of the first type of transaction is the recording of depreciation on a building. Generally, as time expires, the building loses part of its ability to render service. This decline is recognized through the recording of depreciation. Depreciation Expense is debited, and the Allowance for Depreciation of Buildings account is credited. The Allowance for Depreciation of Buildings account is a subdivision of the credit side of the asset account, Buildings. The allowance shows the portion of the cost of the asset that has been debited to Depreciation Expense.

An example of the second type entry is the earning of salaries by employees for which payment has not been made by the end of the accounting period. The Salaries Expense account is

Answer Frame 19[4]

1. False. Adjustments are shown on the work sheet.
2. True. Each adjustment shown does affect both an earnings statement item and statement of financial position item.
3. False. Adjustments are made *after* the trial balance has been taken.
4. False. The *Statement of financial position* effect carries *forward* to the future. The *earnings statement* effect aids the proper determination of net earnings for the current period and is not carried forward to the future.

If you missed any of the above, restudy Frame 19[4] before continuing with the Summary on page 101.

SUMMARY continued

debited, and the Accrued Salaries Payable account is credited.

The third type of situation requiring an adjusting entry consists of the earning of revenues for which collection had been previously secured and recorded in a liability account. As the revenue earned, the liability account is debited and a revenue account is credited. Suppose, for instance, that amounts were received for subscriptions to magazines to be delivered in the following year. At the time the money is received, the Cash account is debited and the Subscriptions Received in Advance account is credited. As the magazines are delivered in the following year, a portion of the original proceeds is recognized as being earned. The debit is to the liability account, Subscriptions Received in Advance, and the credit is to the Subscriptions Revenue account.

The fourth type of adjusting entry (the earning of revenue which is matched by the gradual increase in an unrecorded asset) is typified by the recording of interest earned on investments. At the end of an accounting period interest may have been earned on investments but not yet received. The entry to recognize this situation includes a debit to Accrued Interest Receivable and a credit to Interest Revenue.

Now continue by studying the new terms in the Glossary below. Then work the Student Review Quiz for a self-administered test of the material in the chapter.

GLOSSARY

Accrued (assets and liabilities)–those assets and liabilities which exist at the end of an accounting period but which have not been recorded up to the time at which adjusting entries are to be prepared. They represent rights to receive or obligations to make payments which are not legally due at the statement of financial position date. Examples are accrued interest receivable, accrued rent receivable, accrued salaries (or wages) payable, and accrued interest payable.

Accumulated Depreciation account–synonymous with allowance for depreciation below.

Adjusting entries–journal entries made at the end of the accounting period to bring the accounts to their proper balances before financial statements are prepared.

Aging (of accounts receivable)–a process of classifying accounts receivable according to age intervals such as not yet due, 1 to 30 days past due, 31 to 60 days past due, etc.; a procedure often employed in estimating the size of the allowance for doubtful accounts.

Allowance for depreciation account–a contra asset account (defined as an account shown as a deduction from the asset to which it relates in the statement of financial position); an account which shows the sum of all amounts taken as depreciation on the asset up to the statement of financial position date.

Allowance for Doubtful Accounts account–an account showing the estimated amount of outstanding accounts receivable not expected to be collected; a contra asset account shown as a deduction from accounts receivable in the statement of financial position.

Depreciation accounting–the process of allocating and charging to expense the cost of a limited-life, long-term asset (such as a building) over its useful life.

Depreciation expense–the portion of the cost of a depreciable asset charged to expense in a given accounting period.

Depreciation formula–the procedure employed in calculating periodic depreciation, generally cost less salvage value divided by the number of years of expected useful life, which is the procedure employed to determine the annual depreciation charge under the "straight-line" method.

Revenue received in advance–a flow of assets received from customers in advance of the rendering of services for or the delivery of goods to them; since the revenue has not been earned, the amount collected is a liability; often called *prepaid revenue, unearned revenue,* although preferred terminology would be *advances by customers.*

STUDENT REVIEW QUIZ

1. Which of the following changes in the accounts is handled through an adjusting entry?
   a. Gradual conversion of an asset into an expense.
   b. Equal and gradual growth of an expense and a liability over the accounting period.
   c. Earning of revenue received in advance.
   d. Equal and gradual growth of an asset and a revenue over the accounting period.
   e. All of the above.

2. If total net sales for the period are $18,000 ($17,000 credit sales; $1,000 cash sales), the accounts receivable balance is $10,000, and uncollectible accounts are estimated to be 1 percent of net credit sales, the correct entry to adjust the accounts at the end of the accounting period is:

a.	Allowance for Doubtful Accounts ..	180	
	Bad Debts Expense		180
b.	Bad Debts Expense	170	
	Allowance for Doubtful Accounts		170
c.	Allowance for Doubtful Accounts ..	100	
	Bad Debts Expense		100
d.	Bad Debts Expense	180	
	Allowance for Doubtful Accounts		180
e.	Bad Debts Expense	100	
	Allowance for Doubtful Accounts		100

3. A company's annual accounting period closes on December 31. On January 15, the account of P. L. Forrest (which arose as the result of a sale on December 20) in the amount of $75 is found definitely to be uncollectible. The company estimates and records its bad debts at the end of each year. What is the proper entry?

a.	Bad Debts Expense	75	
	Accounts Receivable– P. L. Forrest		75
b.	Allowance for Doubtful Accounts ..	75	
	Accounts Receivable– P. L. Forrest		75
c.	Bad Debts Expense	75	
	Allowance for Doubtful Accounts		75
d.	Allowance for Doubtful Accounts ..	75	
	Bad Debts Expense		75
e.	None of the above.		

4. On November 30, the close of an annual accounting period, interest in the amount of $500 has been earned but not received. The *correct* entry is:

a.	No entry.		
b.	Cash	500	
	Interest Revenue		500
c.	Accrued Interest Receivable	500	
	Interest Revenue		500
d.	Accounts Receivable	500	
	Interest Revenue		500
e.	Interest Revenue	500	
	Accrued Interest Receivable ...		500

5. Net sales for the period are $20,000 ($18,000 credit sales and $2,000 cash sales). The balance of the Accounts Receivable account is $14,500. The account, Allowance for Doubtful Accounts, has a credit balance of $15. Uncollectible accounts are estimated to be 1 percent of accounts receivable. What entry should be made assuming it is the end of the firm's accounting period?

a.	Bad Debts Expense	200	
	Allowance for Doubtful Accounts		200
b.	Bad Debts Expense	145	
	Allowance for Doubtful Accounts		145

c. Bad Debts Expense 185
  Allowance for Doubtful
  Accounts 185

d. Allowance for Doubtful Accounts .. 130
  Bad Debts Expense 130

e. None of the above.

6. The Unexpired Insurance account shows a balance of $900, representing the payment on July 1 of a three-year insurance premium of $900. The correct adjusting entry on December 31, the close of the annual accounting period, is:

a. Insurance Expense 150
  Unexpired Insurance 150

b. Insurance Expense 300
  Unexpired Insurance 300

c. Unexpired Insurance 150
  Insurance Expense 150

d. Unexpired Insurance 25
  Insurance Expense 25

e. None of the above.

7. Which of the following is *not* correct? The percentage estimate of bad debts should be:
   a. A fixed percentage (constant over time).
   b. Modified with a change in the ratio of cash sales to total sales.
   c. Modified with changes in general economic conditions.
   d. Modified with changes in the credit and collection policy within the firm.
   e. Based upon previous collection experience of the particular firm.

8. On June 30, the close of the monthly accounting period, the employees of the Stamp Company have earned salaries totaling $921 payable on the payday of July 3. The entry required on June 30 is:

a. Salary Expense 921
  Accrued Salaries Payable 921

b. Accrued Salaries Payable 921
  Salary Expense 921

c. Salary Expense 921
  Cash 921

d. Salary Expense 921
  Accounts Payable 921

e. None of the above.

9. Office furniture is purchased on October 1 at a cost of $3,400. Estimated salvage value is $200, and estimated useful life is four years. The entry to record the depreciation on December 31 is (assume this is the close of the annual accounting period):

a. Depreciation Expense—Office
  Furniture 850
  Allowance for Depreciation
  —Office Furniture 850

b. Depreciation Expense—Office
  Furniture 800
  Allowance for Depreciation
  —Office Furniture 800

c. Allowance for Depreciation—
  Office Furniture 800
  Depreciation Expense—
  Office Furniture 800

d. Depreciation Expense—Office
  Furniture 200
  Allowance for Depreciation
  —Office Furniture 200

e. Allowance for Depreciation—
  Office Furniture 200
  Depreciation Expense—
  Office Furniture 200

10. Company X pays its employees on the 15th day of each month. The accounting period ends on December 31. If the adjusting entry on December 31, were neglected, which of the following would be the effect at that date?
   a. The assets of the company would be understated.
   b. The stockholders' equity of the company would be understated.
   c. Net earnings for the period ended would be understated.
   d. The liabilities of the company would be understated.
   e. Net earnings for the period ended would be unaffected.

11. Adjusting entries are made so that the accounts will have proper balances—
   a. At the end of each month.
   b. At the end of each calendar year.
   c. To bring accounts to their proper balances before financial statements are prepared.
   d. All of the above are true.
   e. None of the above is true.

Now compare your answers with the correct answers and explanations given on page 206.

chapter 5

MERCHANDISE INVENTORIES AND SALES REVENUE

LEARNING OBJECTIVES

Study of the material in this chapter is designed to provide knowledge of—

1. What constitutes a sale and a purchase; the time that each is recorded and why; the nature and reasons for, as well as the accounting for and reporting of, sales (purchases) discounts and sales (purchases) returns and allowances.
2. The operating characteristics and advantages and disadvantages of perpetual inventory procedure as a means of accounting for merchandise inventories and the cost of merchandise sold.
3. Common terms under which merchandise is sold, including freight terms; accounting for purchase discounts; cash discounts distinguished from trade discounts.
4. Some basic business documents employed in operating a merchandising business.

Frame 1[5]

INVENTORY PROCEDURES FOR COMPANIES SELLING MERCHANDISE

One of the major assets owned by many firms, especially those engaged in selling merchandise, is the merchandise inventory itself. Accounting procedures have been developed which will help management to maintain control over this asset and thereby help it to protect the asset against loss. Of the commonly used inventory procedures, one will be discussed in this chapter, the other in Chapter 6.

Basic accounting procedures thus far have been treated from the point of view of a company that secures its net earnings only by performing services for its clients and customers. In these chapters accounting procedures are discussed as they apply to a company that earns revenue through a process of buying merchandise and selling that merchandise to its customers.

Sales to customers are the major source of gross revenue for these firms. The purchase cost of the goods sold is a major expense in producing the sales revenue. Accounts with suitable titles that may be used to record the transactions involved in buying and selling the merchandise are introduced and explained in this and the following chapter. When a company buys merchandise and then sells that merchandise to its customers, normally a quantity of goods must be on hand and available for sale. The quantity of goods on hand and available for sale at any time is known as *inventory* or *merchandise inventory*.

Two commonly used procedures of accounting for merchandise as it is purchased, held, and then shipped to customers are perpetual inventory procedure and the periodic inventory procedure. The proper entries to record purchases, transportation-inward costs, and shipments of merchandise depend on which of these two procedures is being used. Perpetual procedure is presented below; periodic procedure in the next chapter.

PERPETUAL INVENTORY PROCEDURE

Cost of goods bought and sold. A perpetual inventory procedure is one in which the quantity and dollar amount of the inventory are determined after each sale and each purchase of goods is recorded. In other words, the dollar amount of the inventory is kept perpetually up to date in the Merchandise Inventory account. Perpetual inventories are commonly used when the inventory items are of high individual value, as exemplified by automobiles, which are easily identifiable by serial numbers. In this way the inventory records serve as a control over the actual goods in that they state the exact amount of goods which should be on hand. Periodic inventory procedure normally is used when the items are of low unit value and are interchangeable, as exemplified by nuts and bolts. When perpetual inventory records are maintained, one convenient method of accounting for the cost of goods bought and sold is described below. The two accounts used are:

1. Merchandise Inventory (an asset).
2. Cost of Goods Sold (an expense).

Both accounts are increased by debits and decreased by credits.

When merchandise is purchased, an asset is increased, and hence the Merchandise Inventory account is debited for the cost of the inventory purchased. Cost means the cost incurred to obtain title to the merchandise and to have it delivered to the buyer. Sometimes the price agreed to by the supplier and the buyer includes the cost of delivery. In this case the entry is illustrated as follows:

1975			
Oct. 12	Merchandise Inventory	4,500	
	Accounts Payable (or Cash)		4,500
	To record purchase of goods at cost of $4,500, including delivery, from M.C.A. Wholesalers.		

The entry to record the purchase is not made until the goods and an invoice have been received from the seller and the buyer is satisfied that the goods ordered were received in good condition and in the proper quantity. The invoice is checked to verify the prices, discount terms,

FIGURE 5.1
Purchase order

BOWEN COMPANY
515 Church Street, Adrian, Michigan

Purchase Order No. 414
Date 10/2/75

To M.C.A. Wholesalers
Address 1817 Fifth Avenue, Buffalo, New York

Terms Net 30
Ship Via Motor Carrier

Please send the following and charge our account:

Description	*Quantity*	*Price per unit*	*Amount*
Folding chairs—Model No. 568–375	450	$10	$4,500
	Total		$4,500

Authorized by *Walter C. Hilliard*
Purchasing Agent

FIGURE 5.2
Purchase invoice

M.C.A. WHOLESALERS
1817 Fifth Avenue, Buffalo, New York

Invoice No. 217
Date 10/10/75

To Bowen Company
Address 515 Church Street, Adrian, Michigan

Your Purchase Order No. 414
Shipped by Northern Trucking Co.
Date Shipped 10/10/75

Description	*Quantity*	*Price per unit*	*Amount*
Model 568–375 folding chairs	450	$10	$4,500
	Total		$4,500

transportation charges, and the extensions and summarization of amounts.

The system of internal control over the purchase of and payment for merchandise is often elaborate. The purpose is to safeguard the assets of the company. Some of the forms typically used in such a system are shown below in a brief illustration involving the Bowen Company, which is designed to explain the "paper work" which resulted in the above entry.

The Bowen Company decides to purchase some chairs from M.C.A. Wholesalers. Four copies of the purchase order shown in Figure 5.1 are prepared. The original is sent to M.C.A. Wholesalers. One copy is retained by the purchasing department. The other two copies are sent to the receiving department and the accounting department. No entry would be made at this point to record the purchase.

When the chairs arrive at the receiving department, they are examined to see if the shipment agrees with the purchase order. Any differences are noted. The receiving department's copy of the purchase order may itself become a receiving report. If so, it is sent to the accounting department with a notation that the goods have been received. Any differences between the shipment and the purchase order are indicated on the receiving report.

When the Bowen Company receives the invoice for the goods from M.C.A. Wholesalers, it is forwarded to the accounting department. The invoice is compared with the accounting department's copy of the purchase order and with the receiving report. The invoice might appear as shown in Figure 5.2.

If no discrepancies in the invoice are apparent, the entry to record the purchase is made.

After the entry is recorded and posted, the purchase data are recorded on a perpetual inventory card such as that shown in Figure 5.3.

FIGURE 5.3
Perpetual inventory card

Folding Chairs—Model 568–375

		Received			*Shipped*			*Balance*		
Date	*Ref.**	*Units*	*Unit Cost*	*Total*	*Units*	*Unit Cost*	*Total*	*Units*	*Unit Cost*	*Total*
10/10	P.I.217	450	$10.00	$4,500.00				450	$10.00	$4,500.00

* P.I. = Purchase Invoice.

Indicate which of the following entries correctly records the purchase of $3,000 of merchandise for cash on October 15, 1975, from M.C.A. Wholesalers. Place a check by the correct answer.

______ 1.	Merchandise Inventory	3,000	
	Accounts Receivable		3,000
	To record purchase of goods from M.C.A. Wholesalers.		
______ 2.	Merchandise Inventory	3,000	
	Accounts Payable		3,000
	To record purchase of goods from M.C.A. Wholesalers.		
______ 3.	Accounts Payable	3,000	
	Merchandise Inventory		3,000
	To record purchase of goods from M.C.A. Wholesalers.		
______ 4.	Merchandise Inventory	3,000	
	Cash		3,000
	To record purchase of goods from M.C.A. Wholesalers.		
______ 5.	Accounts Payable	3,000	
	Cash		3,000
	To record purchase of goods from M.C.A. Wholesalers.		

Check your response in Answer Frame 1[5] on page 110.

Frame 2[5]

Purchase returns and allowances. For any one of several reasons, such as receiving the wrong merchandise, the purchaser may return part or all of the goods received from a vendor. Returning merchandise to the supplier reduces the amount of the asset on hand and also reduces the liability to the supplier. Therefore, the Merchandise Inventory account must be reduced in the amount of the cost of the goods returned, and the account payable must be correspondingly reduced. Since liabilities are reduced by debits and assets by credits, an illustrative entry would be as follows:

Accounts Payable	250	
Merchandise Inventory		250
To record return of goods that cost $250 to M.C.A. Wholesalers.		

If merchandise ordered is received in a damaged condition but the purchaser feels that he will be able to sell the goods at a reduced price, he may agree to retain the goods if the vendor will grant a reduction in the purchase price. If granted, such a reduction is termed a *purchase allowance* and reduces the cost of the asset to the buyer and also reduces his liability to the supplier. (To the vendor it is a sales allowance.)

Which of the following statements correctly describes the effect of a purchase allowance under perpetual inventory procedure? Place a check by the correct answer.

______ 1. Merchandise Inventory would decrease. Accounts Payable would increase.

______ 2. Merchandise Inventory would increase. Accounts Payable would decrease.

______ 3. Merchandise Inventory would decrease. Accounts Payable would decrease.

______ 4. Merchandise Inventory would increase. Accounts Payable would increase.

Check your response in Answer Frame 2[5] on page 110.

Frame 3[5]

Trade and cash discounts. Discounts are of two general types: (1) trade discounts and (2) cash (or purchase) discounts. Any one invoice may be subject to both types of discounts.

Nature and computation of trade discounts. A trade discount is a deduction from the list (resale) price of an article. It is merely a means for the determination of the price of the item purchased. The amount of the trade discount probably will be shown on the seller's invoice but not recorded in his records nor is it to be recorded on the books of the purchaser. Assume an invoice as follows:

Gross list price, 200 swimsuits at $3	$600
Less: Trade discount, 30%	180
Gross Invoice Price	$420

The vendor would record the sale at $420, and the purchaser would record the cost of the merchandise at $420.

A policy of quoting trade discounts is followed for several reasons, such as—

1. To reduce the cost of catalog publication. If separate discount lists are given the salesmen whenever prices change, catalogs may be used for a long period of time. Prices may be changed by simply changing the trade discounts without reprinting the entire catalog.
2. To grant quantity discounts. For example, customers may be allowed a 20 percent discount if they buy up to 100 units and an additional 5 percent discount if they buy up to 300 units.
3. To be able to quote different prices to different types of customers, such as to retailers and wholesalers.

Trade discounts are computed as indicated below. Assume that the list price of an article is $50 subject to trade discounts as indicated:

On total purchases up to 50 units, 20 percent.
On total purchases of from 51 to 100 units, 20 percent and 10 percent.
On total purchases of from 101 to 150 units, 20 percent, 10 percent, and 5 percent.

The price for 150 units would be quoted as $50 less 20 percent, 10 percent, and 5 percent on each and every unit; this is known as a series of trade discounts, or a chain discount.

The computation of the gross invoice price of the 150 units is as follows:

List price—150 @ $50	$7,500
Less: 20 percent of $7,500	1,500
Remainder	$6,000
Less: 10 percent of $6,000	600
Remainder	$5,400
Less: 5 percent of $5,400	270
Gross Invoice Price	$5,130

The gross invoice price to be recorded in the accounting records of the seller and the purchaser is $5,130. Price-determining means are not reflected in recorded sales and purchases amounts.

The amount desired in the foregoing computation is the gross invoice price, not the amount of the discount. Therefore, the procedure will be faster if the list price is multiplied by 100 percent minus the discount rates, as follows:

$7,500 × (100% − 20%) = $7,500 × 0.80	$6,000
$6,000 × (100% − 10%) = $6,000 × 0.90	$5,400
$5,400 × (100% − 5%) = $5,400 × 0.95	$5,130

A single discount equivalent to the series of discounts granted may be computed as follows: take each discount in the series and subtract it from 100 percent. Thus, in the preceding illustration:

$$100\% - 20\% = 80\%\ (0.80)$$
$$100\% - 10\% = 90\%\ (0.90)$$
$$100\% - 5\% = 95\%\ (0.95)$$

Next, multiply the decimal equivalents by one another, $0.80 \times 0.90 \times 0.95 = 0.6840$, which is the percentage gross invoice price.

To convert the percentage gross invoice price (0.6840) to net dollars, multiply the list price by the percentage gross invoice price:

$$\$7{,}500 \times 0.6840 = \$5{,}130$$

To obtain the single *discount* percentage, subtract 68.40 percent from 100 percent = 31.60 percent. The computation of a single equivalent discount is valuable when several invoices, each having the same series of discounts, must be checked.

Answer frame 1[5]

Entry No. 4 is the correct answer. Since a purchase was made, the inventory is increased by the cost of the goods purchased; and since the transaction involved cash, Cash is decreased by the cost.

If you answered incorrectly, review Frame 1[5] before beginning Frame 2[5] on page 108.

Answer frame 2[5]

Answer No. 3 is correct. The Merchandise Inventory account is credited directly for both purchase returns and purchase allowances. The Accounts Payable account balance is reduced correspondingly. An illustrative journal entry for a purchase allowance would appear as follows:

Accounts Payable	500	
Merchandise Inventory		500
To record allowance for defective goods received from M.C.A. Wholesalers.		

If you answered incorrectly, review Frame 2[5] before starting Frame 3[5] on page 109.

Frame 3[5] continued

Is each of the following statements true or false with regard to trade discounts?

_______ 1. A trade discount may be used to induce a customer to buy in larger quantities.

_______ 2. A seller's invoice appears as follows:

List price, 100 pairs men's socks @ $0.50	$50.00
Less: Trade discount, 25%	12.50
Gross Invoice Price	$37.50

The purchaser should enter $50 in his Merchandise Inventory account.

_______ 3. The trade discount is a pricing means that allows the seller to quote different prices to different types of customers.

Check your responses in Answer Frame 3[5] on page 112.

Frame 4[5]

Cash discount terms. Cash discounts are often viewed as being offered to the purchaser by the seller in an attempt to induce prompt payment of an invoice. Theoretically, they also represent adjustments to gross invoice price to arrive at the actual cost—the cash price—of the merchandise. These discounts, usually ranging from 1 to 3 percent of the gross invoice price of the merchandise, may or may not be taken by the buyer. To the purchaser, they are purchase discounts; to the seller, they are sales discounts.

Cash discount terms are often stated as follows:

2/10, n/30—which is read as "two ten, net thirty." Unfortunately, the statement is misleading. The terms actually offered are a 2 percent discount (2 percent of the gross invoice price of the merchandise) if payment is rendered within 10 days following the invoice date. *No* discount is allowed after 10 days following the invoice date, and the gross invoice price is due 30 days from the invoice date. The "n" in the terms should be interpreted as "no discount" rather than as "net" since the residual obtained when the discount is subtracted from the invoice price is properly described as "net."

2/E.O.M., n/60—which is read as "two E.O.M., net sixty." The terms actually mean a 2 percent discount may be deducted if the invoice is paid by the end of the month, no discount may be taken after the end of the month, and the invoice is due 60 days from the date of the invoice.

2/10/E.O.M., n/60—which is usually read as "two ten E.O.M., net sixty." The actual terms offered are a 2 percent discount if the invoice is paid by the 10th of the following month, no discount is allowed after this date, and the gross invoice amount is due 60 days from the date of the invoice.

Recording cash discounts. To illustrate the recording of a cash discount, assume the following facts:

Gross invoice price of merchandise	$5,130.00
Discount offered by seller (2%)	102.60
Net Invoice Amount	$5,027.40

Assuming that the purchase (on account) had been recorded previously, the entry to record the payment of the invoice is:

Accounts Payable	5,130.00	
Merchandise Inventory		102.60
Cash		5,027.40

Under this procedure the purchase discounts taken are treated as reductions in the cost of the merchandise purchased and credited directly to the Merchandise Inventory account.

Indicate whether each of the following statements is true or false.

_______ 1. A cash discount is often viewed as an amount deductible from the gross invoice price granted for prompt settlement of a debt arising out of the acquisition of an asset.

_______ 2. The terms 3/10 E.O.M., n/45 indicate that if the invoice is paid within 10 days after the end of the month in which the invoice is dated, a 3 percent discount may be taken. In any case, payment must be made within 45 days after the invoice date.

_______ 3. A cash discount taken is best treated as a reduction in the cost of the purchases.

_______ 4. The percentage rate of cash discount allowed is often changed as a means of changing prices on merchandise offered for sale.

Check your responses in Answer Frame 4[5] on page 112.

Frame 5[5]

Accounts used for sales of merchandise

Sales revenue. The principal gross revenue for a merchandising firm is gained from the sales of merchandise. Each time a sale is made, a revenue account must be increased by the amount of the total *selling price*. This revenue account is called the Sales account and like any revenue account is increased by credits when sales are made to customers. For example, a $5,000 sale on account would be recorded as follows:

Accounts Receivable	5,000	
Sales		5,000
To record the sale of merchandise.		

When a sale is made, it is expected that the sales revenue will serve not only to cover the *cost of goods sold* and operating expenses but to provide net earnings as well.

Under perpetual inventory procedure a debit entry to the Cost of Goods Sold account at *cost* is also required at the time of the sale. The cost

Answer frame 3^5

1. True. This *is* a characteristic of trade discounts.
2. False. The purchaser does not make the entry as described in this response. Rather, only the gross invoice price ($37.50) is entered in his Merchandise Inventory account. Assuming that the purchase was made on account, he would make the following entry:

Merchandise Inventory	37.50	
Accounts Payable		37.50
To record the purchase of merchandise on account.		

   The need for and nature of these entries on the seller's books and the computation of the amounts will be discussed in a later section.
3. True. This *is* a characteristic of the trade discount.

If you answered any of the above incorrectly, reread Frame 3^5 before going on to Frame 4^5 on page 110.

Answer frame 4^5

1. True. A cash discount is a means for encouraging prompt payment.
2. True. The terms actually read that the purchaser may receive a 3 percent discount if he pays within 10 days after the end of the month of purchase and that the gross amount is due within 45 days of the invoice date.
3. True. The amount of a cash discount taken by a buyer reduces his cost of the merchandise purchased.
4. False. Varying *trade* discounts, not cash discounts, constitutes a means of changing prices.

If you answered any of the above incorrectly reread Frame 4^5 before going on to Frame 5^5 on page 111.

Frame 5^5 continued

of the merchandise sold is transferred from the asset account (Merchandise Inventory) to an expense account (Cost of Goods Sold) because the inventory is reduced physically and the cost of the goods sold is one of the expenses of making the sale. Thus, the Cost of Goods Sold account accumulates the cost of all the merchandise sold during a period. If the cost of the merchandise whose sale was recorded above was $3,500, the entry to record the cost of the sale would be:

Cost of Goods Sold	3,500	
Merchandise Inventory		3,500
To record cost of goods sold.		

The above entries are made only after the accountant has evidence that the merchandise has been packaged and shipped to the customer.

The seller typically prepares a sales invoice after receiving a shipping ticket from the shipping department indicating that the goods have been shipped. The nature of the goods, quantities, and prices must agree with those appearing on the written order received from the customer. A typical sales invoice which would serve as a basis for making the sales entry described above is shown in Figure 5.4.

The information needed to make the cost of goods sold entry would be found on the perpetual inventory card for this particular brand and model of radios (for an illustrative card, see Figure 5.3, page 107).

The total of the credits to revenue accounts for a period of time gives the gross revenue figure necessary to determine the net earnings or loss of the business. From your own experience, however, you may recognize that the amount of gross revenue or sales of a merchandising business is not indicative of the actual value of the

FIGURE 5.4
Sales invoice

DIXON WHOLESALE CO. *476 Mason Street, Detroit, Michigan*		*Invoice No.* 1258 *Date* Dec. 19, 1975	
Customer's Order No. 218 *Sold To* Hanley Company *Address* 2255 Hannon Street, Big Rapids, Michigan *Terms* Net 30		*Date Shipped* Dec. 19, 1975 *Shipped by* York Trucking Co.	
Description	*Quantity*	*Price per unit*	*Amount*
True-tone AM/FM radios Model No. 5868–24393	100	$50	$5,000
	Total		$5,000

goods delivered by it. Why? There are three main reasons:

1. Sales returns.
2. Sales allowances.
3. Sales discounts.

Sales returns. Sales made to a customer and later returned to the seller are known as sales returns. In the earnings statement, sales returns are deducted from gross sales. When customers return merchandise that has previously been recorded in the Sales account, the decrease in sales is recorded by a debit in a separate account called Sales Returns and Allowances. A separate account is used because the amount of such items may be significant information to management, owners, and others. In addition to this entry made at selling price, an entry at cost must also be made debiting the Merchandise Inventory account and crediting the Cost of Goods Sold account to reflect the cost of the goods returned.

To illustrate: Top Quality Wholesale Stores sold merchandise which cost $28,000 for $40,000: $25,000 on account and $15,000 for cash. The entries required are:

1975				
July	20	Accounts Receivable	25,000	
		Cash	15,000	
		Sales		40,000
		To record sales on account and cash sales.		
	20	Cost of Goods Sold	28,000	
		Merchandise Inventory ..		28,000
		To record the cost of goods sold to customers.		

Some time later cash sale customers returned merchandise which cost $70 and which had been sold originally for $100 and received cash refunds. Accounts receivable sale customers returned merchandise which cost $170 and which sold originally for $250 and received full credit for the returns. On the records of Top Quality Wholesale Stores, the following entries are made:

1975				
July	25	Sales Returns and Allowances	350	
		Cash		100
		Accounts receivable		250
		To record sales returns from customers.		
	25	Merchandise Inventory	240	
		Cost of Goods Sold		240
		To record the cost of goods returned by customers.		

Now prepare the entries required on the vendor's books to record the following transactions:

1. Sold merchandise on account. List price: $2,000. Trade discounts granted: 20 percent and 10 percent.
2. Cost of merchandise to vendor: $1,200.
3. Allowed customers to return damaged merchandise:

List price (before trade discounts)	$250
Cost	150

Now turn to Answer Frame 5[5] on page 116 to check your answers.

Frame 6[5]

Sales allowances. Sales allowances are deductions from original sales prices. They may be granted to a customer for a number of reasons. The goods shipped to customers may not have been of the quality ordered or may possess minor defects or flaws which will detract from their salability. Or the goods may have been damaged or may have deteriorated while in transit because

FIGURE 5.5
Debit memorandum

CHANEY COMPANY — *Debit Memorandum No.* 94
1001 Good Luck Road, Riverdale, Maryland — *Date* 7/18/75

To Top Quality Wholesale Stores
Address 1542 Jolly Road, Port Huron, Michigan

Your account has been debited in accordance with our telephone conversation (Invoice No. 516, dated 7/12/75) because of defective merchandise in the amount of $400

of seller negligence. A sales allowance is *not* a discount granted a customer but a price adjustment for some reason. In the earnings statement, sales allowances are deducted from gross sales because they are literally corrections of sales prices. Since no merchandise changes hands, the only entry required to reflect the granting of an allowance is the one in which the Sales Returns and Allowances account is debited at selling price.

Sales returns and sales allowances reduce the originally recorded gross sales revenue; hence, they are debits. The Sales Returns and Allowances account (or accounts) is really a negative revenue account (i.e., a subdivision of the Sales account). It is not an expense account, but it has a debit balance and is treated like an expense as far as debits and credits are concerned.

To continue the Top Quality Wholesale Stores illustration, assume that the Chaney Company, a customer which had purchased merchandise on account, claimed that some of the merchandise shipped to it was defective. The customer thought an allowance of $400 should be granted. Top Quality Wholesale Stores agreed and made the following entry:

1975			
July 29	Sales Returns and Allowances	400	
	Accounts Receivable		400
	To record allowance for defective merchandise.		

Since no merchandise was returned, no other entry was required.

The evidence for making an entry recording the sales returns and allowances is usually the receipt of (and agreement with) a debit memorandum from the customer giving the reason why the return was made or why the allowance should be granted. A typical one supporting the above entry might appear as shown in Figure 5.5.

After agreeing to grant an adjustment of $400, Top Quality Wholesale Stores would send a credit memorandum to the Chaney Company. It might appear as shown in Figure 5.6.

Sales discounts. A third cause for reducing recorded gross revenues is the sales discount. As mentioned previously, when merchandise is sold on account, the seller may offer a discount from the gross invoice price which can be taken only if the account is paid within a specified period of time. If taken, it becomes a purchase discount to the purchaser and a sales discount to the seller. It is customary for the seller to record the dis-

FIGURE 5.6
Credit memorandum

TOP QUALITY WHOLESALE STORES — *Credit Memorandum No.* 63
1542 Jolly Road, Port Huron, Michigan — *Date* 7/21/75

To Chaney Company
Address 1001 Good Luck Road, Riverdale, Maryland

Your account has been credited relative to our invoice No. 156 for defects as per our telephone conversation in the amount of $400

Answer frame 5[5]

The correct entries required are as follows:

Accounts Receivable	1,440	
Sales		1,440
To record sale of merchandise ($2,000 × 0.80 × 0.90 = $1,440)		
Cost of Goods Sold	1,200	
Merchandise Inventory		1,200
To record the cost of the goods sold.		
Sales Returns and Allowances	180	
Accounts Receivable		180
To record selling price of goods returned ($250 × 0.80 × 0.90 = $180).		
Merchandise Inventory	150	
Cost of Goods Sold		150
To record cost of the goods returned to inventory.		

If you answered incorrectly, restudy Frame 5[5] before beginning 6[5] on page 114.

Frame 6[5] continued

counts taken by customers in a Sales Discounts account. In the earnings statement the amount of sales discounts is treated as a reduction of the recorded sales revenue.

Assume that Good Buys, Inc. sells merchandise on which the discount offered is subsequently taken. On the vendor's books the following entries are made:

1975				
July	31	Accounts Receivable–Company X	100	
		Sales		100
		To record sales; terms, 2/10, n/30.		
	31	Cost of Goods Sold	75	
		Merchandise Inventory		75
		To record the cost of the goods sold.		
Aug.	10	Cash	98	
		Sales Discounts	2	
		Accounts Receivable–Company X		100
		To record collection within discount period.		

If the above entries recorded the only sales and sales-related transactions for the period, a partial earnings statement prepared on August 10 would appear as follows:

GOOD BUYS, INC.
Partial Earnings Statement
For the Month Ended August 10, 1975

Sales	$100
Less: Sales discounts	2
Net sales	$ 98
Less: Cost of goods sold	75
Gross Margin	$ 23

Assume that the Gordon Company granted a sales discount upon payment of an account. Its accountant debited Sales instead of the Sales Discounts account. Indicate whether each statement is true or false.

_______ 1. The procedure is not seriously in error even though the Sales Discounts account is not used, since net revenue would be the same.

_______ 2. The procedure is wrong since the net revenue of the business would be incorrectly stated.

Check your responses in Answer Frame 6[5] on page 118.

Frame 7[5]

COMPLETE ILLUSTRATION FOR A MERCHANDISING CONCERN USING PERPETUAL INVENTORY PROCEDURE

In order to summarize the steps involved in the correct operation of a perpetual inventory system, the following illustration is presented. Typical transactions are given and journalized and then posted to the correct accounts.

On January 3, Sunshine Stores purchased merchandise which had an invoice cost of $6,000; terms, 2/10, n/30, with buyer to pay freight costs. The correct entry to record this purchase is:

1975				
Jan.	3	Merchandise Inventory	6,000	
		Accounts Payable		6,000
		To record purchase of merchandise on account; terms, 2/10, n/30.		

On January 5, a bill for $120 was received from the Speedy Delivery Company for the delivery of the merchandise. The bill was paid the same day and would be recorded as follows:

1975				
Jan.	5	Merchandise Inventory	120	
		Cash		120
		To record payment of freight on January 3 purchase of merchandise.		

Sunshine Stores requested and was granted an allowance in the amount of $350 for merchandise received as a part of the January 3 purchase which was discovered to be slightly damaged. Since this allowance reduces the net amount which will be paid for the merchandise, the correct entry is:

1975				
Jan.	7	Accounts Payable	350	
		Merchandise Inventory		350
		Received an allowance for damaged merchandise.		

If the bill already had been paid when the allowance was granted and a cash refund were received, the debit would be to Cash rather than to Accounts Payable. In this case the amount of cash received would not be $350 but rather $350 minus the applicable cash discount, or $350 − (0.02 × $350) = $343.

If the damaged merchandise had been returned to the vendor, the accounts involved would be identical to those shown immediately above; only the amounts would differ.

The correct entry to record the payment of the invoice on January 13 (the last day of the discount period) is as follows:

1975				
Jan.	13	Accounts Payable	5,650	
		Cash		5,537
		Merchandise Inventory		113
		To record payment of bill for January 3 purchase of merchandise.		

Before the payment of the bill, the balance in the Accounts Payable account for the January 3 purchase is $5,650: $6,000 − $350, the allowance granted. The discount applicable thereto is 0.02 × $5,650, or $113, so that the net amount of cash owed is $5,537.

Next, Sunshine Stores sold on account for $2,000 merchandise which cost $1,500. The entries required to record the sale and the inventory reduction are:

1975				
Jan.	15	Accounts Receivable	2,000	
		Sales		2,000
		To record sales on account.		
	15	Cost of Goods Sold	1,500	
		Merchandise Inventory		1,500
		To record cost of goods sold to customers.		

If, at a later date, customers are allowed to return merchandise which cost $300 and which was sold originally for $400, one entry must be made to reduce the accounts receivable and to record the sales return, and a second entry must be made to increase the Merchandise Inventory account (to reflect the return of the goods to inventory) and to decrease the Cost of Goods Sold. The following entries would accomplish this:

1975				
Jan.	20	Sales Returns and Allowances	400	
		Accounts Receivable		400
		To record the sales price of the goods returned by customers.		
	20	Merchandise Inventory	300	
		Cost of Goods Sold		300
		To record the cost of goods returned by customers.		

Answer frame 6[5]

1. True. The net result of this procedure would be the same as the procedure suggested using the Sales Discounts account. The Gordon Company accountant simply took a shortcut to arrive at net revenue.
2. False. *Net* revenue would be correct, but *gross* revenue would not be shown.

If you answered either of the above incorrectly, reread Frame 6[5] before going on to Frame 7[5] on page 117.

Frame 7[5] continued

If, on the other hand, customers are granted sales allowances on damaged merchandise, only one entry is required, the one at sales price. Since no merchandise is returned to inventory, no adjustment to the inventory account is needed. Assume that customers are granted allowances totaling $150 on merchandise which cost $1,800 and which was sold originally for $2,400. The only entry required is the following one:

1975			
Jan. 23	Sales Returns and Allowances	150	
	Accounts Receivable		150
	To record allowance granted to customers for damaged merchandise.		

The preceding entries show the recording of typical transactions that affect the Merchandise Inventory, Sales, Sales Returns and Allowances, and Cost of Goods Sold accounts. When these entries are made and posted currently during the accounting period, the balance in the Merchandise Inventory account—after posting—is the cost of the remaining inventory, an *asset,* that would appear on the statement of financial position if prepared at the then current date. The balance in the Cost of Goods Sold account is an *expense* of the period that would be deducted from sales revenue in the earnings statement.

It is to be remembered that sales allowances and sales discounts granted customers affect revenue only. But sales returns affect both revenue and the cost of the goods sold because the goods, charged to cost of goods sold, are actually returned to the seller.

The accounts of Sunshine Stores would appear as follows after posting the preceding entries:

Merchandise Inventory — *Account No. 108*

Date		Explanation	Folio	Debit	Credit	Balance
1975						
Jan.	1	Beginning balance				48,000
	3	Goods purchased		6,000		54,000
	5	Transportation costs		120		54,120
	7	Purchase allowance granted			350	53,770
	13	Cash discount taken			113	53,657
	15	Cost of goods sold			1,500	52,157
	20	Cost of goods returned		300		52,457

Sales — *Account No. 310*

Date		Explanation	Folio	Debit	Credit	Balance
1975						
Jan.	15	Sales on account			2,000	2,000

Sales Returns and Allowances — *Account No. 311*

Date		Explanation	Folio	Debit	Credit	Balance
1975						
Jan.	20	Sales returns allowed		400		400
	23	Sales allowances granted		150		550

Cost of Goods Sold — *Account No. 410*

Date		Explanation	Folio	Debit	Credit	Balance
1975						
Jan.	15	Cost of goods sold		1,500		1,500
	20	Cost of goods returned			300	1,200

FIGURE 5.7
Inventory listing sheet

INVENTORY LISTING SHEET

Date *December 21, 1975* *Sheet No. 4*

Description of Inventory Item	*Quantity per Inventory Records*	*Actual Quantity*	*Price per Unit*	*Amount*
Tables—Model 259	59			
Tables—Model 124	42			
Chairs, folding, white—Model 622	643			
Chairs, folding, brown—Model 623	224			
Desks, metal—Model 586	76			

The balance of the Merchandise Inventory account ($52,457) is the cost of the inventory which *should* be on hand. This is one of the major reasons why some companies choose to use perpetual inventory procedure. The cost of inventory which *should* be on hand is readily available. Periodically a physical inventory is taken to determine the accuracy of the balance shown. Management may wish to investigate any major discrepancies between the balance shown in the account and the cost based on the physical count. Greater control over inventory is thereby achieved. A physical inventory listing sheet as shown in Figure 5.7 might be used in taking the physical inventory.

The quantities shown in the column, Quantity per Inventory Records, should not be entered until after the inventory is taken. The amounts shown in this column are taken from the supporting records which are maintained under perpetual inventory procedure. Each time an entry is made in the Merchandise Inventory account, the supporting records are also brought up to date.

The supporting records are called perpetual inventory cards or stock cards and usually consist of three sections headed Received, Shipped, and Balance. A perpetual inventory card (with assumed data) for the first item on the inventory listing sheet in Figure 5.7 is shown in Figure 5.8.

FIGURE 5.8
Perpetual inventory card

Table—Model 259

		Received			*Shipped*			*Balance*		
Date	*Ref.**	*Units*	*Unit Cost*	*Total*	*Units*	*Unit Cost*	*Total*	*Units*	*Unit Cost*	*Total*
2/7	P.I.104	500	$20.00	$10,000.00				500	$20.00	$10,000.00
3/2	S.I.207				200	$20.00	$4,000.00	300	20.00	6,000.00
6/3	S.I.418				200	20.00	4,000.00	100	20.00	2,000.00
7/18	P.I.228	300	20.00	6,000.00				400	20.00	8,000.00
8/1	S.I.527				300	20.00	6,000.00	100	20.00	2,000.00
11/2	S.I.741				50	20.00	1,000.00	50	20.00	1,000.00
11/17	C.M.201	9	20.00	180.00				59	20.00	1,180.00

* P.I. = Purchase Invoice; S.I. = Sales Invoice; C.M. = Credit Memorandum.

The amount shown for merchandise inventory in the statement of financial position is the amount shown in the ledger adjusted to the current physical count. Assuming this to be the case, the $52,457 balance shown in the Merchandise Inventory account, page 118, would appear in the statement of financial position.

The balance in the Cost of Goods Sold account of $1,200 would appear as an expense in the earnings statement.

Indicate whether each of the following statements is true or false with regard to why two entries are normally required to record a sale when perpetual inventoy records are maintained.

_______ 1. The two entries are normally used to provide management with additional information.

_______ 2. By using the two entries, it is possible to subtract the balance of the Merchandise Inventory account from the balance of the Sales account to determine the cost of goods sold for the period.

_______ 3. One entry is necessary to record the realization of sales revenue; the second is necessary in order to record the cost of the sale and to reduce the balance of the Merchandise Inventory account.

Now check your answers by turning to Answer Frame 7[5] on page 122.

Frame 8[5]

PREPARATION OF AN EARNINGS STATEMENT

To illustrate the preparation of an earnings statement when perpetual inventory procedure is used, assume that the transactions of the Marshall Sales Company, Inc. have been journalized and posted and are properly summarized in the trial balance in the work sheet in Figure 5.9.

The Merchandise Inventory balance in the pre-closing trial balance is the amount of the inventory on hand at the *end of the year*, December 31, 1975, and is extended to the Statement of Financial Position debit column. The Cost of Goods Sold balance, like all other expenses for the year, is extended to the debit Earnings Statement column. Net earnings are computed and entered in the work sheet in the customary manner.

The earnings statement is prepared from the work sheet and appears in Figure 5.10.

The closing entries for the Marshall Sales Company, Inc. are as follows:

Sales	250,000	
Sales Returns and Allowances		3,500
Sales Discounts		4,500
Expense and Revenue Summary		242,000
To close net sales revenue to Expense and Revenue Summary.		

Expense and Revenue Summary	231,000	
Cost of Goods Sold		155,000
Sales Salaries		37,000
Rent Expense		19,000
Advertising Expense		5,000
Delivery Expense		3,000
Administrative Expenses		12,000
To close the expense accounts to Expense and Revenue Summary.		

Expense and Revenue Summary	11,000	
Retained Earnings		11,000
To close the Expense and Revenue Summary account to Retained Earnings.		

FIGURE 5.9
Work sheet under perpetual inventory procedure

MARSHALL SALES COMPANY, INC.
Work Sheet for the Year Ended December 31, 1975

Account Name	Trial Balance		Earnings Statement		Statement of Financial Position	
	Dr.	Cr.	Dr.	Cr.	Dr.	Cr.
Sundry assets*	200,000				200,000	
Merchandise inventory	46,000				46,000	
Sundry liabilities*		90,000				90,000
Capital stock		125,000				125,000
Retained earnings		20,000				20,000
Sales		250,000		250,000		
Sales returns and allowances	3,500		3,500			
Sales discounts	4,500		4,500			
Cost of goods sold	155,000		155,000			
Sales salaries	37,000		37,000			
Rent expense	19,000		19,000			
Advertising expense	5,000		5,000			
Delivery expense	3,000		3,000			
Administrative expense	12,000		12,000			
	485,000	485,000	239,000	250,000	246,000	235,000
Net earnings for the year			11,000			11,000
			250,000	250,000	246,000	246,000

* Sundry means that several items are combined into this category.

FIGURE 5.10
Earnings statement under perpetual inventory procedure

MARSHALL SALES COMPANY, INC.
Earnings Statement
For the Year Ended December 31, 1975

Sales				$250,000
Less: Sales returns and allowances			$3,500	
Sales discounts			4,500	8,000
Net sales				$242,000
Less: Cost of goods sold				155,000
Gross margin				$ 87,000
Deduct: Operating expenses				
Selling expenses				
Sales salaries	$37,000			
Rent	19,000			
Advertising	5,000			
Delivery	3,000			
Total Selling Expenses		$64,000		
Administrative expenses		12,000		
Total Operating Expenses				76,000
Net Earnings for the Year				$ 11,000

Answer frame 7^5

1. False. Management information is provided, but this is not the reason two entries are necessary under perpetual procedure.
2. False. The Merchandise Inventory account is kept at the *cost* price. The Sales account is kept at the *selling* price. There is no relationship here to cost of goods sold. Rather, cost of goods sold is simply the balance in that account.
3. True. In the next frame you will see how these accounts are treated in the earnings statement.

If you answered any of the above incorrectly, reread Frame 7^5 before going on to Frame 8^5 on page 120.

Frame 8^5 continued

Now let's test your understanding. When customer X returns a chair sold to her for $100 and receives cash in return, which of the following properly describes the effect on an earnings statement to be prepared for that period. Place a check by the correct answer.

_____ 1. Net sales and cost of goods sold both decrease. Net earnings decrease.

_____ 2. Net sales and cost of goods sold do not change. An adjustment is made to net earnings to reduce it by $100.

_____ 3. Cost of goods sold decreases and net sales increases. Net earnings increase.

_____ 4. Net sales decreases and cost of goods sold remains the same. Net earnings decrease.

_____ 5. Cost of goods sold increases and net sales decreases. Net earnings decrease.

Check your response in Answer Frame 8^5 on page 124.

SUMMARY

This chapter discusses the accounting procedures which exist to help control inventories and which are used by a company which earns its revenues through a process of buying merchandise and selling it to its customers.

When sales of merchandise are made, the revenue is recorded by crediting (increasing) the Sales account. Returns and allowances and discounts are recorded by debiting (increasing) Sales Returns and Allowances and Sales Discounts accounts, which are negative, or contra, revenue accounts and which normally have debit balances. The amounts of such items are recorded in separate accounts so as not to obscure potentially useful information.

One of the two commonly employed procedures for accounting for merchandise is perpetual inventory procedure. Under this procedure the Merchandise Inventory account is kept perpetually up to date by recording in it all of the transactions which affect merchandise.

The chapter illustrates the typical entries made and the accounts employed in accounting for merchandise purchased and sold under perpetual inventory procedure.

The perpetual inventory account, Merchandise Inventory, is debited to record the increases in the asset because of purchase costs and transportation-in costs. It is credited to record the decreases in the asset brought about by purchase returns and allowances, purchase discounts, and the sale of goods to customers. The balance in the account at any date is the cost of the inventory which should be on hand.

Use of the perpetual inventory procedure requires two journal entries for each sale, one at selling price and one at cost. Two entries also are required in order to record sales returns. A sales allowance requires only that an entry be made at selling price. Identifying the cost of each sale made and adjusting the inventory records accordingly is too burdensome a process for some situations; hence, the companies in these situations do not use perpetual inventory procedure and do not accumulate the cost of goods sold in a Cost of Goods Sold account during the year. Instead they use periodic inventory procedure and compute the cost of goods sold after a physical inventory has been taken, as will be described in the next chapter.

Trade and cash discounts are often granted in business. Trade discounts are given to adapt one price list to various customers often on the basis of quantity purchased. Trade discounts may run as high as 40 to 50 percent. Cash discounts are given to induce prompt payment by customers. Cash discounts are usually only 1 to 3 percent of the gross invoice price.

Now turn to the Glossary which follows and study the new terms introduced in this chapter. Then work the Student Review Quiz on page 124 for a self-administered test of your comprehension of the material in the chapter.

GLOSSARY

Cash discount–often called a purchase discount by a buyer and a sales discount by a seller. It is a deduction allowed from the gross price of an invoice which can be taken only if the account is paid within a specified period of time. These discounts often range from 1 to 3 percent of the invoice price.

Cost of goods sold–an expense consisting of the cost to the seller of merchandise sold to customers.

Credit memorandum–a business document used by a seller to inform a customer that his Accounts Receivable account on the seller's books is being credited (reduced) for reasons such as errors, returns, or allowances granted; when prepared by the buyer it informs seller that his Accounts Payable account on the buyer's books is being credited (increased), usually in order to correct an error.

Debit memorandum–a business document used by a seller to inform a customer that his Accounts Receivable account on the seller's books is being debited (increased) for some reason, usually a correction of an error; when prepared by a buyer it informs the seller that his Accounts Payable account on the buyer's books is being debited (reduced) for some reason, such as damaged merchandise.

Inventory listing sheet–a form used in taking the physical inventory.

Merchandise inventory–the quantity of goods on hand and available for sale at any time.

Perpetual inventory procedure–an approach to the accounting for merchandise acquired for sale to customers wherein the cost of such merchandise sold and the amount of such merchandise on hand can be determined at any time by reference to the Cost of Goods Sold and Merchandise Inventory accounts.

Purchase invoice–a document prepared by the seller of merchandise and sent to the buyer containing the details of a sale of merchandise such as the number of units sold, the unit price, the total billed price, terms, and manner of shipment. From the buyer's point of view, the document is a purchase invoice; from the seller's point of view, a sales invoice.

Purchase order–a form prepared by a potential buyer ordering merchandise and sent to a potential seller.

Sales account–a revenue account in which is recorded the retail price charged customers for merchandise sold to them; any balance in the account will be a credit balance.

Sales allowances–deductions from the originally agreed-upon sales price for merchandise sold granted by the seller to the buyer because the merchandise was not fully satisfactory to the buyer.

Sales discount–a reduction in the amount due from a buyer granted by the seller for prompt payment by the buyer.

Sales Discounts account–an account used to record the amount of sales discounts granted to customers; a contra to the Sales account and, therefore, normally a debit balance account.

Answer frame 8[5]

The first answer is the correct answer. The return of the chair means a reduction of net sales and of cost of goods sold. Net earnings will decrease by the amount the selling price exceeds the cost of the chair.

If you answered incorrectly, review Frame 8[5] before beginning the Summary on page 122.

GLOSSARY continued

Sales invoice–see purchase invoice above.

Sales returns–from the seller's point of view, merchandise returned by a buyer; from the buyer's point of view, the return is a purchase return.

Sales Returns and Allowances account–a contra (negative) revenue account used to record the retail price of sales returns and the reductions from retail price granted by a seller; represents a reduction in recorded sales revenue and, therefore, is a debit balance account.

Trade discount–a deduction from the list price of an article; a means for determining the gross invoice price of an item to be purchased in a given quantity by a particular category of customer (e.g., retailers and wholesalers).

STUDENT REVIEW QUIZ

1. Given a list price of \$1,000 and a series of trade discounts of 25 percent, 20 percent, and 10 percent and terms of 2/10, n/30, the gross invoice price of this merchandise sale is which of the following?
   a. \$1,000 × (0.75 × 0.80 × 0.90) = \$540.
   b. \$540 × 0.98 = \$529.20.
   c. \$1,000 × 0.98 = \$980.
   d. \$1,000 × (0.25 + 0.10) = \$550.
   e. \$500 × 0.98 = \$490.
2. Based on the data given in (1), prepare the entry which should be made on the buyer's books at the time of the payment of the invoice if paid within the discount period.
3. Assume a situation in which merchandise having a stated list price is sold under terms of a 30 percent trade discount, a 5 percent quantity discount, and a 2 percent cash discount if paid in 10 days. Also assume that the buyer paid the transportation charges. The cash discount should be computed as 2 percent of—
   a. List price.
   b. List price less trade discount.
   c. List price less trade and quantity discounts.
   d. None of the above.
4. A firm receives an invoice in the amount of \$5,000 with terms of 3/10, n/30. It can borrow funds at a 6 percent rate of interest. Compute the annual rate of interest paid if the company pays on the 30th day. Also compute the dollar amount saved if funds are borrowed to pay the invoice and the loan is repaid 20 days later. What is the approximate annual interest rate applied in the cash discount terms if the company paid on the 30th day?
5. Rae's Dress Shop received from Lorraine, Inc. merchandise having an invoice price of \$4,000; terms, 1/15, n/60; and also paid \$20 shipping charges to Speedy Delivery Company. If payment of the Lorraine, Inc. invoice is made within the discount period, the amount of the check should be—
   a. \$4,000 – (\$4,000 × 0.01) = \$3,960.
   b. \$4,000 – \$20 – (\$4,000 × 0.01) = \$3,940.
   c. \$4,000 – \$20 – (\$3,980 × 0.01) = \$3,940.20.
   d. \$4,000 – (\$3,980 × 0.01) = \$3,960.20.
   e. \$4,000 + \$20 – (\$4,020 × 0.01) = \$3,979.80.
6. Which of the following statements is *not* correct? Trade discounts are used—
   a. To encourage prompt payment of an invoice.
   b. To facilitate charging different prices to different types of customers.
   c. To induce purchases in large quantities.
   d. To facilitate the use of the same catalog for a long period of time.

7. The amount of sales discounts is treated in an earnings statement as—
   a. An asset.
   b. An offset to or a reduction of an expense.
   c. Revenue.
   d. An offset to or a reduction of revenue.
   e. A liability.

8. On June 21 the Dorset Company purchased merchandise; upon the delivery of the goods incurred and paid the freight bill of $50. Which of the following entries correctly records the payment of this bill under perpetual procedure?

a.	Transportation-In	50	
	Cash		50
b.	Accounts Payable	50	
	Cash		50
c.	Merchandise Inventory	50	
	Cash		50
d.	Merchandise Inventory	50	
	Accounts Payable		50

9. On September 15 the entry made to record an invoice dated on that date was:

Merchandise Inventory	1,200	
Accounts Payable		1,200
To record purchase of merchandise; terms, 3/10, n/30.		

Which of the following entries would be the correct one if the invoice were paid on September 25? On September 26?

a.	Accounts Payable	1,164	
	Merchandise Inventory	36	
	Cash		1,200
b.	Accounts Payable	1,200	
	Cash		1,200
c.	Accounts Payable	1,200	
	Cash		1,164
	Merchandise Inventory		36
d.	Accounts Payable	1,164	
	Cash		1,164

10. JMC, Inc. buys goods from the MSU Company. When they arrive, some are discovered to be damaged. Which is the correct entry (entries) on MSU's books if an allowance of $50 is granted? If goods with a selling price of $50 are returned? Assume that the goods cost MSU $35.

a.	Accounts Payable	50	
	Merchandise Inventory		50
b.	Sales Returns and Allowances	50	
	Accounts Receivable		50
c.	Sales Returns and Allowances	50	
	Accounts Receivable		50
	Merchandise Inventory	35	
	Cost of Goods Sold		35
d.	Sales Returns and Allowances	35	
	Accounts Receivable		35
	Merchandise Inventory	50	
	Cost of Goods Sold		50
e.	Sales	50	
	Cost of Goods Sold		50

Now compare your answers with the correct answers and explanations given on page 208.

chapter 6

PERIODIC INVENTORY PROCEDURE

LEARNING OBJECTIVES

Study of the material in this chapter is designed to provide knowledge of—

1. The operating characteristics and advantages and disadvantages of periodic inventory procedure as a means of accounting for merchandise inventories and the cost of merchandise sold.
2. The adjusting entries needed to establish the amount in the expense account Cost of Goods sold under the periodic procedure.
3. The work sheet used as an aid in preparing financial statements under periodic procedure.
4. The earnings statement usually prepared for a merchandising firm using periodic procedure, with its basic classifications of operating and nonoperating revenues, operating and nonoperating expenses; criteria for distinguishing between these classifications and examples of each.
5. An alternative method of accounting for purchase discounts.

Frame 1[6]

Some businessmen may believe that the detailed record keeping required throughout the period under perpetual inventory procedure is not desirable for certain (or all) of the merchandise they handle. Each time merchandise is sold, under perpetual procedure, an entry is necessary debiting the Cost of Goods Sold expense account and crediting the Merchandise Inventory account (as well as debiting Accounts Receivable or Cash and crediting Sales). The quantity records must also be adjusted to show the decrease in the number of units on hand, so that the Merchandise Inventory account is maintained at its proper balance throughout the period and the quantity records at all times show the number of units which should be on hand. For companies selling expensive items such as jewelry, furs, and automobiles, the close control possible under perpetual inventory procedure is desirable. The extra costs of record keeping do not outweigh the benefits derived.

Companies dealing in merchandise that has a low value per unit such as nuts and bolts, Christmas cards, pencils, and similar items often believe that the extra costs of record keeping under perpetual procedure more than outweigh the benefits derived. Close control of such items is not as necessary nor is it economically wise. For these firms, periodic inventory procedure may be used. Under this procedure the Merchandise Inventory account is not maintained at its proper balance throughout the period; adjustment is made only at the end of the accounting period. Quantity records (in units) are usually not maintained under periodic procedure (although it is conceivable that they might be). The record keeping is reduced considerably, but so is the control over items. At the end of the period when the physical inventory is taken, there is no account balance against which the physical count may be checked. The balance in the Merchandise Inventory account does not show the cost of inventory which should be on hand at the end of the period.

The mechanics of the periodic inventory procedure are described below.

MECHANICS OF PERIODIC INVENTORY PROCEDURE

The Purchases account. When merchandise is purchased, an asset is acquired. Purchases of merchandise which is to be offered for sale to customers are recorded by debits to a Purchases account instead of debits to the Merchandise Inventory account. The Purchases account is increased by debits because it is really a subdivision of the debit side of the asset account, Merchandise Inventory. But it is usually listed with the earnings statement accounts in the chart of accounts because the balance in the account is closed at the end of every accounting period. By recording purchases in a separate account, management has knowledge of the cost of the merchandise purchased during the accounting period. Under perpetual inventory procedure this information is not readily available.

A purchase of merchandise on account and a purchase for cash by Top Quality Wholesale Stores would be recorded as follows:

Purchases	15,000	
Accounts Payable–Wholesaler A		15,000
To record purchase of merchandise on account.		

Purchases	10,000	
Cash		10,000
To record purchase of merchandise for cash.		

All purchases of merchandise are posted to the Purchases account which appears–with a debit balance–in both the ledger and the trial balance.

Concerning the two transactions above, which of the following properly describes the effect on total assets? Place a check by the correct answer.

______ 1. The first transaction causes total assets to increase, and the second transaction causes no change in total assets.

______ 2. Total assets would decrease in both cases since other assets are used to pay for the merchandise.

______ 3. Neither of the transactions would cause any change in total assets.

______ 4. Total assets would increase in both cases since merchandise inventory is accumulated.

Check your response in Answer Frame 1[6] on page 128.

Frame 2[6]

Transportation-In. When a buyer must incur the cost of delivering goods to him, under periodic inventory procedure he debits the Transportation-In account instead of the Merchandise Inventory account. This account is debited because the amount represents an addition to the cost of the merchandise as shown in the Purchases account; traditionally, transportation-inward costs are recorded in a separate ledger account, not in the Purchases account. The reason for this is that management can thus have available information on the transportation-inward costs incurred during the accounting period. The Transportation-In account appears in the ledger and in the trial balance adjacent to the Purchases account. It, also, is a special subdivision of the debit side of the Merchandise Inventory account. It is not to be confused with the Transportation-Out expense account. This latter account is for the recording of freight on merchandise sold

Answer frame 1[6]

The first answer is correct. The cash transaction causes no change in total assets. One asset, cash, is simply exchanged for another asset, merchandise. In the accounts payable transaction, total assets would increase, and this increase would be matched by an increase in the liability, accounts payable.

If you answered incorrectly, reread Frame 1[6] before going on to Frame 2[6] on page 127.

Frame 2[6] continued

rather than on merchandise purchased. It is a selling expense rather than part of the cost of merchandise purchased.

If a liability for inward transportation cost is incurred, the entry is:

Transportation-In	400	
Accounts Payable—R & D Railroad		400
To record freight bills on merchandise purchased.		

Is each of the following statements concerning transportation-in true or false?

______ 1. To record freight costs and purchases, the Transportation-In and Purchases accounts are debited under periodic procedure.

______ 2. The Transportation-In account is a selling expense.

______ 3. The Transportation-In account could be eliminated if the transportation costs were debited to Purchases.

______ 4. If perpetual procedure were being used, the amounts appearing in the Purchases and Transportation-In accounts would appear in the Merchandise Inventory account.

Check your responses in Answer Frame 2[6] on page 130.

Frame 3[6]

Ending merchandise inventory. The periodic ending inventory does *not* appear in the unadjusted trial balance because as merchandise is purchased during an accounting period, its cost is debited to the Purchases account. As sales are made during a period, the Sales account is credited. *No* entry is made debiting the Cost of Goods Sold account and crediting the Merchandise Inventory account when merchandise is sold as is done under perpetual procedure. When the ending inventory is determined by counting and costing the merchandise on hand at the end of the period, it will be recognized in the accounts at that time by a method to be illustrated later. The ending inventory of one period is the beginning inventory of the succeeding period. Thus, the account representing the inventory at the beginning of a period will appear as a debit in the trial balance taken at the end of that period. During the period, the Merchandise Inventory account remains untouched and, therefore, continues to show only the cost of the beginning inventory in the account throughout the entire period.

When periodic inventory procedure is used as described above, the Purchases account is debited when merchandise is purchased rather than debiting the Merchandise Inventory account. Indicate (by writing true or false) whether each of the following statements correctly or incorrectly explains the reason for this.

______ 1. The cost of goods sold could not be calculated subsequently if the Merchandise Inventory account were debited at the time of purchase.

_______ 2. There is no attempt to maintain the correct amount of merchandise inventory in the Merchandise Inventory account during the period. Therefore, purchases can be debited to the Purchases account and management will have a segregated amount in that account representing merchandise acquisitions made in the current period.

_______ 3. The use of a separate Purchases account helps in maintaining the correct amount of inventory in the Merchandise Inventory account throughout the accounting period.

Check your responses in Answer Frame 3[6] on page 130.

Frame 4[6]

The Cost of Goods Sold account. When periodic inventory procedure is used, the cost of goods sold is computed at the end of the period. The amount computed is recorded by making adjusting entries which involve the Cost of Goods Sold expense account. Before entries are made in the Cost of Goods Sold expense account, the data for the cost of goods available for sale are recorded in three accounts: Merchandise Inventory, Purchases, and Transportation-In. When the balances of these accounts are transferred to the Cost of Goods Sold expense account, the resulting balance therein is the cost of goods which were available for sale during the period. In order to reduce this to the amount of the cost of goods sold, the cost of the ending inventory is removed and transferred to the asset account, Merchandise Inventory. By this series of entries the ending inventory and the cost of goods sold are shown as balances in the accounts in the ledger.

To illustrate the entries to be posted to the Cost of Goods Sold account, assume the following account debit balances at the end of the current year:

Merchandise inventory (beginning of period)	$15,000
Purchases	27,000
Transportation-in	400

The cost of the goods which were available for sale during the period is first transferred to the Cost of Goods Sold account by means of the following two entries:

Cost of Goods Sold	15,000	
Merchandise Inventory		15,000
To transfer the beginning inventory to Cost of Goods Sold.		

Cost of Goods Sold	27,400	
Purchases		27,000
Transportation-In		400
To transfer the net cost of purchases to Cost of Goods Sold.		

Thus, goods which cost $42,400 were available for sale during the period. This amount must be reduced by the cost of the ending inventory (the goods available but *not* sold) in order to arrive at the cost of the goods which were sold during the period.

If a physical count reveals that goods with a cost of $18,000 are on hand at the end of the period, the following entry must be made to record the ending inventory and to reduce the balance in the Cost of Goods Sold account to the proper amount:

Merchandise Inventory	18,000	
Cost of Goods Sold		18,000
To transfer the net cost of goods *not* sold to the Merchandise Inventory account.		

Thus, the cost of the goods sold during the period was $42,400 – $18,000, or $24,400.

It should be noted that establishment of the cost of goods sold sometimes is accomplished with one entry. In this entry the ending inventory is recorded, the accounts which reflect the cost of the goods available for sale (beginning inventory, net purchases, and transportation-in) are removed, and the balance is the cost of the goods sold.

Answer frame 2[6]

1. True. These accounts rather than Merchandise Inventory are used.
2. False. Transportation-out is a selling expense; Transportation-in is a cost of acquiring merchandise for sale.
3. True. The overall effect of keeping the two accounts is the same as debiting both purchases and transportation costs to the Purchases account. But certain information regarding inward freight costs would not be as readily available.
4. True. The invoice cost of the inventory is not only the dollar amount paid for the goods. Freight should also be included to arrive at the cost of the inventory. The Purchases and Transportation-In accounts would not appear if perpetual procedure were being used. The cost of merchandise and freight would be debited to the Merchandise Inventory account.

If you answered any of the above incorrectly, reread Frame 2[6] before going on to Frame 3[6] on page 128.

Answer frame 3[6]

1. False. If the Merchandise Inventory account were debited directly, the cost of goods sold would be determined simply by subtracting the ending inventory figure from the last balance in the Merchandise Inventory account. This, however, would be an improper handling of the situation in accounting for inventories under periodic procedure.
2. True. If the transactions were all put into the Merchandise Inventory account, it would be difficult for management to sort out the information needed. For example: How much was purchased during this period? How much was returned?
3. False. First of all, it is under perpetual procedure that the correct amount of inventory on hand is maintained in the accounts during the period. Second, when the correct amount of inventory is to be maintained in the accounts, all elements of the cost of merchandise are debited to the Merchandise Inventory account.

If you answered any of the above incorrectly, reread Frame 3[6] before going on to Frame 4[6] on page 129.

Frame 4[6] continued

If such an entry were used in the above example, it would appear as follows:

Merchandise Inventory	18,000	
Cost of Goods Sold	24,400	
Purchases		27,000
Transportation-In		400
Merchandise Inventory		15,000
To establish the ending inventory, remove goods available for sale, and record cost of goods sold.		

The Cost of Goods Sold account is eventually closed to the Expense and Revenue Summary account along with the other expense accounts. The entry to accomplish this is as follows:

Expense and Revenue Summary	24,400	
Cost of Goods Sold		24,400
To close the Cost of Goods Sold account to Expense and Revenue Summary account.		

After posting the above entries, which of the following amounts correctly states the balance in the Cost of Goods Sold account? Place a check by the correct answer.

______ 1. $0.

______ 2. $3,000.

______ 3. $18,000.

______ 4. $24,400.

Check your response in Answer Frame 4[6] on page 132.

Frame 5[6]

A traditional form of disclosing the sales revenue, cost of goods sold, and expenses (summarized) for a merchandising concern in its earnings statement is shown in Figure 6.1.

The ending inventory amount of $18,000 in this illustration will appear as the beginning inventory for the next period.

FIGURE 6.1
Earnings statement under periodic inventory procedure

TOP QUALITY WHOLESALE STORES COMPANY
Earnings Statement for the Year Ended December 31, 1975

Gross sales			$40,100
Less: Sales returns and allowances		$ 750	
Sales discounts		702	1,452
Net sales			$38,648
Cost of goods sold:			
Inventory, January 1, 1975		$15,000	
Purchases	$27,000		
Add: Transportation-in	400		
Net cost of purchases		27,400	
Cost of goods available for sale		$42,400	
Deduct: Inventory, December 31, 1975		18,000	
Cost of goods sold			24,400
Gross margin			$14,248
Deduct: Expenses*			7,000
Net Earnings for the Year			$ 7,248

* In a more detailed earnings statement the expenses would be classified as selling and administrative, or at least detailed.

Which of the following statements explains why the 1975 ending inventory is the 1976 beginning inventory and will appear in the Merchandise Inventory account at the end of 1976 (before adjusting and closing entries are prepared)? Place a check by the correct answer.

_______ 1. It will be set up in the accounts at that time as part of the entries made to determine the cost of goods sold for the period.

_______ 2. It represents the cost of goods on hand at the end of this period which is carried into the next accounting period. All costs of acquiring merchandise during that next period will be charged to the Purchases and Transportation-In accounts.

Check your response in Answer Frame 5[6] on page 132.

Frame 6[6]

Purchase returns and allowances. Merchandise purchased and later returned to the supplier is a purchase return. Purchase allowances are reductions from the original price granted the purchaser by the seller when no merchandise is returned. Typical reasons for purchase allowances include improper quality and damage in transit.

Purchase returns and allowances may be grouped into one account and deducted from purchases to arrive at the net cost of merchandise purchased. Because they are deductions from purchases, that is, because they reduce the cost of the merchandise acquired, purchase returns and allowances are recorded as credits. The account credited is called Purchase Returns and

Answer frame 4[6]

The first answer is the correct answer. The account looks like this (all data except dollar amounts are assumed):

Cost of Goods Sold — *Account No. 418*

Date		Explanation	Folio	Debit	Credit	Balance
1975						
Dec.	31		J 22	15,000		15,000
	31		J 22	27,400		42,400
	31		J 23		18,000	24,400
	31		J 23		24,400	-0-

If you answered incorrectly, reread Frame 4[6] before going on to Frame 5[6] on page 131.

Answer frame 5[6]

The second statement is correct. The ending inventory of one period is the beginning inventory in the next period. Under *periodic* procedure of inventory accounting, the cost of merchandise purchased during the period is recorded in the Purchases and Transportation-in accounts, not the Merchandise Inventory account. Therefore, the balance in the inventory account will remain unchanged until the cost of goods sold for the period is determined.

If you answered incorrectly, reread Frame 5[6] before going on to Frame 6[6] on page 131.

Frame 6[6] continued

Allowances; it appears in the ledger and the trial balance.

To illustrate, assume that a purchaser returns $490 of goods to a seller and also requests and is granted a $110 price reduction due to a minor blemish in certain of the items purchased and not returned.

Which of the following entries correctly records this situation on the books of the purchaser under periodic inventory procedure? Place a check by the correct answer.

_______ 1. Purchase Returns and Allowances 600
  Purchases 600
 Returned merchandise, $490; price adjustment, $110.

_______ 2. Accounts Payable—Wholesaler A 600
  Purchase Returns and Allowances 600
 Returned merchandise, $490; price adjustment, $110.

_______ 3. Accounts Payable—Wholesaler A 380
  Purchase Returns and Allowances 380
 Returned merchandise, $490; price adjustment, $110.

_______ 4. Accounts Payable—Wholesaler A 490
  Purchase Returns and Allowances 110
 Returned merchandise, $490; price adjustment, $110.

Check your response in Answer Frame 6[6] on page 134.

Frame 7[6]

Purchase discounts. As mentioned in Chapter 5, merchandise is often purchased under terms which permit the buyer to deduct a stated discount if the invoice is paid within a specified period of time. The traditional way of handling these credit purchase transactions is to debit the Purchases account for the gross invoice price upon the receipt of the goods and later when the invoice is paid to credit the Purchase Discounts account for discounts taken. Purchase discounts are considered reductions of the cost of purchases, and the account is a contra account to the Purchases account. A contra account shows a separately classified offset or reduction of another account. The balance in a contra account is deducted directly from the balance in the account to which it is contra in one of the formal accounting statements, such as the earnings statement. Occasionally, however, purchase discounts are treated as an element of miscellaneous revenue—a treatment which can be justified only as an expedient. Revenue is not generated by the buying of merchandise. The following illustrates the correct accounting treatment:

1975			
Aug. 15	Purchases	2,000	
	Accounts Payable— Baxter Company		2,000
	To record invoice; terms, 2/10, n/30.		
25	Accounts Payable— Baxter Company	2,000	
	Cash		1,960
	Purchase Discounts		40
	To record payment within the discount period.		

If an earnings statement were prepared at this point, the Purchases account and its contra account would be shown as follows:

Purchases	$2,000	
Less: Purchase discounts	40	$1,960

Suppose that the above merchandise were partially damaged. The purchaser, prior to paying for the goods, called the Baxter Company and obtained a purchase allowance of $50.

Which of the following correctly gives the amount he would pay the Baxter Company in settling his account within the discount period? Place a check by the correct answer.

_____ 1. $1,950.

_____ 2. $1,911.

_____ 3. $1,910.

Check your response in Answer Frame 7[6] on page 134.

Frame 8[6]

Under either perpetual or periodic procedure an alternative method can be used for purchase discounts. The alternative method involves the use of a Discounts Lost account. The original recording of the purchase is made at *net invoice price.* Assuming goods with a *gross* invoice price of $1,000 are purchased under terms of 2/10, n/30, the transaction would be recorded as follows:

July 10	Purchases (or Merchandise Inventory if perpetual procedure)	980	
	Accounts Payable		980
	To record the purchase of merchandise for $1,000; terms, 2/10, n/30.		

If the discount is taken, the entry is a debit to Accounts Payable and a credit to Cash for $980.

Answer frame 6[6]

Entry No. 2 is correct. Two things happened in this transaction: (1) $490 worth of merchandise was returned to Wholesaler A and (2) a $110 price concession was secured on the goods not returned. Each of these figures must be deducted from Wholesaler A's account payable and also eventually from the Purchases account balance as shown in the earnings statement.

If you answered incorrectly, reread Frame 6[6] before going on to Frame 7[6] on page 133.

Answer frame 7[6]

Response No. 2 is the correct response. The amount upon which the discount is based is no longer $2,000, but $1,950. The 2 percent discount amounts to $39. This gives the net amount due of $1,911.

If you answered incorrectly, reread Frame 7[6] before starting Frame 8[6] on page 133.

Frame 8[6] continued

If the discount is not taken, the entry is as follows:

July 25	Discounts Lost	20	
	Accounts Payable	980	
	Cash		1,000
	To record the payment for goods purchased. The discount period had expired.		

Some persons prefer this procedure because it focuses attention on the discounts missed rather than those taken. Discounts lost normally are classified among the "other expenses" in the earnings statement. Also, the recorded cost of the merchandise is its net invoice price whether the discount is taken or not. The first method discussed will be used in all of the questions and the Student Review Quiz in this chapter and in all other chapters except where otherwise indicated.

Cost of goods sold. The net cost of purchased merchandise can be determined by the balances of four accounts that appear in the ledger. This is expressed as the formula: Net Cost of Purchases = Purchases (a debit) + Transportation-In (a debit) − Purchase Returns and Allowances (a credit) − Purchase Discounts (a credit).

To expand the example begun in Frame 4[6], assume the following account balances:

Purchases	$27,000 Dr.
Transportation-in	400 Dr.
Purchase returns and allowances	600 Cr.
Purchase discounts	40 Cr.

The net cost of purchases, then, is $26,760: $27,000 + $400 − $600 − $40.

When net purchases are added to the beginning inventory figure, the cost of the goods which were available for sale during the period is obtained. The cost of goods sold can then be determined by subtracting the cost of the ending inventory from the cost of goods available for sale.

Since the company above had a beginning inventory of $15,000 and an ending inventory of $18,000 (Frame 4[6]), the cost of goods sold would be determined as shown in Figure 6.2.

Then, in expanded form, the equation for determining the cost of goods sold is: Beginning Inventory + (Purchases + Transportation-In − Purchase Returns and Allowances − Purchase Discounts) − Ending Inventory = Cost of Goods Sold.

The four items enclosed in parentheses equal the net cost of purchases, and this amount plus the cost of the beginning inventory equals the cost of goods available for sale. As noted earlier, this cost of goods available for sale is first computed and then separated into two parts at year-end, the cost of goods sold and the ending inventory.

FIGURE 6.2
Determination of cost of goods sold under periodic procedure

Beginning inventory			$15,000
Purchases		$27,000	
Add: Transportation-in		400	
Total		$27,400	
Less: Purchase returns and allowances	$600		
Purchase discounts	40	640	
Net cost of purchases			26,760
Cost of goods available for sale			$41,760
Less: Ending Inventory			18,000
Cost of goods sold			$23,760

Is each of the following true or false?

_______ 1. The dollar amount of the beginning inventory plus the net cost of goods purchased less the dollar amount of the inventory at the end of the period equals the cost of goods sold during the period.

_______ 2. The cost of goods sold figure during a period may be greater than the dollar amount of the beginning inventory plus the net cost of purchases.

_______ 3. The cost of goods sold during an accounting period is the amount of purchases plus transportation-in less purchase discounts and less purchase returns and allowances.

Check your responses in Answer Frame 8[6] on page 136.

Frame 9[6]

COMPLETE ILLUSTRATION FOR A MERCHANDISE CONCERN USING PERIODIC PROCEDURE

The steps in the accounting cycle treated up to this point are now summarized for a company that uses *periodic* inventory procedure to determine the cost of goods sold. The transactions of the Lyons Store, Inc. are presented for the month of January, 1975. The transactions are explained, journalized, and posted to the accounts; a work sheet (showing the adjusting entries) and statements are prepared; the accounts are then closed.

The complete cycle is presented to preserve continuity and is as follows:

THE TRANSACTIONS
(The Entries Are Recorded in Figure 6.3)

January 2, 1975:

The owners invested cash of $8,000 and $7,000 of merchandise inventory in exchange for $15,000 of capital stock in the corporation.

The Cash account is increased. The Inventory account is increased.

Stockholders' equity, represented by the Capital Stock account, is increased.

January 5, 1975:

Purchased merchandise, $3,000, on account from the Reliable Wholesale Company; terms, 2/10, n/30.

The merchandise available for sale is increased by a debit to the Purchases account.

The Accounts Payable–Reliable Wholesale Company account is increased.

Answer frame 8[6]

1. True. The calculation outlined would yield the cost of goods sold for the period. Since the operation of a periodic inventory system involves so many accounts in the determination of the cost of goods sold, a complete illustration of this method is presented in Frame 13[6].
2. False. The cost of goods sold cannot be larger than the sum of the beginning inventory and the net cost of purchases. If all the merchandise were sold, the two figures would be equal. But in most cases, there is an inventory at the close of the accounting period. The cost of goods sold figure, therefore, will be smaller than the net cost of purchases plus beginning inventory.
3. False. *The net cost of purchases* during an accounting period *is* the amount described in this answer. It is equal to the cost of goods sold only in the unlikely event that there is no beginning or ending inventory.

If you answered any of the above incorrectly reread Frame 8[6] before going on to Frame 9[6] on page 135.

Frame 9[6] continued

January 6, 1975:

Purchased merchandise, $1,200, from the Moonbrook Company; paid $700 cash, the remaining $500 being due in 10 days, net.

The Purchases account is increased. The Cash account is decreased. The Accounts Payable–Moonbrook Company account is increased.

January 7, 1975: (Journalize this transaction on page 138.)

Returned $100 of merchandise to the Moonbrook Company because it was damaged.

Accounts Payable–Moonbrook Company is decreased. The Purchase Returns and Allowances account is increased.

January 9, 1975:

Sold merchandise for cash, $3,200.

The Cash account is increased. The Sales account is increased.

January 11, 1975:

Sold merchandise on account to the T. James Company, $2,200; terms, 2/10, n/30.

The Accounts Receivable–T. James Company account is increased. The sales account is increased.

January 14, 1975: (Journalize this transaction.)

Lyons Store, Inc. paid the Reliable Wholesale Company for the merchandise purchased January 5 and took the purchase discount of $60.

Accounts Payable–Reliable Wholesale Company is decreased. The Cash account is decreased, and the Purchase Discounts account is increased $60.

January 15, 1975:

Paid salesclerks' salaries, $300.

The Sales Salaries account (an expense) is increased. The Cash account is decreased.

January 16, 1975:

Paid the balance due the Moonbrook Company.

Accounts Payable–Moonbrook Company is decreased. The Cash account is decreased.

January 18, 1975:

Purchased merchandise, $1,100, on account from the Reliable Wholesale Company; terms, 3/10, n/30.

The Purchases account is increased. The Accounts Payable–Reliable Wholesale Company account is increased.

January 19, 1975:

Sold merchandise on account to the Baker Company, $1,900; terms, n/30.

The account, Accounts Receivable–Baker Company, is increased. The Sales account is increased.

January 20, 1975:

Received a check from the T. James Company for the sale of January 11. The T. James Company took the proper discount.

The Cash account is increased. The Sales Discounts account is increased. The Accounts Receivable–T. James Company account is decreased.

January 22, 1975:

Purchased merchandise, $700, on account from the Moonbrook Company; terms, 2/10, n/30.

The Purchases account is increased. The Accounts Payable–Moonbrook Company account is increased.

January 24, 1975: (Journalize this transaction.)

The Baker Company returned $20 of merchandise sold to it on January 19, 1975.

The Sales Returns and Allowances account is increased. The Accounts Receivable–Baker Company account is decreased.

January 27, 1975:

Paid the Reliable Wholesale Company for the purchase of January 18 and deducted the proper discount.

The Accounts Payable–Reliable Wholesale Company account is decreased. The Cash account is decreased. The Purchase Discounts account is increased.

January 28, 1975: (Journalize this transaction.)

Paid for transportation-in, $75.

The Transportation-In account is increased. The Cash account is decreased.

January 29, 1975:

Cash sales, $6,300.

The Cash account is increased. The Sales account is increased.

January 31, 1975:

Paid salesclerks' salaries, $350.

The Sales Salaries account is increased. The Cash account is decreased.

January 31, 1975:

Lyons Store, Inc. paid rent for January, $150 cash.

The Rent Expense account is increased, since the asset purchased has already expired. The Cash account is decreased.

The entries for these transactions are given in Figure 6.3. Supply any missing data by referring back to the transactions.

FIGURE 6.3

LYONS STORE, INC.
GENERAL JOURNAL

Page 1

Date		Account and Explanation	L.F.	Debit	Credit
1975					
Jan.	2	Cash	1	8,000	
		Merchandise Inventory	4	7,000	
		Capital Stock			15,000
		Owners' investment, consisting of $8,000 cash and $7,000 inventory.			
	5	Purchases	12	3,000	
		Accounts Payable—Reliable Wholesale Company	5		3,000
		Purchased merchandise on account; terms, 2/10, n/30.			
	6	Purchases	12	1,200	
		Cash	1		700
		Accounts Payable—Moonbrook Company	6		500
		Purchased merchandise, $700 for cash and $500 on account; terms, n/10.			
	7	______________________	6	———	
		______________________	13		———
		Returned damaged merchandise.			
	9	Cash	1	3,200	
		Sales	9		3,200
		Sold merchandise for cash.			
	11	Accounts Receivable—T. James Company	2	2,200	
		Sales	9		2,200
		Sold merchandise on account; terms, 2/10, n/30.			
	14	______________________	5	———	
		______________________	1		———
		______________________	14		———
		Paid invoice of January 5, less the 2 percent discount.			
	15	Sales Salaries	16	300	
		Cash	1		300
		Paid salaries of salesclerks.			
	16	Accounts Payable—Moonbrook Company	6	400	
		Cash	1		400
		Paid the balance due ($500 less return of $100).			
	18	Purchases	12	1,100	
		Accounts Payable—Reliable Wholesale Company	5		1,100
		Merchandise purchased; terms 2/10, n/30.			
	19	Accounts Receivable—Baker Company	3	1,900	
		Sales	9		1,900
		Sold merchandise on account; terms, n/30.			
	20	Cash	1	2,156	
		Sales Discounts	11	44	
		Accounts Receivable—T. James Company	2		2,200
		Received check for sale of January 11, less discount of $44.			

FIGURE 6.3 (continued)

GENERAL JOURNAL (continued) *Page 2*

Date		*Account and Explanation*	*L.F.*	*Debit*	*Credit*
1975					
Jan.	22	Purchases	12	700	
		Accounts Payable—Moonbrook Company	6		700
		Merchandise purchased; terms 2/10, n/30.			
	24	______________	10	—	
		______________	3		—
		Merchandise sold to Baker Company, January 19, returned for credit.			
	27	Accounts Payable—Reliable Wholesale Company	5	1,100	
		Cash	1		1,078
		Purchase Discounts	14		22
		Paid the invoice of January 18, $1,100 less 2 percent.			
	28	______________	15	—	
		______________	1		—
		Transportation-in for January.			
	29	Cash	1	6,300	
		Sales	9		6,300
		Sold merchandise for cash.			
	31	Sales Salaries	16	350	
		Cash	1		350
		Paid salaries of salesclerks.			
	31	Rent Expense	17	150	
		Cash	1		150
		Paid rent for January, 1971.			

Check your responses with the correct ones in Answer Frame 9[6] on page 140.

Frame 10[6]

Ledger accounts. The general ledger accounts in Figure 6.4 show the results of posting the preceding journal entries. Explanations are omitted in most cases. Note that in the accounts receivable and accounts payable sections of the ledger the name of the customer or the creditor is placed after the title of Accounts Receivable. This is necessary in order to maintain a record with each customer and each creditor.

Answer frame 9^6

The correct answers to the missing journal entries in the accounting cycle illustration are:

Jan.	7	Accounts Payable–Moonbrook Company	100	
		Purchase Returns and Allowances		100
	14	Accounts Payable–Reliable Wholesale Company	3,000	
		Cash		2,940
		Purchase Discounts		60
	24	Sales Returns and Allowances	20	
		Accounts Receivable–Baker Company		20
	28	Transportation-In	75	
		Cash		75

Be sure you understand these answers before starting Frame 10^6 on page 139.

Frame 10^6 continued

Supply the required information by filling in the blank spaces provided. For the moment, disregard all entries carrying the folio reference J 3. They will be explained later.

FIGURE 6.4

LYONS STORE, INC.
GENERAL LEDGER

Cash — *Account No. 1*

Date		Explanation	Folio	Debit	Credit	Balance
1975						
Jan.	2		J 1	8,000		8,000
	6		J 1		700	7,300
	9		J 1	3,200		10,500
	14		J 1		____	____
	15		J 1		300	7,260
	16		J 1		400	6,860
	20		J 1	2,156		9,016
	27		J 2		1,078	7,938
	28		J 2		____	____
	29		J 2	6,300		14,163
	31		J 2		350	13,813
	31		J 2		150	13,663

Accounts Receivable—T. James Company — *Account No. 2*

Date		Explanation	Folio	Debit	Credit	Balance
1975						
Jan.	11		J 1	2,200		2,200
	20		J 1		2,200	–0–

Accounts Receivable—Baker Company — *Account No. 3*

Date		Explanation	Folio	Debit	Credit	Balance
1975						
Jan.	19		J 1	1,900		1,900
	24		J 2		20	1,880

FIGURE 6.4 (continued)

GENERAL LEDGER (continued)

Merchandise Inventory *Account No. 4*

Date		Explanation	Folio	Debit	Credit	Balance
1975						
Jan.	2		J 1	7,000		7,000
	31	Cost of goods sold	J 3		7,000	-0-
	31		J 3	8,000		8,000

Accounts Payable—Reliable Wholesale Company *Account No. 5*

Date		Explanation	Folio	Debit	Credit	Balance
1975						
Jan.	5		J 1		3,000	3,000
	14		J 1	———		———
	18		J 1		1,100	1,100
	27		J 2	1,100		-0-

Accounts Payable—Moonbrook Company *Account No. 6*

Date		Explanation	Folio	Debit	Credit	Balance
1975						
Jan.	6		J 1		500	500
	7		J 1	100		400
	16		J 1	400		-0-
	22		J 2		700	700

Capital Stock *Account No. 7*

Date		Explanation	Folio	Debit	Credit	Balance
1975						
Jan.	2		J 1	15,000		15,000

Retained Earnings *Account No. 8*

Date		Explanation	Folio	Debit	Credit	Balance
1975						
Jan.	31	Expense and Revenue Summary	J 3		7,843	7,843

Sales *Account No. 9*

Date		Explanation	Folio	Debit	Credit	Balance
1975						
Jan.	9		J 1		3,200	3,200
	11		J 1		2,200	5,400
	19		J 1		1,900	7,300
	29		J 2		6,300	13,600
	31	Expense and revenue summary	J 3	13,600		-0-

Sales Returns and Allowances *Account No. 10*

Date		Explanation	Folio	Debit	Credit	Balance
1975						
Jan.	24		J 2	20		20
	31	Expense and revenue summary	J 3		20	-0-

Sales Discounts *Account No. 11*

Date		Explanation	Folio	Debit	Credit	Balance
1975						
Jan.	20		J 1	44		44
	31	Expense and revenue summary	J 3		44	-0-

FIGURE 6.4 (continued)

GENERAL LEDGER (continued)

Purchases — *Account No. 12*

Date		Explanation	Folio	Debit	Credit	Balance
1975						
Jan.	5		J 1	—		—
	6		J 1	—		—
	18		J 1	—		—
	22		J 2	700		6,000
	31	Cost of goods sold	J 3		6,000	–0–

Purchase Returns and Allowances — *Account No. 13*

Date		Explanation	Folio	Debit	Credit	Balance
1975						
Jan.	7		J 1		100	100
	31	Cost of goods sold	J 3	100		–0–

Purchase Discounts — *Account No. 14*

Date		Explanation	Folio	Debit	Credit	Balance
1975						
Jan.	14		J 1		60	60
	27		J 2		22	82
	31	Cost of goods sold	J 3	82		–0–

Transportation-In — *Account No. 15*

Date		Explanation	Folio	Debit	Credit	Balance
1975						
Jan.	28		J 2	75		75
	31	Cost of goods sold	J 3		75	–0–

Sales Salaries — *Account No. 16*

Date		Explanation	Folio	Debit	Credit	Balance
1975						
Jan.	15		J 2	300		300
	31		J 2	350		650
	31	Expense and revenue summary	J 3		650	–0–

Rent-Expense — *Account No. 17*

Date		Explanation	Folio	Debit	Credit	Balance
1975						
Jan.	31		J 2	150		150
	31	Expense and revenue summary	J 3		150	–0–

Cost of Goods Sold — *Account No. 18*

Date		Explanation	Folio	Debit	Credit	Balance
1975						
Jan.	31	Net purchases and January 1 inventory	J 3	12,893		12,893
	31	Inventory January 31	J 3		8,000	4,893
	31	Expense and revenue summary	J 3		4,893	–0–

FIGURE 6.4 (continued)

GENERAL LEDGER (continued)

Expense and Revenue Summary *Account No. 19*

Date		Explanation	Folio	Debit	Credit	Balance
1975						
Jan.	31	Cost of goods sold	J 3	4,893		(4,893)
	31	Net sales	J 3		13,536	8,643
	31	Operating expenses	J 3	800		7,843
	31	Net earnings to retained earnings	J 3	7,843		-0-

Now check your answers in Answer Frame 10[6] on page 144.

Frame 11[6]

The work sheet. The accounts comprising the trial balance are listed on the work sheet from the ledger accounts before adjusting and closing entries are journalized and posted in order to facilitate the preparation of financial statements. A pair of columns is provided for the adjusting entries needed to establish the cost of goods sold, another pair is for the earnings statement items, and the last pair of columns is for the statement of financial position items. Each of the debits and credits in the trial balance, plus or minus any debits or credits in the Adjustments columns, is carried into the debit or credit column of the appropriate statement columns.

The Adjustments columns are inserted between the trial balance and the financial statements columns since the data entered in the Adjustments modify the trial balance data prior to their extension into the statement columns. Thus, the balances in the Merchandise Inventory account (representing the beginning inventory), the Purchases account, and all of the purchase-related accounts (such as Transportation-In, Purchase Discounts, and Purchase Returns and Allowances) are transferred to the Cost of Goods Sold account. The entry made consists of debits to Cost of Goods Sold, Purchase Discounts, and Purchase Returns and Allowances and credits to Merchandise Inventory, Purchases, and Transportation-In. The ending inventory is established by debiting Merchandise Inventory and crediting Cost of Goods Sold. All of these debits and credits should appear in the Adjustments columns of the work sheet. Either a series of simple entries can be made transferring the various items making up cost of goods sold to the Cost of Goods Sold account individually or one compound entry can be made.

All revenue accounts in the work sheet are carried to the credit Earnings Statement column. All revenue contra accounts and all expense accounts, including the Cost of Goods Sold account, are carried to the debit Earnings Statement column.

The amount needed to balance the Earnings Statement columns is the net earnings or net loss amount for the period. It is carried to the appropriate Statement of Financial Position column to show the increase (credit) or decrease (debit) in the stockholders' equity. The work sheet is described in greater detail in Chapter 7.

Answer frame 10[6]

The correct answers to the accounting cycle illustration ledger postings are:

Cash		
Jan. 14	Credit $2,940	Balance $7,560
Jan. 28	Credit $75	Balance $7,863
Accounts Payable—Reliable Wholesale Company:		
Jan. 14	Debit $3,000	Balance -0-
Purchases:		
Jan. 5	Debit $3,000	Balance $3,000
Jan. 6	Debit $1,200	Balance $4,200
Jan. 18	Debit $1,100	Balance $5,300

Be sure you understand these answers before starting Frame 11[6] on page 143.

Frame 11[6] continued

Supply the missing trial balance figures and complete the work sheet in Figure 6.5. The entry to establish the ending merchandise inventory of $8,000 has already been entered in the work sheet.

FIGURE 6.5
Work sheet with periodic inventories

LYONS STORE, INC.
Work Sheet for the Month Ended January 31, 1975

Account No.	*Account Name*	*Trial Balance*		*Adjustments*		*Earnings Statement*		*Statement of Financial Position*	
		Dr.	*Cr.*	*Dr.*	*Cr.*	*Dr.*	*Cr.*	*Dr.*	*Cr.*
1	Cash	—							
3	Accounts receivable—Baker Co.	1,880							
4	Merchandise inventory—Jan. 1	7,000							
6	Accounts payable—Moonbrook Co.		—						
7	Capital stock		15,000						
9	Sales		13,600						
10	Sales returns and allowances	20							
11	Sales discounts	44							
12	Purchases	—							
13	Purchase returns and allowances		—						
14	Purchase discounts		82						
15	Transportation-in	—							
16	Sales salaries	650							
17	Rent expense	150							
		29,482	29,482						
	Cost of goods sold				8,000				
	Merchandise inventory, Jan. 31			8,000					
				21,075	21,075				
	Net earnings for January								
						13,600	13,600	23,543	23,543

Now check your solution with the completed work sheet in Answer Frame 11[6] on page 146.

Frame 12[6]

Entries at the end of the period. The period-end journal entries for Lyons Store, Inc. are shown in Figure 6.7; the ledger accounts are given in Figure 6.4, pages 140–43. The beginning inventory and the accounts comprising net purchases are transferred to the Cost of Goods Sold expense account. The ending inventory is debited to the Merchandise Inventory account and credited to the Cost of Goods Sold account. The Cost of Goods Sold and all other expense and revenue accounts are closed to the Expense and Revenue Summary account. The balance of the Expense and Revenue Summary account is closed to the Retained Earnings account.

The period-end journal entries are taken directly from the items in the Adjustments and Earnings Statement columns of the work sheet. Note that the journal entries in Figure 6.7 combine related items. You are to supply the missing information in Figure 6.7.

FIGURE 6.7

LYONS STORE, INC.
GENERAL JOURNAL

Page 3

Date		*Account and Explanation*	*L.F.*	*Debit*	*Credit*
1975					
Jan.	31	Cost of Goods Sold	18	——	
		Purchase Returns and Allowances	13	——	
		Purchase Discounts	14	——	
		Merchandise Inventory	4		——
		Purchases	12		——
		Transportation-In	15		——
		To transfer the beginning inventory and the accounts comprising net purchases to Cost of Goods Sold expense account.			
	31	Merchandise Inventory	4	8,000	
		Cost of Goods Sold	18		8,000
		To place the January 31 inventory in the asset account, and to credit Cost of Goods Sold with the cost of the goods not sold.			
	31	Expense and Revenue Summary	19	——	
		Cost of Goods Sold	18		——
		To close Cost of Goods Sold to Expense and Revenue Summary. (This could be closed with the other expense accounts.)			
	31	Sales	9	13,600	
		Sales Returns and Allowances	10		20
		Sales Discounts	11		44
		Expense and Revenue Summary	19		13,536
		To close accounts comprising net sales to Expense and Revenue Summary.			
	31	Expense and Revenue Summary	19	800	
		Sales Salaries	16		650
		Rent Expense	17		150
		To close store operating expenses to Expense and Revenue Summary.			
	31	Expense and Revenue Summary	19	7,843	
		Retained Earnings	8		7,843
		To close net earnings for January to Retained Earnings.			

Check your answers with the correct ones in Answer Frame 12[6] on page 148.

Answer frame 11[6]

Answers to the work sheet in the accounting cycle illustration are as follows:

LYONS STORE, INC.
Work Sheet for the Month Ended January 31, 1975

Ac-count No.	Account Name	Trial Balance Dr.	Trial Balance Cr.	Adjustments Dr.	Adjustments Cr.	Earnings Statement Dr.	Earnings Statement Cr.	Statement of Financial Position Dr.	Statement of Financial Position Cr.
1	Cash	13,663						13,663	
3	Accounts receivable—Baker Co.	1,880						1,880	
4	Merchandise inventory—Jan. 1	7,000			7,000				
6	Accounts payable—Moonbrook Co.		700						700
7	Capital stock		15,000						15,000
9	Sales		13,600				13,600		
10	Sales returns and allowances	20				20			
11	Sales discounts	44				44			
12	Purchases	6,000			6,000				
13	Purchase returns and allowances		100	100					
14	Purchase discounts		82	82					
15	Transportation-in	75			75				
16	Sales salaries	650				650			
17	Rent expense	150				150			
		29,482	29,482						
	Cost of goods sold			12,893	8,000	4,893			
	Merchandise inventory, Jan. 31*			8,000				8,000	
				21,075	21,075	5,757	13,600		
	Net earnings for January					7,843			7,843
						13,600	13,600	23,543	23,543

* If desired, the $8,000 in the Adjustments column and in the Statement of Financial Position column may be placed on the same line as the $7,000 beginning inventory figure.

If only one entry was used to establish the cost of goods sold, the only amount which would appear in the adjustments columns for the cost of goods sold would be $4,893 in the debit column; this is the cost of goods sold (Figure 6.6).

FIGURE 6.6
Determination of the cost of goods sold under periodic procedure

Inventory, January 1			$ 7,000
Purchases		$6,000	
Add: Transportation-in		75	
Total		$6,075	
Less: Purchase returns and allowances	$100		
Purchase discounts	82	182	
Net cost of purchases			$ 5,893
Cost of goods available for sale			$12,893
Deduct: Inventory, January 31			8,000
Cost of goods sold			$ 4,893

Be sure you understand the data in Answer Frame 11[6] before starting Frame 12[6] on page 145.

Frame 13[6]

Revenue and expense classification. This section is a review and expansion of the revenue and expense classification material already presented and discussed briefly.

Revenues are divided into two classes:

1. *Operating revenue*—the sales of products or services or both regularly offered for sale.
2. *Nonoperating revenue*—revenue not directly connected with the chief products or services regularly sold. An example is interest revenue.

Expenses are divided into two classes:

1. *Operating expenses*—those incurred in the normal buying, selling, and administrative functions of a business.
2. *Nonoperating expenses*—those not directly connected with the acquisition and sale of the commodities or services regularly offered for sale. An example of a nonoperating expense is interest expense.

Operating expenses for a mercantile concern are subdivided into two classifications:

1. *Selling expenses*—those incurred directly in the sale and delivery of a commodity. Examples include salesmen's salaries and commissions, sales travel expense, delivery wages, advertising, the cost of outward transportation paid by the seller, and taxes applicable to the sales division.
2. *Administrative expenses*—those incurred in managing a business. Examples include salaries of officers, salaries of office employees, office supplies expense, rent applicable to administration, welfare and recreation, and taxes applicable to administration.

An earnings statement which shows these classifications together with a gross margin figure is called a multiple-step earnings statement.

Statements prepared from work sheet. The earnings statement (Figure 6.8) and the state-

FIGURE 6.8
Earnings statement under periodic procedure

LYONS STORE, INC.
Earnings Statement
For the Month Ended January 31, 1975

Gross sales				$13,600
Less: Sales returns and allowances			$ 20	
Sales discounts			44	64
Net sales				$13,536
Cost of goods sold				
Inventory, January 1, 1975			$ 7,000	
Purchases		$6,000		
Add: Transportation-in		75		
Total		$6,075		
Less: Purchase returns and allowances	$100			
Purchase discounts	82	182		
Net cost of purchases			5,853	
Cost of goods available for sale			$12,893	
Deduct: Inventory, January 31, 1975			8,000	
Cost of goods sold				4,893
Gross margin				$ 8,643
Deduct: Operating expenses:				
Selling expenses				
Sales salaries			$ 650	
Rent expense			150	
Total selling expenses				800
Net Earnings for January				$ 7,843

Answer frame 12[6]

The correct answers to the accounting cycle illustration are:

Jan. 31	Cost of Goods Sold	12,893	
	Purchase Returns and Allowances	100	
	Purchase Discounts	82	
	Merchandise Inventory		7,000
	Purchases		6,000
	Transportation-In		75
31	Expense and Revenue Summary	4,893	
	Cost of Goods Sold		4,893

Be sure you understand the above answers before starting Frame 13[6] on page 147.

Frame 13[6] continued

FIGURE 6.9

LYONS STORE, Inc.
Statement of Financial Postion
January 31, 1975

Assets		*Liabilities and Stockholders' Equity*		
Current Assets		Current Liabilities		
Cash	$13,663	Accounts payable		$ 700
Accounts receivable	1,880	Stockholders' Equity		
Merchandise inventory	8,000	Capital stock	$15,000	
		Retained earnings	7,843	
		Total Stockholders' Equity		$22,843
Total Assets	$23,543	Total Liabilities and Stockholders' Equity		$23,543

ment of financial position (Figure 6.9) for Lyons Store, Inc. are prepared directly from the work sheet in Figure 6.5, page 144. Note that in the ledger, an account receivable is kept with each customer. In the statement of financial position, all accounts receivable are added together and appear as one amount. This is also true for accounts payable.

From the earnings statement, the following equations may be developed:

1. Net Sales = Gross Sales − Sales Returns and Allowances − Sales Discounts.
2. Cost of Goods Sold = Inventory at Beginning of Period + (Purchases + Transportation-In − Purchase Returns and Allowances − Purchase Discounts) − Inventory at End of Period.
3. Gross Margin = Net Sales − Cost of Goods Sold.
4. Net Earnings from Operations = Gross Margin − Operating (Selling and Administrative) Expenses.
5. Net Earnings = Net Earnings from Operations + Other Revenue − Other Expense.

Net loss for a period. If total expenses are greater than the gross margin and other revenue for a period, a *net loss* results and the earnings statement will indicate a loss. When there is a net loss for the period, a debit balance will appear in the Expense and Revenue Summary account after the expense and revenue accounts have been closed to it; this debit balance will be closed by a debit to Retained Earnings and a credit to

Expense and Revenue Summary. Stockholders' equity will be reduced because of the loss.

In the work sheet the Earnings Statement debit column will exceed the Earnings Statement credit column by the amount of the loss. The loss will be placed in the Earnings Statement credit column and in the Statement of Financial Position debit column in order to balance the work sheet.

Is each of the following a true or false statement?

______ 1. A net loss is the opposite of net earnings.

______ 2. The net loss for an accounting period is the excess of expenses over revenues.

______ 3. When a net loss occurs, the Earnings Statement debit column total will be smaller than the credit column total in a work sheet.

Check your responses in Answer Frame 13[6] on page 150.

SUMMARY

Periodic inventory procedure is used by companies dealing in merchandise with a low per unit value such as nuts, bolts, nails, pencils and many similar items, since close control of these items is unnecessary and perpetual inventory procedure is not economically wise. Under periodic inventory procedure the Merchandise Inventory account is not adjusted after each purchase or sale; adjustment is made only at the end of the accounting period.

Under periodic inventory procedure no attempt is made to maintain the balance in the Merchandise Inventory account at an amount equal to the cost of the goods actually on hand at all times. The balance in this account represents the beginning inventory, and this amount remains in the account until adjusting entries are made at the end of the accounting period.

A work sheet may be used as an aid in preparing financial statements. When periodic inventory procedure is being used, it is necessary to insert two columns for adjustments between the Trial Balance columns and the Earnings Statement columns. The entries to record the cost of goods sold (presented in general journal form above) are recorded in the Adjustments columns of the work sheet. A complete illustration of a work sheet incorporating these adjustments is found in Frame 11[6] on page 144.

Now turn to the Glossary on page 150 and study the definitions of new terms introduced in this chapter. Then work the Student Review Quiz on page 151, for a self-administered test of your comprehension of the material in the chapter.

Answer frame 13[6]

1. True. Net earnings increase the balance in retained earnings, while a net loss decreases it.
2. True. When expenses exceed revenues there is a net loss.
3. False. Items of expense are debits; items of revenue are credits. Therefore, when a net loss occurs, the Earning Statement debit column total will be greater than the credit column total.

If you missed any of the above, restudy Frame 13[6] before turning to the Summary on page 149.

GLOSSARY

Administrative expenses–operating expenses incurred in managing a business.

Cost of goods sold–a business expense which when properly adjusted shows the cost of the goods sold and delivered to customers in a given period; under periodic procedure, it is computed as Beginning Inventory + (Purchases + Transportation-In − Purchase Returns and Allowances − Purchase Discounts) − Ending Inventory.

Discounts Lost account–an account used to show discounts missed under either perpetual or periodic procedure when purchases are recorded at net invoice price.

Gross Margin = Net Sales − Cost of Goods Sold.

Net Earnings = Net Earnings from Operations + Other Revenue − Other Expenses.

Net Earnings from Operations = Gross Margin − Operating Expenses.

Net Sales = Gross Sales − Sales Returns and Allowances − Sales Discounts.

Nonoperating expenses–expenses incurred which are not directly connected with the acquisition and sale of the commodities or services regularly offered for sale, as for example, interest expense.

Nonoperating revenue–revenue not directly connected with the sale of products or services regularly offered for sale, as for example, interest revenue.

Operating expenses–expenses incurred in the normal buying, selling, and administrative functions of a business.

Operating revenue–revenue resulting from the sale of products or services regularly offered for sale.

Periodic inventory procedure–a method of accounting for merchandise acquired for sale to customers wherein the cost of such merchandise sold and the amount of such merchandise on hand are determined only through the taking of a physical inventory.

Purchase Discounts account–an account used under periodic inventory procedure to record the amount of discounts taken on purchases for prompt payment of invoices; treated as a reduction in the cost of purchases and, therefore, is a credit balance account.

Purchase Returns and Allowances account–an account used under periodic inventory procedure to record the cost of merchandise returned to a seller and to record reductions in the selling price of merchandise purchased granted by the seller usually because the merchandise delivered is not fully satisfactory to the buyer; the items recorded are reductions in the cost of purchases and, therefore, the account has a credit balance.

Purchases account–an account used under periodic inventory procedure to record the cost of merchandise purchased during the current accounting period; any balance in the account should be a debit balance.

Selling expenses–operating expenses directly incurred in the sale and delivery of merchandise or in the rendering of services to customers.

Transportation-In account–an account used under periodic inventory procedure to record transportation costs incurred in the acquisition of merchandise; an addition to the cost of merchandise purchased and, therefore, a debit balance account.

STUDENT REVIEW QUIZ

1. Which of the following accounts usually has a credit balance?
   a. Sales Returns and Allowances.
   b. Purchases.
   c. Transportation-In.
   d. Purchase Discounts.
   e. None of the above.

2. Given the following information:

Beginning inventory	$5,000	Transportation-in	$700
Ending inventory	$3,000	Purchase returns and allowances	$400
Purchases	$9,000	Purchase discounts	$200

   Which of the following statements is *correct?*
   a. Net cost of purchases equals $9,100.
   b. Cost of goods available for sale equals $14,100.
   c. Cost of goods sold equals $11,100.
   d. All of the above are true.
   e. Only two of the above, specifically (*a*) and (*b*) are true.

3. The following facts are given:
   a. Beginning inventory, $8,000.
   b. Ending inventory, $11,000.
   c. Purchases, $12,000.

   Under periodic inventory procedure, which of the above figures would appear in the pre-closing trial balance? Which of them would appear in the post-closing trial balance?

   Under perpetual inventory procedure, which of the above figures would appear in the pre-closing trial balance? In the post-closing trial balance?

4. A company allowed a credit of $150 to Enwright Corporation for defective merchandise returned. The merchandise cost $95. Periodic inventory procedure is used. The required entry in A's journal is:

a.	Merchandise Inventory	150	
	Accounts Receivable–Enwright Corporation		150
b.	Merchandise Inventory	95	
	Cost of Goods Sold		95
c.	Sales Returns and Allowances	150	
	Accounts Receivable–Enwright Corporation		150
d.	Merchandise Inventory	150	
	Sales Returns and Allowances		150
e.	Sales	150	
	Accounts Receivable–Enwright Corporation		150

5. X Company received an invoice from Ramp Supply Company for merchandise purchased, $3,000. Assuming periodic inventory procedure is used, the required entry on X's books is:

a.	Merchandise Inventory	3,000	
	Accounts Payable–Ramp Supply Company		3,000
b.	Purchases	3,000	
	Accounts Payable–Ramp Supply Company		3,000
c.	Equipment	3,000	
	Accounts Payable–Ramp Supply Company		3,000
d.	Accounts Payable–Ramp Supply Company	3,000	
	Merchandise Inventory		3,000

6. On June 1, the following entry was made to record an invoice received on that date:

Purchases	1,000	
Accounts Payable		1,000
To record purchase on which the terms were 2/10, n/30.		

What entry would be *correct* if the invoice were paid on June 10?

a.	Accounts Payable	1,000	
	Cash		1,000
b.	Accounts Payable	980	
	Purchase Discounts	20	
	Cash		1,000
c.	Accounts Payable	980	
	Cash		980
d.	Accounts Payable	1,000	
	Cash		980
	Purchase Discounts		20

7. On July 3 the following entry was made:

Purchases	800	
Accounts Payable		800
To record purchase of merchandise on which terms were 3/10 E.O.M.		

Assuming the invoice is paid on July 29, the entry would be:

a.	Accounts Payable	800	
	Cash		800
b.	Accounts Payable	800	
	Cash		776
	Purchase Discounts		24
c.	Cash	800	
	Accounts Payable		800
d.	Accounts Payable	776	
	Purchase Discounts	24	
	Cash		800
e.	None of the above.		

8. Assume that a company paid Mandel Trucking Company $110 for transporting a shipment of merchandise from the Zek Manufacturing Company. Which entry would be *correct* if periodic inventory procedures were being used?

a.	Transportation-In	110	
	Accounts Payable–Zek Manufacturing Company		110
b.	Purchases	110	
	Accounts Payable–Zek Manufacturing Company		110
c.	Merchandise Inventory	110	
	Accounts Payable–Zek Manufacturing Company		110
d.	Transportation-In	110	
	Cash		110
e.	Merchandise Inventory	110	
	Cash		110

9. Assume that a company sold merchandise (selling price, $300; cost, $198) to the Witts End Motel on account. Indicate which of the following entries would be correct under perpetual inventory procedure and which would be correct under periodic inventory procedure.

a.	Cost of Goods Sold	198	
	Merchandise Inventory		198
	Accounts Receivable–Witts End Motel	300	
	Sales		300
b.	Cost of Goods Sold	198	
	Sales		198
c.	Accounts Receivable–Witts End Motel	300	
	Sales		300
d	Cost of Goods Sold	300	
	Sales		300
e.	Accounts Receivable–Witts End Motel	300	
	Merchandise Inventory		300
	Cost of Goods Sold	198	
	Sales		198

10. If the ending inventory is overstated—

a. Cost of goods sold is understated and net earnings for the period are overstated.
b. Cost of goods sold is understated and net earnings for the period are understated.
c. Cost of goods sold is overstated and net earnings are overstated.
d. Cost of goods sold is overstated and net earnings are understated.
e. Cost of goods sold is understated and gross margin is understated.

11. Which of the following correctly describes the makeup of the cost of goods sold section of the earnings statement under periodic inventory procedure?

a. Beginning Inventory + Purchases − Transportation-In − Purchase Returns and Allowances − Purchase Discounts − Ending Inventory.
b. Beginning Inventory + Purchases − Transportation-In − Purchase Returns

and Allowances − Purchase Discounts + Ending Inventory.

c. Beginning Inventory + Purchases + Transportation-In + Purchase Returns and Allowances − Purchase Discounts − Ending Inventory.

d. Beginning Inventory + Purchases + Transportation-In − Purchase Returns and Allowances − Purchase Discounts − Ending Inventory.

Now compare your answers with the correct answers and explanations given on page 209.

chapter 7

THE WORK SHEET AND THE ACCOUNTING CYCLE ILLUSTRATED

LEARNING OBJECTIVES

The learning objectives to be achieved by studying this chapter include:

1. An understanding of the uses of a work sheet with columns for Trial Balance, Adjustments, Earnings Statement, and Statement of Financial Position.
2. The ability to prepare a work sheet in conventional format.
3. An understanding of the steps in the entire accounting cycle (an expanded version of the one covered in Chapter 3).

Frame 1[7]

THE WORK SHEET

A useful internal tool. The work sheet was discussed briefly in Chapter 3. It is a useful working aid prepared by accountants to classify data for use in future work. The work sheet summarizes the data to be used in preparing the earnings statement, statement of financial position, adjusting journal entries, and closing journal entries. It is used only internally by the accountant rather than being a formal accounting statement which is prepared for outsiders.

Work sheet technique for cost of goods sold. One format which is often used is an eight-column work sheet with pairs of columns headed Trial Balance, Adjustments, Earnings Statement, and Statement of Financial Position. With the inclusion of columns for the adjustments, the establishment of the correct amount for cost of goods sold expense can be included among the other adjusting entries as shown in Figure 7.1.

An explanation of adjustments in the work sheet of Figure 7.1 are:

A—To transfer cost of goods available for sale (beginning inventory and purchases) to cost of goods sold.
B—To set up the ending inventory as an asset and reduce cost of goods sold accordingly.

The debit to Merchandise Inventory to establish the ending balance can be placed opposite that caption in the trial balance or it may be placed below the trial balance captions as a new item.

Adjusted Trial Balance columns. A pair of columns headed Adjusted Trial Balance may be inserted immediately following the Adjustments columns. The purpose of these columns is to total horizontally the figures appearing in the Trial Balance and Adjustments columns before extend-

FIGURE 7.1
A typical eight-column partial work sheet

Account No.	Account Name	Trial Balance Dr.	Trial Balance Cr.	Adjustments Dr.	Adjustments Cr.	Earnings Statement Dr.	Earnings Statement Cr.	Statement of Financial Position Dr.	Statement of Financial Position Cr.
	Merchandise inventory	4,000		B 3,000	A 4,000			3,000	
	Purchases	6,000			A 6,000				
	Cost of goods sold			A 10,000	B 3,000	7,000			

ing them to the other columns. Also, since the totals of these two columns must be equal, they provide a check upon the accuracy of the work done in entering the adjustments.

THE CASSADAGA COMPANY—AN ILLUSTRATION

To show how adjusting entries fit into the work sheet, a brief illustration is now presented. For the sake of simplicity, the adjustments are limited to those that affect expense accounts. These include recognition of (*a*) recorded assets that have expired and become expenses and (*b*) the obligation to pay for assets received which have expired by the time of recording and are thus recorded as expenses. The trial balance shown in Figure 7.2 is for the Cassadaga Company on June 30, 1975.

FIGURE 7.2

CASSADAGA COMPANY
Trial Balance
June 30, 1975

Account No.	Account Name	Debits	Credits
101	Cash	$ 4,270	
102	Merchandise inventory, June 1	7,200	
103	Accounts receivable	3,000	
104	Store supplies	720	
105	Unexpired insurance	480	
120	Store fixtures	2,400	
201	Accounts payable		$ 5,300
301	Capital stock		10,000
310	Retained earnings		3,000
401	Sales		16,000
512	Purchases	12,200	
513	Purchase returns and allowances		200
514	Sales salaries expense	1,100	
515	Advertising expense	700	
517	General selling expense	1,130	
521	Office salaries expense	600	
522	General administrative expense	700	
		$34.500	$34,500

The following data are the bases for the adjustments to the account balances in the trial balance:

A—Of the unexpired insurance premiums, $40 expired during the month of June. (Use Account No. 519, Insurance Expense.)

B—A physical inventory showed store supplies with a cost of $120 on hand at June 30. (Store Supplies Expense is Account No. 516.)

C—Bad Debts Expense (Account No. 520) for the month is estimated at 1 percent of sales. (Use Account No. 103-A for the allowance.)

D—The store fixtures were acquired on June 2 and are estimated to have a useful life of 10 years. (Use Account No. 518 for the depreciation expense and 120-A for the allowance.)

E—At June 30, office salaries of $120 have been earned by the employees since the last payday. The next payday falls on July 3. (Use Account No. 202, Accrued Office Salaries Payable.)

F—Included in general selling expense is $130 of travel expense advances to salesmen to cover travel expected in July. (Use Account No. 106, Travel Advances.)

G—The inventory of merchandise at June 30 has a cost of $11,000. (Use Account No. 524, Cost of Goods Sold.)

Procedure for completing the work sheet. The trial balance and additional data just given are to be used to complete the eight-column work sheet on pages 158–59. Carefully follow each step as outlined to complete the work sheet.

1. Enter the necessary adjustments to record the data given in items A through G on page 155. For example, to record the information given in item A, $40 must be removed from the asset account, Unexpired Insurance, and charged to an expense account, Insurance Expense (Account No. 519). To record this in the work sheet, enter a credit of $40 in the Adjustments credit column on the Unexpired Insurance account line. At the bottom of the work sheet, immediately below the trial balance totals, write in the name of the account, Insurance Expense, and on this line in the debit column of the Adjustments columns enter the $40 of expense for the month. Place a letter A in front of both the debit and credit. Then, on the 10th line from the bottom of your work sheet, enter the letter A in the account name column. Immediately adjacent to this letter write the explanation of the entry made in the Adjustments columns of the work sheet. This will facilitate the making of the actual adjusting entries in the general journal later. Make the entries necessary for items B through F, following the procedure just outlined.
2. Item G actually requires two entries. First, the beginning inventory and the net purchases (purchases less purchase returns and allowances) should be transferred to the Cost of Goods Sold expense account (Account No. 524). This entry can be lettered G. A second entry is then required which will remove from the Cost of Goods Sold account the goods which remain on hand, the ending inventory. This entry can be lettered H. As an alternative, the required debit for the ending inventory may be entered on the work sheet on a separate line following the trial balance totals. Now total the Adjustments columns to make sure the debits equal the credits.

After you understand these steps completely, proceed with the next step.

3. Now extend the totals of the balances of the amounts entered in the Trial Balance columns and the Adjustments columns into the proper Earnings Statement or Statement of Financial Position columns. In making these extensions, a debit in the Trial Balance columns and a debit in the Adjustments columns are added together and carried across as a debit to either the Earnings Statement or Statement of Financial Position columns, depending upon the nature of the item. Similarly, a credit in the Trial Balance columns and a credit in the Adjustments columns are added together and extended as a credit into either the Earnings Statement or Statement of Financial Position columns. On the other hand, if one amount is a debit and the other a credit, the smaller must be subtracted from the larger and the balance, which is of the same type as the larger amount, must be carried across to the proper Earnings Statement or Statement of Financial Position column. The proper extension procedure may be summarized as follows:
   a. Assets are debit balances and are extended to the debit Statement of Financial Position column.
   b. Liabilities and stockholders' equity accounts with credit balances are extended to the credit Statement of Financial Position column.
   c. Expenses (debit balances) are extended to the debit Earnings Statement column.

   d. Revenues (credit balances) are extended to the credit Earnings Statement column.

4. The net earnings (or loss) for the period are (is) computed by adding the debit and the credit Earnings Statement columns and finding the difference between these two totals. Sum the Earnings Statement columns and place the total of each column at the bottom of the column on the same line as the totals of the Adjustments columns. If there are net earnings for the period, the *credit* total will be greater; if there is a net loss, the *debit* total will be the greater. If there are net earnings, transfer them to stockholders' equity on the next line by—
   a. Entering the amount of net earnings in the *debit* Earnings Statement column, and
   b. Entering the amount of net earnings in the *credit* Statement of Financial Position column because earnings increase stockholders' equity by increasing retained earnings. If there is a net loss, enter the amount of the net loss in the credit Earnings Statement column and in the debit Statement of Financial Position column.
5. Add the Earnings Statement columns; their totals should be in agreement. Add the Statement of Financial Position columns; their totals should be in agreement.

CASSADAGA COMPANY
Work Sheet for the Month Ended June 30, 1975

Account No.	Account Name	Trial Balance Dr.	Trial Balance Cr.	Adjustments Dr.	Adjustments Cr.	Earnings Statement Dr.	Earnings Statement Cr.	Statement of Financial Position Dr.	Statement of Financial Position Cr.
101	Cash	4,270							
102	Merchandise inventory	7,200							
103	Accounts receivable	3,000							
104	Store supplies	720							
105	Unexpired insurance	480							
120	Store fixtures	2,400							
201	Accounts payable		5,300						
301	Capital stock		10,000						
310	Retained earnings		3,000						
401	Sales		16,000						
512	Purchases	12,200							
513	Purchase returns and allowances		200						
514	Sales salaries expense	1,100							
515	Advertising expense	700							
517	General selling expense	1,130							
521	Office salaries expense	600							
522	General administrative expense	700							
		34,500	34,500						
	Totals forward								

Account No.	Account Name	Trial Balance		Adjustments		Earnings Statement		Statement of Financial Position	
		Dr.	Cr.	Dr.	Cr.	Dr.	Cr.	Dr.	Cr.
	Totals brought forward								
	Adjustments:								

Now turn to Answer Frame 1[7] on pages 160–62 and compare your solution with the correct one.

Answer frame 1[7]

This answer frame contains the completed work sheet and detailed explanations of each adjustment. Study this carefully to be sure that you fully understand this procedure.

CASSADAGA COMPANY
Work Sheet for the Month Ended June 30, 1975

Account No.	Account Name	Trial Balance Dr.	Trial Balance Cr.	Adjustments Dr.	Adjustments Cr.	Earnings Statement Dr.	Earnings Statement Cr.	Statement of Financial Position Dr.	Statement of Financial Position Cr.
101	Cash	4,270						4,270	
102	Merchandise inventory	7,200		H 11,000	G 7,200			11,000	
103	Accounts receivable	3,000						3,000	
104	Store supplies	720			B 600			120	
105	Unexpired insurance	480			A 40			440	
120	Store fixtures	2,400						2,400	
201	Accounts payable		5,300						5,300
301	Capital stock		10,000						10,000
310	Retained earnings		3,000						3,000
401	Sales		16,000				16,000		
512	Purchases	12,200			G 12,200				
513	Purchase returns and allowances		200	G 200					
514	Sales salaries expense	1,100				1,100			
515	Advertising expense	700				700			
517	General selling expense	1,130			F 130	1,000			
521	Office salaries expense	600		E 120		720			
522	General administrative expense	700				700			
		34,500	34,500						
519	Insurance expense			A 40		40			
516	Store supplies expense			B 600		600			
520	Bad debts expense			C 160		160			
103-A	Allowance for doubtful accounts				C 160				160
518	Depreciation expense,			D 20		20			
	store fixtures								20
120-A	Allowance for depreciation of								120
	store fixtures				D 20			130	
202	Accrued office salaries payable				E 120				
106	Travel advances			F 130					
524	Cost of goods sold			G 19,200	H 11,000	8,200			
	Totals			31,470	31,470	13,240	16,000	21,360	18,600
	Net earnings for June					2,760			2,760
						16,000	16,000	21,360	21,360

Adjustments:
- A—Portion of insurance which expired during June.
- B—Portion of store supplies which were used during June.
- C—To recognize the estimated uncollectibles on accounts receivable arising during month.
- D—Portion of asset, store fixtures, which expired during June.
- E—Office salaries which have accrued during June since the last payday.
- F—Remove travel advances from expense account and set them up as assets.
- G—To transfer beginning inventory and net purchases to cost of goods sold.
- H—To set up the ending inventory and adjust the cost of goods sold expense accordingly.

Detailed explanations of adjustments A through H follow. You may wish to refer only to those you recorded incorrectly.

A. *Insurance Expense.* Item A, in effect, states that of the $480 paid in advance for insurance protection, $40 represents the cost of such protection for the month of June. Since the month of June has passed, this amount is no longer paid in advance. Thus, it can no longer render benefits in the future and must be charged to an expense account. The entry to accomplish this debits Insurance Expense $40 and credits Unexpired Insurance $40. The insurance expense will appear in the earnings statement, and the $440 of unexpired insurance premiums will appear as an asset in the statement of financial position.

B. *Store Supplies Expense.* Item B indicates that of the supplies previously recorded in the Store Supplies asset account, $600 were used during June. Therefore, their cost must be transferred from asset to expense. The entry to show this change debits Store Supplies Expense for the increase of $600 and credits Store Supplies for the decrease of $600. The store supplies expense of $600 will appear on the earnings statement, and the remaining $120 in the Store Supplies account will be shown as an asset on the June 30 statement of financial position.

C. *Bad Debts Expense.* Item C measures the expense of bad debts from sales made during June. It indicates that 1 percent of the sales are estimated to be uncollectible. In other words, the Bad Debts Expense should have a debit balance of 1 percent of $16,000, or $160, after the adjustment. The entry to recognize the estimated uncollectibles is a debit to Bad Debts Expense and a credit to the Allowance for Doubtful Accounts. The debit shows the increase in the expense. The credit shows the decrease in the asset, accounts receivable, since the balance in the Allowance for Doubtful Accounts account is subtracted from the total of the receivables in the statement of financial position.

D. *Depreciation Expense.* Item D presents the data needed to compute the amount of the expense that is incurred by the gradual use of the store fixtures. The store fixtures cost $2,400. They have an estimated useful life of 10 years with no residual scrap value. Thus, the annual depreciation expense is $240, computed by dividing the cost by the estimated life ($2,400 ÷ 10). For the month of June, the expense is 1/12 of the annual expense, or $20. The entry to show the expiration of a part of the asset and its recognition as an expense through use during June is a debit of $20 to Depreciation Expense–Store Fixtures account. The depreciation expense appears on the earnings statement. The Allowance for Depreciation of Store Fixtures account is a contra account. It may also be viewed as a subdivision of the credit side of the Store Fixtures asset account. Disclosure of the asset reduction to $2,380 is presented in the statement of financial position as follows:

Store Fixtures (at cost)	$2,400	
Less: Allowance for depreciation	20	$2,380

E. *Accrual of Office Salaries.* Item E states that employee services, for which the company has agreed to pay $210, have been received from employees since the last payday. Thus, the company has an unrecorded liability to pay for these services received. Because such services generally produce no lasting benefit to the employer, they are recorded as expired assets, expenses, at the time of recording. It should be clearly recognized that employee services are assets. They are recorded as expenses because they have expired by the time of recording. Thus the entry needed at this time is a debit to Office Salaries Expense and a credit to Accrued Office Salaries Payable in the amount of $120. The increase in the expense account of $120 plus the $600 balance already in the Office Salaries Expense account is shown as one expense item of $720 in the earnings statement for June. The $120 of accrued office salaries payable appears as a liability on the June 30 statement of financial position.

F. *Travel Advances.* Of the $1,130 shown as general selling expense in the trial balance, $130 of travel advances will not become an expense until July. This amount is, therefore, set up as an asset at the end of June. In July, it will be transferred back into the General Selling Expense account.

G. *Cost of Goods Sold.* Entry G transfers the beginning inventory of $7,200 to Cost of Goods Sold along with net purchases. The Purchase Returns and Allowances account has served its purpose (indicating the amount of such returns and allowances) and in this entry is, in effect, closed to Purchases since the debit to the Cost of Goods Sold account consists of $7,200 of beginning inventory plus $12,000 of net purchases ($12,200 of purchases less $200 purchase returns and allowances).

Answer frame 1[7] continued

H. *Cost of Goods Sold.* Upon the completion of the recording of entry G above, all of the cost of the merchandise available for sale has been charged to the expense account, Cost of Goods Sold. But not all of the goods were sold. The existence of an *ending* inventory proves this. Hence, it would be a mistake to charge all of the goods to expense, and thus, an entry is made to remove from Cost of Goods Sold the cost of the ending inventory. Entry H accomplishes this.

When you are satisfied with your understanding, you should begin Frame 2[7] below.

Frame 2[7]

In extending the net earnings or the loss for the period into the Statement of Financial Position columns, the net earnings or loss should not be added to the Retained Earnings account line but should simply be extended to the Statement of Financial Position column on a separate line. The net earnings or loss for the period increases or decreases stockholders' equity, and the effect of the increase or decrease is shown in the statement of financial position.

Financial statements prepared from work sheet. The earnings statement is prepared from the data in the Earnings Statement columns of the work sheet. The statement of financial position is prepared from the data in the Statement of Financial Position columns of the work sheet.

Adjusting and closing entries. The adjusting and closing journal entries can be entered in the journal now that the work sheet has been completed.

On the general journal form record the required adjusting entries as shown on the work sheet.

CASSADAGA COMPANY
GENERAL JOURNAL
(Adjusting Entries)

Page 4

Date		*Account Titles*	*L.F.*	*Dr.*	*Cr.*

GENERAL JOURNAL (continued)

Date	Account Titles	L.F.	Dr.	Cr.

Now go to Answer Frame 2^7 on page 164 to check your responses.

Frame 3^7

To further test your understanding of the material covered determine whether each of the following statements is true or false.

_______ 1. The work sheet summarizes the data included in the adjusting and closing entries.

_______ 2. If there are net earnings for the period, the amount of the total in the credit Earnings Statement column is larger than the total in the debit Earnings Statement column before the net earnings for the period are entered.

_______ 3. If there are net earnings, they are shown in the debit column of the Earnings Statement columns and on the Statement of Financial Position columns.

_______ 4. Expenses are extended to the credit Earnings Statement column.

_______ 5. If there is a net loss for a given period, the debit total will exceed the credit total in the Earnings Statement columns before the net loss figure is entered.

Now turn to Answer Frame 3^7 on page 164 to check your answers.

Answer frame 2[7]

Page 4

Date		Account Titles	L.F.	Dr.	Cr.
1975					
June	30	Insurance Expense	519	40	
		Unexpired Insurance	105		40
		Expense for insurance protection during June.			
	30	Store Supplies Expense	516	600	
		Store Supplies	104		600
		Supplies used during June.			
	30	Bad Debts Expense	520	160	
		Allowance for Doubtful Accounts	103-A		160
		For uncollectible accounts equal to 1 percent of sales.			
	30	Depreciation Expense—Store Fixtures ...	518	20	
		Allowance for Depreciation of Store Fixtures	120-A		20
		Depreciation for the month of June.			
	30	Office Salaries Expense	521	120	
		Accrued Office Salaries Payable	202		120
		Expense and liability incurred since last payday.			
	30	Travel Advances	106	130	
		General Selling Expense	517		130
		To remove travel advances from expense and set them up as assets.			
	30	Cost of Goods Sold	524	19,200	
		Purchase Returns and Allowances	513	200	
		Merchandise Inventory	102		7,200
		Purchases	512		12,200
		To transfer beginning inventory and net purchases to cost of goods sold.			
	30	Merchandise Inventory	102	11,000	
		Cost of Goods Sold	524		11,000
		To set up the ending inventory and reduce cost of goods sold accordingly.			

Note: The posting references are not part of the journalizing but have been inserted to show the completed journal after posting.

When you are satisfied with your understanding, begin Frame 3[7] on page 163.

Answer frame 3[7]

1. True. The adjusting and closing entries usually are journalized from data contained in the work sheet. The adjustments and Earnings Statement columns contain the data needed for adjusting and closing entries.
2. True. This means that revenues exceed expenses for the period.
3. False. They are shown in the debit column of the Earnings Statement columns and the *credit* column of the Statement of Financial Position columns.
4. False. They are extended to the *debit* column of the Earnings Statement columns.
5. True. This means that expenses exceed revenues for the period.

If you missed any of the above, you should restudy Frame 3[7] before turning to Frame 4[7] on page 165.

Frame 4[7]

Closing entries illustrated. The closing journal entries for the Cassadaga Company are shown below. Closing entries may be combined or compounded in a variety of ways. All revenue accounts may be closed in one entry, all expense accounts closed in one entry, and, finally, one entry made to close the balance to retained earnings. This approach is illustrated below.

Using the work sheet in Answer Frame 1[7], provide the information missing in the closing entries below:

Page 5

CASSADAGA COMPANY
GENERAL JOURNAL
(Closing Entries)

Date		Account Titles	Folio	Dr.	Cr.
1975					
(1) June	30	Sales	401	16,000	
		____________ ...	525		16,000
		To close the revenue account.			
(2)	30	Expense and Revenue Summary	525	13,240	
		Cost of Goods Sold	524		8,200
		Sales Salaries Expense	514		1,100
		Advertising Expense	515		700
		____________ ...	516		600
		General Selling Expense	517		1,000
		Depreciation Expense—Store Fixtures	518		20
		____________ ...	519		40
		Bad Debts Expense	520		160
		Office Salaries Expense	521		720
		General Administrative Expense ...	522		700
		To close expenses.			
(3)	30	Expense and Revenue Summary	525	——	
		Retained Earnings	525		——
		To close the Expense and Revenue Summary account.			

Now turn to Answer Frame 4[7] on page 166 to check your responses.

Frame 5[7]

Summary of uses of work sheet. To summarize, the above illustration shows that the work sheet serves as the basis for preparing:

1. The earnings statement.
2. The statement of financial position.
3. Adjusting journal entries.
4. Closing journal entries.

The work sheet does not eliminate the need for making adjusting and closing entries in the journal and posting them to the ledger. Each serves a different purpose. The work sheet is a tool that helps the accountant classify data so that adjusting entries, closing entries, and statements can be prepared. The journal and the ledger are permanent records of the business transactions while the work sheet is a temporary summarizing tool. In many businesses the work sheet is used in the preparation of monthly financial statements but with formal adjusting and closing entries recorded only once each year when the accounts are formally closed.

The general ledger illustrated. For sake of simplicity, the illustration presented covers one month and assumes formal closing of the accounts at the end of June. After posting the adjusting and closing entries, the general ledger would appear as shown on page 166.

Answer frame 4^7

The responses for the general journal entries are:

(1) Expense and Revenue Summary.

(2) Store Supplies Expense; Insurance Expense.

(3) 2,760 (Dr.); 2,760 (Cr.).

If you answered incorrectly, restudy Frame 4^7 before starting Frame 5^7 on page 165.

Frame 5^7 continued

Provide the missing information by referring to Answer Frame 2^7 on page 164 for the adjusting entries and to Frame 4^7 on page 165 for the closing entries.

CASSADAGA COMPANY
GENERAL LEDGER

Cash — *Account No. 101*

Date		Explanation	Folio	Debit	Credit	Balance
1975						
June	30	Balance (shown on the trial balance in Frame 1^7)				4,270

Merchandise Inventory — *Account No. 102*

Date		Explanation	Folio	Debit	Credit	Balance
1975						
June	1	Balance (see trial balance—Frame 1^7)				7,200
	30	Cost of goods sold	J 4		____	____
	30	Balance—ending inventory	J 4	____		____

Accounts Receivable — *Account No. 103*

Date		Explanation	Folio	Debit	Credit	Balance
1975						
June	30	Balance (see trial balance—Frame 1^7)				3,000

Allowance for Doubtful Accounts — *Account No. 103-A*

Date		Explanation	Folio	Debit	Credit	Balance
1975						
June	30	Adjustment	J 4		____	____

Store Supplies — *Account No. 104*

Date		Explanation	Folio	Debit	Credit	Balance
1975						
June	30	Balance (see trial balance—Frame 1^7)				720
	30	Adjustment	J 4		____	____

Unexpired Insurance — *Account No. 105*

Date		Explanation	Folio	Debit	Credit	Balance
1975						
June	30	Balance (see trial balance—Frame 1^7)				480
	30	Adjustment	J 4		40	440

GENERAL LEDGER (continued)

Travel Advances — *Account No. 106*

Date		Explanation	Folio	Debit	Credit	Balance
1975						
June	30	Adjustment	J 4	130		130

Store Fixtures — *Account No. 120*

Date		Explanation	Folio	Debit	Credit	Balance
1975						
June	30	Balance (see trial balance—Frame 1[7])				2,400

Allowance for Depreciation—Store Fixtures — *Account No. 120-A*

Date		Explanation	Folio	Debit	Credit	Balance
1975						
June	30	Adjustment	J 4		20	20

Accounts Payable — *Account No. 201*

Date		Explanation	Folio	Debit	Credit	Balance
1975						
June	30	Balance (see trial balance—Frame 1[7])				5,300

Accrued Office Salaries Payable — *Account No. 202*

Date		Explanation	Folio	Debit	Credit	Balance
1975						
June	30	Adjustment	J 4		120	120

Capital Stock — *Account No. 301*

Date		Explanation	Folio	Debit	Credit	Balance
1975						
June	30	Balance (see trial balance—Frame 1[7])				10,000

Retained Earnings — *Account No. 310*

Date		Explanation	Folio	Debit	Credit	Balance
1975						
June	30	Balance (see trial balance—Frame 1[7])				3,000
	30	From expense and revenue summary	J 5		——	——

Sales — *Account No. 401*

Date		Explanation	Folio	Debit	Credit	Balance
1975						
June	30	Balance (see trial balance—Frame 1[7])				16,000
	30	To close	J 5	16,000		-0-

Purchases — *Account No. 512*

Date		Explanation	Folio	Debit	Credit	Balance
1975						
June	30	Balance (see trial balance—Frame 1[7])				12,200
	30	To transfer to cost of goods sold	J 4		12,200	-0-

GENERAL LEDGER (continued)

Purchase Returns and Allowances — *Account No. 513*

Date		Explanation	Folio	Debit	Credit	Balance
1975						
June	30	Balance (see trial balance—Frame 1[7])				200
	30	To transfer to cost of goods sold	J 4	200		–0–

Sales Salaries Expense — *Account No. 514*

Date		Explanation	Folio	Debit	Credit	Balance
1975						
June	30	Balance (see trial balance—Frame 1[7])				1,100
	30	To close	J 5		1,100	–0–

Advertising Expense — *Account No. 515*

Date		Explanation	Folio	Debit	Credit	Balance
1975						
June	30	Balance (see trial balance—Frame 1[7])				700
	30	To close	J 5		700	–0–

Store Supplies Expense — *Account No. 516*

Date		Explanation	Folio	Debit	Credit	Balance
1975						
June	30	Adjustment	J 4	600		600
	30	To close	J 5		600	–0–

General Selling Expense — *Account No. 517*

Date		Explanation	Folio	Debit	Credit	Balance
1975						
June	30	Balance (see trial balance—Frame 1[7])				1,130
	30	Adjustment	J 4		130	1,100
	30	To close	J 5		1,000	–0–

Depreciation Expense—Store Fixtures — *Account No. 518*

Date		Explanation	Folio	Debit	Credit	Balance
1975						
June	30	Adjustment	J 4	20		20
	30	To close	J 5		20	–0–

Insurance Expense — *Account No. 519*

Date		Explanation	Folio	Debit	Credit	Balance
1975						
June	30	Adjustment	J 4	____		____
	30	To close	J 5		____	____

Bad Debts Expense — *Account No. 520*

Date		Explanation	Folio	Debit	Credit	Balance
1975						
June	30	Adjustment	J 4	160		160
	30	To close	J 5		160	–0–

GENERAL LEDGER (continued)

Office Salaries Expense — *Account No. 521*

Date		Explanation	Folio	Debit	Credit	Balance
1975						
June	30	Balance (see trial balance—Frame 1[7])				600
	30	Adjustment	J 4	120		720
	30	To close	J 5		720	-0-

General Administrative Expense — *Account No. 522*

Date		Explanation	Folio	Debit	Credit	Balance
1975						
June	30	Balance (see trial balance—Frame 1[7])				700
	30	To close	J 5		700	-0-

Cost of Goods Sold — *Account No. 524*

Date		Explanation	Folio	Debit	Credit	Balance
1975						
June	30	Net purchases and beginning inventory	J 4	19,200		19,200
	30	Ending inventory	J 4		11,000	8,200
	30	To close	J 5		8,200	-0-

Expense and Revenue Summary — *Account No. 525*

Date		Explanation	Folio	Debit	Credit	Balance
1975						
June	30	Sales	J 5		16,000	16,000
	30	Expenses	J 5	13,240		2,760
	30	To close	J 5	2,760		-0-

Now refer to Answer Frame 5[7] on page 170 to check your responses.

Frame 6[7]

To further test your understanding, indicate whether each of the following statements is true or false.

______ 1. The work sheet is prepared from the earnings statement and the statement of financial position.

______ 2. Adjusting and closing entries must be journalized before the work sheet can be prepared.

______ 3. The work sheet is published for persons outside the company to use.

______ 4. After closing, all of the revenue and expense accounts have zero balances.

Now check your answers by turning to Answer Frame 6[7] on page 170.

Answer frame 5[7]

The missing debits, credits, and balances in the ledger accounts are:

Account No.	Explanation	Folio	Debit	Credit	Balance
	(See Answer Frame 2[7])			7,200	–0–
102	(See Answer Frame 2[7])		11,000		11,000
103A	(See Answer Frame 2[7])			160	160
104	(See Answer Frame 2[7])			600	120
310	(See Answer Frame 4[7])			2,760	5,760
	(See Answer Frame 2[7])		40		40
519	(See Answer Frame 4[7])			40	–0–

If you missed any of the above, review Frames 2[7] through 5[7] before beginning Frame 6[7] on page 169.

Answer frame 6[7]

1. False. The earnings statement and statement of financial position are prepared from the work sheet.
2. False. The work sheet is prepared before these entries are journalized. The necessary adjusting and closing entries are more easily determined by the accountant when he has the work sheet before him.
3. False. The work sheet is *not* a formal accounting statement as are the earnings statement, statement of financial position, and statement of retained earnings. It is more of a "scratch pad" for the accountant's own use.
4. True. One of the main purposes for closing is to "empty" the revenue and expense accounts so they are ready to accumulate amounts pertaining to the next accounting period.

If you missed any of the above, it may be worthwhile for you to work through the entire chapter again unless the error was merely a careless one. Then begin Frame 7[7] below.

Frame 7[7]

THE ACCOUNTING CYCLE

The entire accounting procedure of a business concern is known as the accounting cycle. The steps in the accounting cycle are as listed.

Provide the missing words. The first letter of the correct word is given.

1. Recognize business t________________.
2. R________________ the transactions on documents or mechanisms.
3. A ________________ accounting-wise the transactions recorded on the documents or mechanisms into debit and credit terms.
4. J________________ the transactions.
5. Post the journal entries to the ledger a________________.
6. Take a t________________ balance.
7. Complete the w________________ sheet.
8. Prepare the e________________ statement.

9. Prepare the statement of f_________________ p____________ ____________.
10. J__________________ the adjusting entries.
11. Post the a__________________ entries.
12. Journalize the c__________________ entries.
13. P____________ the closing entries.
14. Take a p__________________ trial balance.

Now turn to Answer Frame 7[7] on page 172 to check your answers.

SUMMARY

The work sheet summarizes the data to be used in preparing the earnings statement, statement of financial position, adjusting journal entries, and closing journal entries. The accountant may use any format he desires. Some of the more common formats are discussed in this chapter.

One format used consists of eight columns headed: Trial Balance, Adjustments, Earnings Statement, and Statement of Financial Position. The entries necessary to establish the cost of goods sold, under periodic inventory procedure, are entered in the Adjustments columns.

A pair of columns headed Adjusted Trial Balance may be inserted immediately following the Adjustments columns. These columns are designed to summarize the figures appearing in the Trial Balance and Adjustments columns before extending them to the other columns and to check upon the arithmetic accuracy of the work done.

The steps in the accounting cycle are as follows: recognize business transactions, record the transactions on documents or mechanisms, analyze the transactions, journalize the transactions, post the journal entries to the ledger accounts, take a trial balance, prepare a work sheet, prepare the earnings statement, prepare the statement of financial position, journalize the adjusting and closing entries, post the adjusting and closing entries, and take a post-closing trial balance.

GLOSSARY

Adjusted Trial Balance columns—columns which may be inserted in the work sheet immediately following the Adjustments columns. Their purpose is to provide a summary of the figures appearing in the Trial Balance and Adjustments columns before extending them to the other columns.

Adjustments Columns—columns which are inserted in a work sheet after the Trial Balance columns to provide space for entering necessary adjustments or changes in account balances at the end of the accounting period.

STUDENT REVIEW QUIZ

1. Which of the following statements is (are) *true* concerning the work sheet?
   a. It is a formal accounting statement which is distributed to stockholders and creditors.
   b. The accounting process could not possibly be completed without preparing a work sheet.
   c. The work sheet may not contain more than eight columns.
   d. An explanation of each adjustment must appear toward the bottom of the work sheet.
   e. Since the work sheet is an informal tool, the accountant can use any format he wants to use or choose not to prepare a work sheet at all.
2. Delivery equipment was acquired September 1 for $2,700 with no estimated salvage value and an estimated useful life of nine years. The company uses the straight-line method of depreciation. The correct adjusting entry on *September 30* is:

a.

Depreciation Expense—Delivery Equipment	300	
Allowance for Depreciation—Delivery Equipment		300

Answer frame 7[7]

1. transactions.
2. Record.
3. Analyze.
4. Journalize.
5. accounts.
6. trial.
7. work.
8. earnings.
9. financial position.
10. Journalize.
11. adjusting.
12. closing.
13. Post.
14. post-closing.

When you are satisfied with your comprehension of the steps in the accounting cycle, continue by turning to the Summary on page 171.

STUDENT REVIEW QUIZ continued

b. Depreciation Expense—
Delivery Equipment 25
Allowance for Depreciation
—Delivery Equipment 25

c. Depreciation Expense—
Delivery Equipment 100
Allowance for Depreciation
—Delivery Equipment 100

d. Depreciation Expense—
Delivery Equipment 270
Allowance for Depreciation
—Delivery Equipment 270

e. None of the above.

3. The Trial Balance column of the work sheet shows store fixtures of $4,000. Estimated depreciation for the period is $400. The store fixtures amount in the Statement of Financial Position columns of the work sheet will be:
   a. A $3,600 debit.
   b. A $3,600 credit.
   c. A $4,400 debit.
   d. A $4,000 debit.
   e. A $4,000 credit.

4. Supplies on hand are shown at $315 in the Trial Balance columns of the work sheet. The Adjustments columns show that $290 of these supplies were used during the month. The amount shown as supplies on hand in the Statement of Financial Position columns is:
   a. $25 debit.
   b. $315 debit.
   c. $290 debit.
   d. $25 credit.
   e. $290 credit.

5. The Rogers Company reports net earnings of $4,100 for the current year. This amount will be shown on the work sheet in the—
   a. Debit Earnings Statement column and debit Statement of Financial Position column.
   b. Credit Earnings Statement column and credit Statement of Financial Position column.
   c. Debit Earnings Statement column and credit Statement of Financial Position column.
   d. Credit Earnings Statement column and debit Statement of Financial Position column.
   e. Debit Adjustments column and credit Adjustments column.

6. Which of the following statements is (are) *incorrect?*

a. The work sheet eliminates the need for adjusting and closing journal entries.
b. The work sheet serves as the basis for preparing the earnings statement.
c. The work sheet serves as the basis for preparing the statement of financial position.
d. The work sheet serves as the basis for journalizing adjusting journal entries.

7. The allowance for depreciation account—
a. Is a liability account with a credit balance.
b. Is a special subdivision of the credit side of the related asset account.
c. Is an asset account with a credit balance.
d. Allows the value of the related asset to be reduced and shifted to the earnings statement as an additional revenue of that period.

8. Company Y shows a debit balance of $400 in the account, Unexpired Insurance. This represents one third of the cost of the original coverage of the policy. The original entry to record the premium due on the policy was:

a.	Unexpired Insurance	1,200	
	Accounts Payable		1,200
b.	Insurance Expense	800	
	Unexpired Insurance		800
c.	Insurance Expense	1,200	
	Unexpired Insurance		1,200
d.	Insurance Expense	400	
	Unexpired Insurance		400

9. The Williams Company follows periodic inventory procedure in accounting for the cost of the merchandise it sells. For a particular period, its beginning inventory was $1,200 and its ending inventory $2,000. Which of the following responses *correctly* describes the treatment to be accorded both the beginning and ending inventories?

The beginning inventory appears in the—
a. Adjustments debit column.
b. Adjustments debit column and Statement of Financial Position debit column.
c. Adjustments credit column and Statement of Financial Position debit column.
d. Adjustments credit column.
e. None of the above answers is correct.

The ending inventory appears in the—
f. Statement of Financial Position debit column and Adjustments debit column.
g. Statement of Financial Position credit column.
h. Statement of Financial Position debit column.
i. Statement of Financial Position debit column and Adjustments credit column.

10. Which of the following statements is *false?*
a. The main purpose of making adjusting entries is to bring the accounts to their proper balances before financial statements are prepared.
b. If the credits in the adjusting entries exceed the debits, the company has realized net earnings.
c. Adjusting entries may be journalized in the same journal as the regular entries made during the accounting period.
d. The work sheet aids in the classification of data for earnings statement and statement of financial position preparation.

Now compare your answers with the correct answers and explanations given on page 210.

chapter 8

ACCUMULATING AND CONTROLLING MASS DATA

LEARNING OBJECTIVES

Study of the material in this chapter is designed to achieve several learning objectives, including an understanding of–

1. The basic elements and advantages of a manual accounting system that utilizes various special journals in addition to a general journal.
2. How to use subsidiary ledgers to show detailed information not shown in a controlling account.
3. The specific design features of special journals for sales, purchases, cash receipts, cash disbursements, and payroll, and how these journals are maintained and posted.
4. The circumstances in which a voucher system may be utilized to good advantage and how such a system works, with special attention to how the voucher register and check register are designed, maintained, and posted.
5. Miscellaneous matters such as posting directly from documents, using documentary ledgers, and recording in journals and ledgers simultaneously.

Frame 1[8]

The orderly and efficient handling of the raw financial data contained in business transactions is absolutely essential to the successful operation of a business. The masses of data contained in the transactions of even a small business are largely unintelligible until processed–that is, recorded, analyzed, classified, summarized, and reported. Such processing aids in establishing management control over business operations and must be undertaken if financial reports and statements are to be prepared.

More specifically, the following purposes are accomplished by the orderly and efficient processing of accounting data:

1. The results of operations and the financial position of the firm can be determined and reported on a timely basis in annual financial statements and interim financial reports.
2. Bills can be paid when due.
3. Shipments of merchandise can be made in proper quantities and types.
4. The conduct of other business can be orderly and in accord with objectives rather than disorganized.
5. Reports required by governmental agencies can be prepared.

Accounting data may be recorded initially in a number of different ways, including through use of pens and pencils, typewriters, adding machines, cash registers, bookkeeping machines, and computers. There should be a systematic flow of accounting data from the source activity to the ledger accounts. The method of initially recording and summarizing business data is influenced by the nature of the business activity, the materiality of the amounts, the means available for processing, and the reports desired.

The initial evidence of business activity usually is found largely on source documents, such as sales slips, cash register tapes or readings, and invoices. The functions of source documents are to communicate information, to serve as a record of completed transactions, and to serve as a source of data for reports to management.

BASIC ELEMENTS OF A MANUAL ACCOUNTING SYSTEM

Because of the number of transactions involved, an accounting system which includes only one book of original entry—the general journal—will be inadequate for even a relatively small business. The first step toward more efficient processing of data usually consists of the development of several special journals. These will allow for a division of labor and also for a reduction of posting time because of the grouping of similar types of transactions. Many different formats or types of journals could be used. The ones presented here are illustrative only. The special journals illustrated are the sales, purchases, cash receipts, cash disbursements, and payroll journals. A voucher system utilizing a voucher register and check register is also introduced. Those journals actually used by a particular company are functions of the types of transactions encountered and of the imagination of the person designing them.

Special journals are also used to facilitate control. For example, one of the primary reasons for using specialized journals to record sales and purchases is to aid in the accounting for accounts receivable and accounts payable so that debit-credit information and balances are available for each creditor and each customer. The cash receipts and cash disbursements journals (and the voucher system) provide handy information regarding receipts and disbursements so that control may exist over these cash flows—for example, so that checks will not be written if there are insufficient funds on deposit to cover them.

Before discussing these further, it is necessary to review a topic closely related to the posting of amounts from the special journals to the ledger accounts.

CONTROLLING ACCOUNTS AND SUBSIDIARY LEDGERS

A controlling account is an account in the general ledger that is supported by a detailed classification of accounting information in a subsidiary record. For example, an up-to-date record must be maintained with each customer to show the business done with him and the amount owed by him at any given time; therefore, outside the general ledger, an account is maintained with each individual customer, showing the debits and credits to his account and the balance due from him. The sum of the balances due from all customers equals the balance of the Accounts Receivable controlling account in the general ledger.

The individual account maintained for each customer is known as a subsidiary account or subsidiary ledger account; all of the individual customers' accounts constitute the *subsidiary accounts receivable ledger*, or customers' ledger. A subsidiary ledger, then, is a group of related accounts showing the details of the balance of a controlling account in the general ledger. Subsidiary ledgers are separated from the general ledger in order (*a*) to relieve the general ledger of a mass of detail and thereby shorten the general ledger trial balance, (*b*) to permit different persons to perform different tasks simultaneously in maintaining the ledgers, and (*c*) to ensure that the recording process is carried out efficiently and accurately. A subsidiary ledger may be used whether or not special journals are used.

When a transaction occurs (such as a sale on account) that affects a controlling account and a subsidiary ledger account, it is journalized in such a fashion that it will be posted (*a*) to the appropriate general ledger account (such as Accounts Receivable) and (*b*) to a subsidiary ledger account (such as that maintained for customer G. M. Jones). The usual manner of journalizing is to enter the transaction in a special column in a journal.

The key to effective operation and control of a subsidiary ledger is found in the posting procedure. The use of special columns in the journals makes it possible to post each transaction to an individual account in a subsidiary ledger during the period. Since the column totals are posted to the controlling accounts at the end of the period (usually a month), a comparison of the controlling account balance with the sum of the individual subsidiary account balances aids in determining that all amounts have been posted to the subsidiary accounts.

A few examples of frequently maintained subsidiary ledgers and the names of the related general ledger controlling accounts are:

Subsidiary Ledger	*General Ledger Controlling Account*
Accounts receivable ledger (an account for each customer)	Accounts Receivable
Accounts payable ledger (an account for each vendor)	Accounts Payable
Equipment ledger (an account or record for each item of equipment of each type or class)	Office Equipment Delivery Equipment Store Fixtures, etc.

The number of subsidiary ledgers maintained will vary according to the information requirements of each company. Control accounts and subsidiary ledgers generally will be maintained for control purposes where there is a high volume of transactions affecting a given account and where information as to these details is needed on a continuing basis.

Indicate whether each of the following statements is true or false.

_______ 1. The balance in the controlling account in the general ledger and the total of the accounts in the underlying subsidiary ledger must be in agreement after all postings have been made for an accounting period.

_______ 2. Reduction in posting time is one reason for using special journals.

_______ 3. Two firms, each with knowledgeable management, may have different subsidiary ledgers.

_______ 4. Specialized journals permit effective division of labor.

Now check your responses in Answer Frame 1[8] on page 178.

Frame 2[8]

GROUPING OF SIMILAR TRANSACTIONS IN JOURNALS

Special journals are designed to systematize the original recording of the major recurring transactions. One journal is set up to record the journal entries for purchases of merchandise on account. Another journal is set up to record the journal entries for sales on account. A cash receipts journal is provided for entry of cash receipts transactions, and a cash disbursements journal is provided for entry of cash disbursements transactions. A payroll journal is set up to record the data on payroll transactions. The general journal remains for all transactions that cannot be entered readily in one of the special journals. All six are records of original entry containing data that will be posted to ledger accounts (with the possible exception of the payroll journal). In the folio column of the accounts, abbreviations are used to identify the source of the posting, for example, PJ for purchases journal, and CDJ for cash disbursements journal as might be included in a set of five journals:

Journal	*Abbreviation*
Sales journal	SJ
Purchases journal	PJ
Cash disbursements journal	CDJ
Cash receipts journal	CRJ
General journal	GJ

The sales journal. Sales, normally, are made on a cash or open account basis. The sales journal in Figure 8.1 is designed to be used to record only sales on account. Cash sales would be recorded in the cash receipts journal. Sales of other assets would be recorded in the cash re-

FIGURE 8.1

SALES JOURNAL — *Page 1*

Date		Description	Invoice Number	Accounts Receivable Dr. 111 / Sales Cr. 301 — Amount	√
1975					
Apr.	3	Arthur Benson	100	30.00	√
	4	Peter Cote	101	25.00	√
	12	Kenneth Johnson	102	130.00	√
	19	Peter Cote	103	10.00	√
	30	Anthony Demambro	104	55.00	√
				250.00	
				(111) (301)	

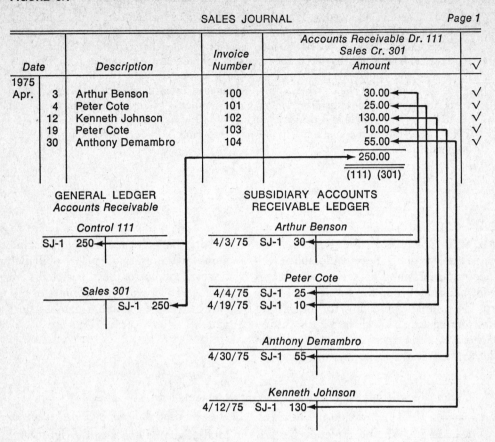

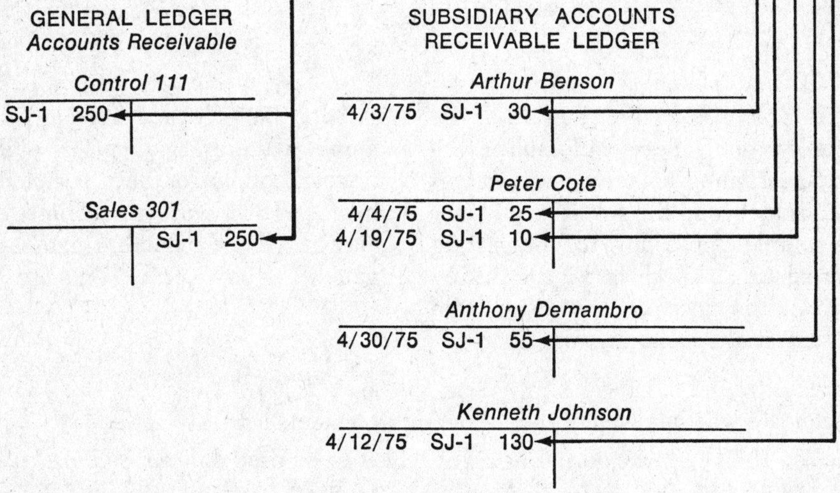

ceipts journal (if cash is received at time of sale) or in the general journal. Figure 8.1 contains the simplest form of sales journal, having only one column entitled Accounts Receivable Dr. and Sales Cr. Many variations in the design of a sales journal are possible. Special columns could be inserted for items such as state sales taxes, federal excise taxes, and sales returns and allowances. And a departmental breakdown can be obtained by providing a Sales Cr. column for each department in a company.

Posting sales. The posting of sales from the sales journal in Figure 8.1 involves entering the total of the money column headed Accounts Receivable Dr. and Sales Cr. as a credit in the general ledger Sales account. The folio reference of SJ-1 (sales journal, page 1) is also entered in the Sales account, and the number (301) is written in the sales journal under the total of the money column to show that the $250 was posted as a credit to Sales. Since there generally is no subsidiary ledger for sales, the individual items comprising sales (the $30, $25, $130, etc.) are not posted in sales accounts.

Posting accounts receivable. To post accounts receivable from the sales journal in Figure 8.1, the total of the money column ($250) is posted as a debit to the Accounts Receivable control account in the general ledger with a folio reference of SJ-1. The number (111) is entered under the total of the money column in the sales journal to show that the amount has been posted to account number 111. The individual amounts in the money column are posted to each individual customer's account in the subsidiary ledger so that the account will show the amount currently due from him. As each individual amount is posted, a check mark (√) is placed in the column headed (√) opposite the amount to show that it has been posted. When the posting of the accounts receivable has been completed, the Accounts Receivable control account will show a

Answer frame 1[8]

1. True. The subsidiary ledger is merely a breakdown of the amounts in the controlling account. The balances, therefore, must be in agreement.
2. True. Column totals are posted in many instances rather than individual items.
3. True. The firms may have different types of transactions. For example, one firm may receive many notes receivable and the other few, if any.
4. True. One person could, for example, be engaged in posting the sales journal to the accounts receivable subsidiary ledger while another is posting the purchases journal to the accounts payable subsidiary ledger.

If you missed any of the above questions, restudy Frame 1[8] before proceeding to Frame 2[8] on page 176.

Frame 2[8] continued

balance of $250, which is equal to the sum of the balances in the Accounts Receivable subsidiary ledger accounts, assuming no previous balances in the control account or in the subsidiary ledger accounts. The complete procedure for the posting of a sales journal can be seen in Figure 8.1 by following each of the lines leading away from the dollar amounts in the sales journal.

Subsidiary ledger accounts usually are not numbered but are kept in alphabetical order, since accounts for new customers are likely to be added while other accounts for old customers may be deleted when business relations are terminated.

Indicate whether each of the following statements is true or false.

______ 1. The sales journal in Figure 8.1 is to be used only for sales on account.

______ 2. When completely posted, the total of the balances in the subsidiary accounts receivable accounts should be equal to the balance in the Accounts Receivable control account.

______ 3. Conceivably, a sales journal could have more than one column.

______ 4. The general journal is the only record of original entry, since all of the other journals are special journals.

Now check your answers by turning to Answer Frame 2[8] on page 180.

Frame 3[8]

The cash receipts journal. The cash receipts journal, which might be used in combination with the sales journal already illustrated, is shown in Figure 8.2. Any number of different designs may be used for this journal also. For example, if some of the items appearing in the Sundry (which means miscellaneous) Accounts Cr. column are frequently credited, it would be advisable to set up a separate column for each of these items.

Since the amounts appearing in the Sundry Accounts Cr. column usually pertain to different accounts, the column total is not posted and a check mark (√) is placed immediately below the amount. The individual items are posted to the accounts indicated (that is, to accounts 138 and 303 in Figure 8.2).

The cash receipts journal in Figure 8.2 has not been posted, since no posting marks are shown there.

FIGURE 8.2

CASH RECEIPTS JOURNAL — *Page 5*

101 Cash Dr.	726 Sales Discounts Dr.	Date		Description	301 Sales Cr.	111 Accounts Receivable Cr.		Sundry Accounts Cr.		
						Amount	√	Acct. No.	Amount	√
		1975								
10,700.00		Apr.	1	Cash sales	10,700.00					
29.40	.60		6	Arthur Benson—Invoice No. 100		30.00				
10,775.00			7	Cash sales	10,775.00					
6,000.00			10	Sold investments at cost to Wells Corporation				138*	6,000.00	
10,600.00			14	Cash sales	10,600.00					
25.00			19	Peter Cote—Invoice No. 101		25.00				
127.40	2.60		20	Kenneth Johnson—Invoice No. 102		130.00				
11,045.00			25	Cash sales	11,045.00					
200.00			26	Dividends received on Krantz Company common stock				303†	200.00	
49,501.80	3.20				43,120.00	185.00			6,200.00	

* 138 Investments.
† 303 Dividend Revenue.

Answer frame 2[8]

1. True. Since every amount entered in the sales journal is included in a total that is debited to Accounts Receivable and credited to Sales, a cash sale could not be properly entered in the accounts if it was entered in the sales journal.
2. True. This is because the subsidiary ledger accounts are merely the control account broken down into individual customers' accounts.
3. True. If, for example, a business is divided into departments and departmental information is desired, there could be two or more columns for sales by departments. Also, there could be columns for sales taxes, federal excise taxes, and for sales returns and allowances. Sundry columns could also be included.
4. False. The special journals are also books of original entry. A transaction could be recorded in a special journal and only in that journal.

If you answered incorrectly, review Frame 2[8] before continuing in Frame 3[8] on page 178.

Frame 3[8] continued

Assume that the general ledger and accounts receivable subsidiary ledger shown below are as they appear after the sales journal (Figure 8.1) has been posted. Determine the information that should be posted to these ledgers from the cash receipts journal by filling in the blank spaces below. Also, indicate by inserting in the cash receipts journal in Figure 8.2, the posting marks that would be entered there as the journal is posted.

PARTIAL GENERAL LEDGER

Cash — *Account No. 101*

Date		Explanation	Folio	Debit	Credit	Balance
1975						
Apr.	1	Beginning balance (assumed)				10,000.00

Accounts Receivable — *Account No. 111*

Date		Explanation	Folio	Debit	Credit	Balance
1975						
Apr.	30		SJ-1	250.00		250.00

Investments — *Account No. 138*

Date		Explanation	Folio	Debit	Credit	Balance
1975						
Apr.	1	Beginning balance (assumed)				18,000.00

Common Stock — *Account No. 250*

Date		Explanation	Folio	Debit	Credit	Balance
1975						
Apr.	1	Beginning balance (assumed)				20,000.00

Retained Earnings — *Account No. 251*

Date		Explanation	Folio	Debit	Credit	Balance
1975						
Apr.	1	Beginning balance (assumed)				8,000.00

PARTIAL GENERAL LEDGER (continued)

Sales — *Account No. 301*

Date		Explanation	Folio	Debit	Credit	Balance
1975						
Apr.	30		SJ-1		250.00	250.00

Dividend Revenue — *Account No. 303*

Date		Explanation	Folio	Debit	Credit	Balance

Sales Discounts — *Account No. 726*

Date		Explanation	Folio	Debit	Credit	Balance
1975						

SUBSIDIARY ACCOUNTS RECEIVABLE LEDGER

Arthur Benson

Date		Explanation	Folio	Debit	Credit	Balance
1975						
Apr.	3		SJ-1	30.00		30.00

Peter Cote

Date		Explanation	Folio	Debit	Credit	Balance
1975						
Apr.	4		SJ-1	25.00		25.00
	19		SJ-1	10.00		35.00

Anthony Demambro

Date		Explanation	Folio	Debit	Credit	Balance
1975						
Apr.	30		SJ-1	55.00		55.00

Kenneth Johnson

Date		Explanation	Folio	Debit	Credit	Balance
1975						
Apr.	12		SJ-1	130.00		130.00

Now turn to Answer Frame 3[8] on page 182 to check your answers.

Frame 4[8]

A combined sales and cash receipts journal. It is possible to combine the sales and cash receipts journals illustrated earlier, as shown in Figure 8.3. This allows total sales to be posted as one amount rather than two.

But posting and journalizing convenience is not the only consideration. Remember that one of the reasons for creating special journals is so that several persons can work with them at the same time. Having separate cash receipts and sales journals does allow more persons to work with the data in the journals at the same time. A decision in any particular case has to be made so as to maximize overall efficiency in working with journals.

Answer frame 3[8]

The items that should have been inserted in the blank spaces are:

Account	*Date*	*Folio*	*Debit*	*Credit*	*Balance*
Cash	30	CRJ-5	49,501.80		59,501.80
Accounts receivable	30	CRJ-5		185.00	65.00
Investments	10	CRJ-5		6,000.00	12,000.00
Sales	30	CRJ-5		43,120.00	43,370.00
	1975				
Dividend Revenue	Apr. 26	CRJ-5		200.00	200.00
	1975				
Sales Discounts	Apr. 20	CRJ-5	3.20		3.20
Arthur Benson	6	CRJ-5		30.00	–0–
Peter Cote	19	CRJ-5		25.00	10.00
Kenneth Johnson	20	CRJ-5		130.00	–0–

You should have placed the number 101 under the total of the Cash Dr. column in the cash receipts journal, 726 under the total of the Sales Discounts Dr. column, 301 under the total of the Sales Cr. column, and 111 under the total of the Accounts Receivable Cr. column to indicate that these amounts have been posted to the accounts so numbered. Under the $6,200 total in the Sundry Accounts Cr. column, you should have placed a check mark (√) indicating that the total is not to be posted. Beside each of the amounts in the Accounts Receivable Cr. column and in the Sundry Accounts Cr. column (in the column provided) you should enter a check mark (√) to indicate that each amount was posted.

Study Frame 3[8] again carefully if you missed any of the above because specific attention to detailed posting instructions will be considerably less in the illustrations that follow. Then proceed to Frame 4[8] on page 181.

Frame 4[8] continued

FIGURE 8.3

COMBINED SALES AND CASH RECEIPTS JOURNAL *Page 11*

101 Cash Dr.	*726 Sales Discounts Dr.*	*111 Accounts Receivable Dr. Amount*	√	*Date*		*Description*	*Invoice No.*	*301 Sales Cr.*	*111 Accounts Receivable Cr. Amount*	√	*Sundry Accounts Cr. Acct. No.*	*Amount*	√
				1975									
10,700.00				Apr.	1	Cash sales		10,700.00					
		30.00	√		3	Arthur Benson	100	30.00					
		25.00	√		4	Peter Cote	101	25.00					
29.40	.60				6	Arthur Benson	100		30.00	√			
10,775.00					7	Cash sales		10,775.00					
6,000.00					10	Sold investments at cost					138*	6,000.00	√
		130.00	√		12	Kenneth Johnson	102	130.00					
10,600.00					14	Cash sales		10,600.00					
		10.00	√		19	Peter Cote	103	10.00					
25.00					19	Peter Cote	101		25.00	√			
127.40	2.60				20	Kenneth Johnson	102		130.00	√			
11,045.00					25	Cash sales		11,045.00					
200.00					26	Dividends received					303†	200.00	√
		55.00	√		30	Anthony Demambro		55.00					
49,501.80	3.20	250.00						43,370.00	185.00			6,200.00	
(101)	(726)	(111)						(301)	(111)			(√)	

* 138 Investments.
† 303 Dividend Revenue.

Indicate whether each of the following statements is true or false.

______ 1. Every company should use a combined cash receipts and sales journal rather than separate journals.

______ 2. The greater the number of specialized journals a company has, the greater the number of persons that can work with them at one time.

______ 3. In posting the special journal in Figure 8.3, both debits and credits would be entered in the subsidiary accounts receivable accounts.

______ 4. All of the items entered in the Cash Dr. column in Figure 8.3 resulted from cash sales.

Now check your responses in Answer Frame 4[8] on page 184.

Frame 5[8]

The purchases journal. If a company engages in frequent transactions involving the purchase of merchandise for resale, the recording of such transactions could be facilitated by use of a purchases journal such as the one shown in Figure 8.4.

The total of the one money column in this journal is posted to the Purchases account (periodic inventory procedure is assumed) as a debit and to the Accounts Payable account as a credit at the end of the month. In this way, all of the purchases on account for the month are posted in a single debit and a single credit. The individual amounts in the column are posted to the individual vendors' accounts in the accounts payable subsidiary ledger.

Most business firms are aware that in order to have an acceptable level of control over cash disbursements they must pay all bills by check (in this way, proper officers can authorize payment and sign the check). Assuming this to be the case here, all purchases are treated as being made on account and are therefore recorded in the purchases journal (even if the length of delay in payment is only long enough to write the check). The payment is then shown in the cash disbursements journal.

There are, of course, many alternative designs of purchases journals that could be used. If there are, for example, separate departments, a separate purchases column could be included for each department. A column could be included for

FIGURE 8.4

PURCHASES JOURNAL *Page 10*

Date		*Terms*	*Invoice Number*	*Creditor*	*Purchases Dr. 801 Accounts payable Cr. 201* Amount	√
1975						
Apr.	1	2/10, n/30	862	Smith Corporation	196.00	√
	7	1/15, n/60	121	Lasky Company	99.00	√
	12	2/20, n/60	561	Booth Corporation	4,900.00	√
	15	2/10, n/30	1042	Gooch Corporation	2,940.00	√
	21	3/15, n/60	633	Wyngarden Company	9,700.00	√
	26	2/10, n/30	734	Mertz Company	98.00	√
	30	2/10, n/30	287	Nelson Company	3,920.00	√
	30	2/20, n/60	568	Booth Corporation	1,470.00	√
					23,323.00	
					(801) (201)	

Answer frame 4[8]

1. False. While it may be advantageous for some firms to use a combined sales and cash receipts journal, other firms may not find it so. The decision hinges on how many different persons need to work with the information in the journals at any one time.
2. True. This is one reason why some companies choose to use separate cash receipts and sales journals.
3. True. Notice that the journal has both an Accounts Receivable Dr. column and an Accounts Receivable Cr. column with entries in both.
4. False. Only four of the items resulted from cash sales. The others were from payments on account, the sale of investments, and dividends received.

If you missed any of the above, reread Frame 4[8] before beginning Frame 5[8] on page 183.

Frame 5[8] continued

purchase returns and allowances if they are frequently encountered. And since a Purchase Returns and Allowances account normally is credited with the debit being to Accounts Payable, a separate Accounts Payable Dr. column would have to be included.

All amounts of purchases have been entered net of discount in the illustration. This procedure is described briefly in Chapter 6. Any discounts missed are considered penalties due to inefficiency and are recorded in a Discounts Lost account.

Indicate whether each of the following statements about the purchases journal in Figure 8.4 is true or false.

______ 1. Ten amounts have been posted from the purchases journal.

______ 2. Four amounts were posted to the general ledger.

______ 3. Eight amounts would be posted to a subsidiary ledger whether a purchases journal was used or not.

______ 4. If only a general journal had been used, a total of 16 postings would have been made.

Turn to Answer Frame 5[8] on page 186 to check your responses.

Frame 6[8]

The cash disbursements journal. Since it is assumed that all cash disbursements are made by check, the cash disbursements journal in Figure 8.5 contains a column in which to record the number of each check written. As might be expected, most of the checks drawn are in payment of accounts payable and, in this instance, in payment of employee salaries. Separate columns are included in which to record any discounts lost and to record the acquisition and expensing of supplies. All other items will have to be recorded in the Sundry Accounts Dr. column.

In companies with many employees, a separate payroll bank checking account probably would be established. Then the cash disbursements journal would show only one amount for payroll, the total amount of salaries payable. The entry would debit Payroll Cash and credit Cash (general checking account). A separate payroll check register, similar to that in Figure 8.9 on page 194, might then be maintained to record the payment of salaries out of the payroll checking account.

The payroll journal. Sometimes a formal payroll journal is maintained to record data for payroll accounting. A payroll journal usually con-

FIGURE 8.5

CASH DISBURSEMENTS JOURNAL — *Page 5*

201 Accounts Payable Dr. Amount	√	*219 Salaries Payable Dr.*	*821 Discounts Lost Dr.*	*822 Supplies Expense Dr.*	*Sundry Accounts Dr.* Acct. No.	Amount	√	*Date*		*Description*	*Check No.*	*101 Cash Cr.*
				42.00				1975 Apr.	2	Brooklyn Square Paint Company	524	42.00
					123*	1,200.00	√		3	Insurance policy to cover May 1975—April 30, 1976	525	1,200.00
					140†	500.00	√		4	Furniture—office	526	500.00
					823‡	200.00	√			Rent for April 1975	527	200.00
196.00	√								8	Smith Corporation—Invoice No. 862	528	196.00
				10.00					14	Allan Park Stationery Company	529	10.00
99.00	√								18	Lask Company—Invoice No. 121	530	99.00
4,900.00	√								21	Booth Company—Invoice No. 561	531	4,900.00
9,700.00	√								27	Wyngarden Company—Invoice No. 633	532	9,700.00
2,940.00	√		60.00						28	Gooch Corporation—Invoice No. 1042	533	3,000.00
		1,553.60							30	Clarke Frankson	534	1,553.60
		1,172.90								Mead Stacy	535	1,172.90
		803.10								Jason Evans	536	803.10
		720.20								Marshall Watson	537	720.20
		403.00								Cleveland Avoy	538	403.00
		341.02								James Jackson	539	341.02
		366.60								Stuart Bently	540	366.60
		377.14								Robert Aleo	541	377.14
17,835.00		5,737.56	60.00	52.00		1,900.00						25.584.56
(201)		(219)	(821)	(822)		(√)						(101)

* 123—Unexpired Insurance.
† 140—Furniture and Equipment.
‡ 823—Rent Expense.

tains a debit column for category of salary or wage expense (e.g., administrative, salesmen's, officers', clerical, warehouse, etc.). Credit columns are included for such accounts as Federal Income Tax Withheld, State Income Tax Withheld, F.I.C.A. (social security) Taxes Withheld, Union Dues Withheld, and Salaries Payable, which are all liabilities representing amounts that must be paid out either to employees or to others on the employees' behalf. Figure 8.6 shows such a journal. Payment of the liability for salaries payable and for the various amounts withheld from the employees' paychecks will be made periodically and recorded in the cash disbursements journal.

Some companies maintain a payroll journal only as a memorandum record, which means no postings are made from it. In these firms, the entry for the payroll would have to be made in some other journal such as the general journal. The entry would be made to the accounts listed in the headings of the columns in Figure 8.6 and in the amounts of the totals of these columns.

Answer frame 5[8]

1. True. Eight individual amounts were posted, together with the column total which was posted twice.
2. False. The column total was posted twice to the general ledger. The other eight items were posted to the accounts payable subsidiary ledger.
3. True. In this particular instance the number of postings to the subsidiary ledger would not be affected.
4. False. A total of 24 amounts would have been posted. Eight items would have been posted to the Purchases account, eight to the Accounts Payable account, and another eight to the individual accounts payable subsidiary ledger accounts.

If you missed any of the above, reread Frame 5[8] before beginning Frame 6[8] on page 184.

FIGURE 8.6

PAYROLL JOURNAL — Page 2

810 Administrative Salaries Expense Dr.	811 Salesmen's Salaries Expense Dr.	812 Office Clerical Salaries Expense Dr.	813 Warehouse Salaries Expense Dr.	Date		Employee	215 Federal Income Tax Withheld Cr.	216 State Income Tax Withheld Cr.	217 F.I.C.A. Taxes Withheld Cr.	218 Union Dues Withheld Cr.	219 Salaries Payable Cr.
				1975							
2,000.00				Apr.	30	Clarke Frankson	355.40	64.60	117.00		1,463.00
1,500.00						Mead Stacy	220.70	40.40	87.75		1,151.15
	1,000.00					Jason Evans	124.70	28.20	58.50		788.60
	900.00					Marshall Watson	112.60	27.60	52.65		707.15
		500.00				Cleveland Avoy	56.20	16.80	29.25	2.00	395.75
		420.00				James Jackson	43.70	14.80	24.57	2.00	334.93
			450.00			Stuart Bently	46.70	15.40	26.33	1.50	360.07
			465.00			Robert Aleo	49.70	16.20	27.20	1.50	370.40
3,500.00	1,900.00	920.00	915.00				1,009.70	224.00	423.25	7.00	5,571.05
(810)	(811)	(812)	(813)				(215)	(216)	(217)	(218)	(219)

Frame 6[8] continued

Indicate whether each of the following statements is true or false.

_____ 1. The cash disbursements journal in Figure 8.5 has not been completely posted.

_____ 2. A total of 14 postings was made from the cash disbursements journal illustrated.

_____ 3. Not all of the invoices in the cash disbursements journal illustrated were paid within the allowed discount period.

_____ 4. The column totals in the payroll journal may not be posted in some accounting systems.

Now check your responses in Answer Frame 6[8] on page 188.

Frame 7[8]

The general journal and other journals. Every transaction that will not fit conveniently into the special journals is entered in the general journal. The general journal would be needed to record the adjusting and closing entries even if all other entries could be fitted into the format of one or another of the special journals used.

Various other special journals could be used, such as a purchases returns and allowances journal and a sales returns and allowances journal. The proper combination for a particular company depends on the volume of transactions, the frequency of the occurrence of certain types of transactions, management's information needs, and the number of persons having to work with the data at any one time.

Summary of the advantages of using special journals. To summarize, the following advantages are obtained from the use of special journals.

1. *Time is saved in journalizing.* Only one line is used for each transaction (usually); a full description is not necessary. The amount of writing is reduced because it is not necessary to repeat the account names printed at the top of the special column or columns.
2. *Time is saved in posting.* Many data are posted as totals of columns rather than as individual items.
3. *Detail is eliminated from the general ledger.* Column totals are posted to the general ledger, and the detail is left in the journals.
4. *Division of labor is promoted.* Several persons can work simultaneously on the accounting records. This specialization and division of labor pinpoints responsibility and aids in the location of errors.
5. *Use of accounting machines is facilitated.* The mass of routine transactions recorded in special journals frequently makes the use of accounting machines economical.
6. *Management analysis is aided.* The journals themselves can be useful to management in analyzing classes of transactions (such as credit sales).

Indicate whether each of the following statements is true or false regarding the advantages to be obtained from the use of special journals.

_______ 1. General ledger accounts become much less detailed.

_______ 2. Journalizing and posting time is reduced.

_______ 3. Accounting machines and special journals may be used in an effective combination.

_______ 4. Special journals generally tend to limit the number of persons that can work on the accounting records at the same time.

Now turn to Answer Frame 7[8] on page 188 to check your responses.

Frame 8[8]

VOUCHER SYSTEM

In very small companies where the owner has an intimate knowledge of all transactions and where he personally signs all checks, there need be no great concern over the proper handling of cash disbursements. In larger companies where the owners or top management officers have no direct part in the payment process, close control over this function should be provided via a formalized element in the system of internal control. While the owner who has an intimate knowledge of all transactions might use special journals to reduce journalizing and posting time, he would not have need for the formalized system of internal control (called a voucher system) presented here. The voucher system utilizes two special journals which have not yet been described.

With a voucher system, management seeks to

Answer frame 6[8]

1. False. It has been completely posted as is indicated by the posting marks (check marks for individual items posted either to the general ledger or to the subsidiary ledgers) and account numbers for the totals of columns.
2. False. Only 13 postings were made. The check mark under the Sundry Accounts Dr. column indicates that this amount is not posted.
3. True. The payment to the Gooch Corporation, Invoice No. 1042, on April 28 was made after the discount period had expired. As a result, the total payment was $3,000, not $2,940.
4. True. In some accounting systems the payroll journal is not posted directly but merely provides information for an entry made in another journal, such as the general journal, or possibly the voucher register as is discussed later in this chapter.

If you missed any of the above questions, check the above answers carefully to make sure that you understand why your answer was incorrect, and then continue in Frame 7[8] on page 187.

Answer frame 7[8]

1. True. Since only special column totals (and individual items in sundry columns) are posted to the general ledger, much detail is omitted from the general ledger accounts.
2. True. Journalizing in one line and entry of amounts only and posting by column totals yields some saving in journalizing and posting time.
3. True. Accounting machines and special journals may often be used together effectively.
4. False. Special journals generally make it possible for more individuals to work on the accounting records simultaneously.

If you missed any of the above, review Frame 7[8] before proceeding to Frame 8[8] on page 187.

Frame 8[8] continued

establish that the cash disbursed was disbursed in the proper amounts, to the proper parties, for valid, authorized reasons, and at the proper time. Such control is achieved in the following manner: each transaction that will involve the payment of cash is entered on a voucher and recorded in a voucher register some time before payment is made. A voucher is a form with spaces provided for data concerning the liability being set up (such as invoice number, invoice date, creditor's name and address, description of the goods or services received, terms of payment and amount due). It also has spaces for signatures of those approving the obligation for payment. Each voucher goes through a rigorous process of examination and eventual approval or disapproval. By the time a voucher is approved for payment, one can be quite certain that the liability for payment is legitimate, since various persons have attested to the propriety and accuracy of the claim, and supporting documents (invoices) are attached.

The voucher system does not include a formal subsidiary accounts payable ledger. The file of unpaid vouchers serves as the subsidiary vouchers (accounts) payable ledger.

When the voucher system is used, the term "vouchers payable" is usually substituted for the term "accounts payable" in the accounts. When financial statements are prepared, however, the more conventional term, accounts payable, is preferable.

Management is further assured that cash disbursements transactions are being handled in accordance with its directives by a separation of duties. For example, the person or persons who authorize the incurrence of liabilities should not also prepare and distribute the checks. The receipt of assets or services giving rise to a liability must be acknowledged and approved by (*a*) the receiving department or (*b*) others who do not have authority to prepare and distribute checks. The persons who have authority to sign checks should do so only when approved vouchers authorizing each check are presented. The possibilities of errors and of recording unauthorized liabilities or cash disbursements are therefore minimized.

Determine whether each of the following statements is true or false.

______ 1. Under a voucher system each transaction that will involve the payment of cash will eventually be entered on a voucher and in the voucher register.

______ 2. The voucher system provides a uniform method for the recording of liabilities that will result in cash disbursement.

______ 3. An account called Vouchers Payable will normally appear in the chart of accounts for a company using a voucher system.

______ 4. The voucher system provides internal control over cash disbursements by centralizing in one person the functions of authorizing the incurrence of liabilities and the preparation and distribution of checks.

Now turn to Answer Frame 8[8] on page 190 to check your answers.

Frame 9[8]

Types of vouchers. In a broad sense a voucher is any written document that serves as a receipt or as evidence of authority to act. In a narrow sense—as applied to a voucher system—a voucher is a form or document that substantiates a liability and thus serves as the basis for an accounting entry. Vouchers are usually numbered consecutively, and all vouchers are carefully accounted for.

One form of voucher is presented in Figure 8.7. Here it is assumed that one voucher is prepared for each invoice received from each creditor and that the proper supporting documents—invoice and receiving ticket—are in order.

The procedures followed (note especially the initials of persons auditing the voucher and approving it for payment) in this basic form of voucher system show clearly that a voucher system is a method of internal control over the payment of liabilities. Emphasis is placed on the time of payment rather than on the identity of the creditor. In the administration and control of cash, the primary matters are the time and the amount of the disbursement.

In some lines of business the terms of discount and of payment run from the date of the invoice. When this is the case a voucher should be prepared for each invoice, as in Figure 8.7, and should be filed according to the date on which the discount period terminates or payment is due. Such a file is often called a tickler file.

When discount terms and payment terms are computed from the end of the month, it is possible to modify the voucher and reduce the number of vouchers prepared and, therefore, the number of entries made in the voucher register. All invoices received from each creditor may be accumulated and listed on one voucher at the end of the month, since all will probably be paid by one check. The details of the various invoices may be summarized and entered on one voucher.

Answer frame 8[8]

1. True. All transactions that will involve the payment of cash will be entered on a voucher and recorded in the voucher register. For most short-term liabilities this is done at the time of the transaction creating the liability.
2. True. The uniformity is achieved by requiring that each transaction involving the payment of cash be entered on a voucher and in a voucher register.
3. True. The account Vouchers Payable will usually be substituted for the Accounts Payable account when a voucher system is used.
4. False. The internal control over cash disbursements is achieved by assigning the functions mentioned to several persons, not combining them in one person. The person who has the authority to approve the incurrence of a liability should not also prepare and distribute the checks. If all of these functions were combined in one person, it would not be difficult for him to prepare checks payable to himself under an assumed name in payment for merchandise or services never delivered or rendered.

If you missed any of the above, reread Frame 8[8] before turning to Frame 9[8] on page 189.

FIGURE 8.7
A voucher

ATWELL SUPPLY COMPANY
Atwell Plaza
Atwell, Texas 78712

VOUCHER

VOUCHER NO. 141
OUR P.O. NO. 2514
VENDOR'S INVOICE 416
PAID BY CHECK NO. 587
DATE PAID 7/18/75

Payable To: Gregory Corporation
48 Cadillac Square
Detroit, Michigan 48226

DATE		ACCT. NO.	DESCRIPTION	QUANTITY	UNIT PRICE	TOTAL
July	14	126	X-16 Transistors	100	$2.00	$200.00
			TOTAL			$200.00
			DISCOUNT	2%		4.00
			NET PAYABLE			$196.00

TERMS 2/10, n/30
EXPLANATIONS:

AUDITED AS TO CORRECTNESS	APPROVED FOR PAYMENT	ENTERED IN VOUCHER REGISTER	DATE ENTERED
a.T.	*L.S.W.*	*R.E.L.*	7/14/75

Frame 9[8] continued

Indicate whether each of the following statements is true or false.

______ 1. The system of preparing one voucher for each creditor each month is most feasible when discount and payment terms are computed from the date of an invoice.

______ 2. The system of preparing a voucher for each invoice is preferable when terms run from the end of the month and many purchases are made from each of the same creditors each month.

______ 3. The preparation of one voucher for each creditor each month eliminates many entries from the voucher register.

______ 4. In a sense, a voucher can be said to vouch for the validity or legitimacy of a transaction requiring the disbursement of cash.

Now check your responses in Answer Frame 9[8] on page 192.

Frame 10[8]

Special journals used in a voucher system

Voucher register. A voucher register is a multicolumn journal containing special debit columns for the accounts most frequently debited when a liability is incurred. Stated in a different manner, a voucher register contains a chronological and serial record of all vouchers prepared. It includes a brief description of the transactions and indicates the accounts involved. One line is allotted to each voucher.

A special Vouchers Payable Cr. column in the voucher register summarizes all vouchers approved for payment. The total of the Vouchers Payable column in the voucher register is posted to the liability controlling account Vouchers Payable at the end of each month (or, possibly, more frequently).

Figure 8.8 is presented to show the entry of vouchers in the special journal for vouchers in cases where one voucher is prepared for each invoice. As each voucher is prepared and entered in the voucher register, the voucher is placed in the unpaid voucher file. As each is paid, the voucher (or a duplicate copy of it) is transferred to the paid voucher file. A notation of the payment is made in the Date Paid and Check Number columns of the voucher register as illustrated.

Check register. A check register (or check record) is a special journal containing a chronological and serial record of all checks issued. One line is allotted to each check. An efficient system of internal control over cash requires that all disbursements be made by check. No check may be issued unless it is authorized by an approved voucher; therefore, the interrelationship between the voucher register and the check record is established. Rigorous compliance enhances close control over cash disbursements.

A special debit column in the check register summarizes all vouchers paid. After the total of this column is posted as a debit to the Vouchers Payable controlling account in the general ledger, the balance of the account should equal the total of the vouchers in the unpaid vouchers file. The voucher register and the check register are the two primary journals in a voucher system from which postings are made to the Vouchers Payable controlling account. And when a voucher system is employed, these two registers replace the more traditional purchases and cash disbursements journals.

The check register, Figure 8.9, sets forth the entry to record the issuance of a check in payment of a voucher. A check register usually has only one column (although it may have more).

Answer frame 9[8]

1. False. Since under this system all of the invoices from a creditor during a month are listed on one voucher, it would not be a practical system to use if discount and payment terms run from the various within-the-month invoice dates rather than from the end of the month.
2. False. This system is preferable when terms run from the invoice date. If they run from the end of the month, several invoices may be recorded on one voucher (one voucher per creditor per month).
3. True. Since a number of invoices may be summarized on one voucher, this system reduces the number of entries to be made in the voucher register as opposed to the system which uses one voucher for each invoice.
4. True. A voucher does indeed attest to the validity or authenticity of a transaction requiring a cash disbursement.

If you answer incorrectly, restudy Frame 9[8] and then continue in Frame 10[8] on page 191.

Frame 10[8] continued

FIGURE 8.8

VOUCHER REGISTER

Line No.	Voucher Date 1975		Voucher No.	Payee	Explanation	Terms	Date Paid		Check No.	Vouchers Payable Cr. 101	General Ledger Account Name
1	May	2	223	Hanley Company	Ring binders	2/10, n/30	May	12	1350	980.00	
2		4	224	Moore Transport	Transportation, binders	2/10, n/30		5	1347	13.00	
3		6	225	White Stationery Company	Office supplies	2/10, n/30		12	1351	102.00	
4		8	226	Specialty Advertisers	Advertising			8	1348	1,200.00	
5		10	227	Blanch Company	Note and interest			10	1349	1,010.00	
6		12	228	Internal Revenue Service	Income tax withheld, April 1975			12	1352	2,200.00	
7		14	229	Swanson Company	Filler paper	2/10, n/30		26	1356	3,920.00	
8		16	230	Rizzo Company	Office desk	n/30		25	1355	640.00	
9		18	231	Warren Company	Spiral binders	2/10, n/30		28	1357	4,900.00	
10		20	232	First National Bank	Interest on mortgage note			20	1353	154.00	
11		22	233	Falcone Company	Books	n/30				10,000.00	
12		24	234	Petty cash	Reimbursement			24	1354	132.00	
13		26	235	Swanson Company	Discount lost (No. 229).			26	1356	80.00	
14		28	236	Celoron Company	Drawing sets	2/20, n/30				9,800.00	
15		31	237	Payroll account	Salaries and wages			31	1358	21,600.00	FICA Tax Liability
16											Federal Income Tax Withheld
										56,731.00	

The total of this one money column is posted as a debit to Vouchers Payable and a credit to Cash. If invoices are entered at gross amount (before discount deductions) in the voucher register, a Purchase Discounts Cr. column should be provided in the check register. In this latter instance, separate columns would be necessary for the debit to Vouchers Payable and the credit to Cash, since the dollar amounts posted to these two accounts would be different by the amount of the discounts taken.

When vouchers are prepared for the net amount of an invoice and the invoice is paid after the discount privilege period has expired, another voucher should be prepared for the amount of the discount (see line 13 in Figure 8.8).

Page No. 15
Month May, 1975

Accounts Cr.										General Ledger Accounts Dr.		
Acct. No.	Amount Cr.	√	Discounts Lost Dr. 122	Merchandise Purchases Dr. 131	Transportation-In Dr. 144	Salaries and Wages Dr. 158	Office Expense Dr. 175	Advertising Expense Dr. 262	Interest Expense Dr. 306	Account Name	Acct. No.	Amount Dr.
				980.00								
					13.00							
							102.00					
								1,200.00				
									10.00	Notes Payable	103	1,000.00
										Federal Income Tax Withheld	108	2,200.00
				3,920.00								
										Office Equipment	42	640.00
				4,860.00	40.00							
									154.00			
				10,000.00								
					31.88		60.12	40.00				
			80.00									
				9,800.00								
107	400.00					24,000.00						
108	2,000.00											
	2,400.00		80.00	29,560.00	84.88	24,000.00	162.12	1,240.00	164.00			3,840.00

FIGURE 8.9

CHECK REGISTER

Page No. 24
Month May, 1975

Line No.	Date 1975		Payee	Voucher No.	Check No.	Vouchers Payable Dr., Cash Cr.
1	May	5	Moore Transport	244	1347	13.00
2		8	Specialty Advertisers	226	1348	1,200.00
3		10	Blanch Company	227	1349	1,010.00
4		12	Hanley Company	223	1350	980.00
5		12	White Stationery Company	225	1351	102.00
6		12	Internal Revenue Service	228	1352	2,200.00
7		20	First National Bank	232	1353	154.00
8		24	Petty Cash	234	1354	132.00
9		25	Rizzo Company	230	1355	640.00
10		26	Swanson Company	235 229	1356	4,000.00
11		28	Warren Company	231	1357	4,900.00
12		31	Payroll account	237	1358	21,600.00
						36,931.00

Indicate whether each of the following statements is true or false.

_______ 1. The check register shown in Figure 8.9 contains a chronological and sequential listing of the vouchers prepared by the company.

_______ 2. The voucher register in Figure 8.8 has been completely posted.

_______ 3. The voucher register shown in Figure 8.8 contains a chronological and sequential record of all of the vouchers prepared by the company.

_______ 4. Each item in the column headed Vouchers Payable Cr. in Figure 8.8 will be posted to the subsidiary vouchers payable ledger.

_______ 5. The totals of the columns headed General Ledger Accounts Cr. and General Ledger Accounts Dr. in Figure 8.8 will not be posted to any general ledger account.

Now check your responses with the correct answers in Answer Frame 10[8] on page 196.

Frame 11[8]

Files maintained in a voucher system

Unpaid and paid voucher files. Two files are always maintained when a voucher system is used: the unpaid voucher file, referred to earlier as the tickler file, and the paid voucher file.

The unpaid voucher file contains all vouchers that have been prepared and approved as proper liabilities but which have not yet been paid. When credit terms run from the invoice date, they are filed according to their due dates. When credit terms run from the end of the month, the invoices of each creditor are grouped and included in one voucher. The vouchers are then arranged by due date. It is important that they are carefully filed, since if one gets out of order an allowable discount may be missed.

The paid voucher file contains all vouchers which have been paid. They are filed by their voucher number in numerical order. Filed in this manner, they constitute a permanent and convenient reference for anyone desiring to check the details of previous cash disbursements.

When a voucher system is in use, the unpaid voucher files serves as (or takes the place of) the subsidiary accounts payable ledger. But when credit terms run from the invoice date, so that invoices are not grouped by creditor, it does not provide information on total amounts owed to particular creditors quickly and conveniently. This information may be obtained by regrouping the vouchers by creditor, but this can often be cumbersome. Sometimes, therefore, it is useful to keep duplicate copies of the invoices filed alphabetically.

Procedure for preparing a voucher. Since the voucher system is a method of recording liabilities that will result in cash disbursements, the preparation of a voucher begins with the receipt of an invoice from a vendor, or with approved evidence that a liability has been incurred and that cash will need to be disbursed. The procedure followed from that point is typically as follows. Basic data such as the invoice number, invoice date, creditor's name and address, description of the goods or services, terms of payment, and amount due are entered on the voucher from the invoice. The invoice, voucher, and receiving report are sent to the persons responsible for verifying the correctness of the description of the goods as to quantity and quality, the extensions and footings, and other details. Each of these persons initials the voucher when he or she is satisfied as to its correctness. When the voucher and accompanying documents are received by the accounting department, a notation is made on the voucher as to the proper accounts to be debited (and, occasionally, credited). After a final review by an authorized person, the proper entry is made in the voucher register and the voucher filed in the unpaid voucher file.

Under the voucher system an invoice or other business document is *not* the basis for making a journal entry; rather, it is the basis for preparing a voucher. The voucher is the basis for making the journal entry in the voucher register. All vouchers are entered in sequence by number in the voucher register.

Indicate whether each of the following statements is true or false.

______ 1. Before a voucher is recorded in the voucher register, its accuracy and validity should be verified.

______ 2. The basis for making a journal entry in the voucher register is the invoice.

______ 3. An invoice or other document is the basis for the preparation of a voucher.

______ 4. The unpaid vouchers file contains evidence to support the validity of past cash disbursements.

Now check your responses in Answer Frame 11[8] on page 196.

Answer frame 10[8]

1. False. It contains a list of checks drawn, not vouchers prepared.
2. False. As explained in previous discussion, when the column totals are posted the account number is listed in parentheses under the total of the column, and when individual amounts are posted from the general ledger columns, check marks (√) are entered beside the amount. This has not been done in the voucher register shown.
3. True. This is essentially what a voucher register contains.
4. False. There is no specific subsidiary ledger for Vouchers Payable in which formal debits and credits can be entered. Rather, the unpaid voucher file serves as the underlying subsidiary record or supporting data.
5. True. Items in these columns need to be posted individually, since different accounts are involved.

If you missed any of the above reread Frame 10[8] before continuing in Frame 11[8] on page 195.

Answer frame 11[8]

1. True. If an error or a possible improper cash payment is not discovered prior to the time of entry of the voucher in the voucher register, it is highly unlikely that it will ever be discovered.
2. False. Entries in the voucher register are based on vouchers, not invoices.
3. True. An invoice or other document will usually be available to support the drawing up of a voucher.
4. False. Unpaid vouchers have not yet been paid; therefore, they cannot constitute evidence supporting the authenticity of past disbursements.

If you answered incorrectly, review Frame 11[8] before continuing on in Frame 12[8] below.

Frame 12[8]

Procedure for paying a voucher. When the voucher is due for payment, it is removed from the unpaid voucher file. A check is prepared for the amount payable. The check, voucher, and other supporting documents are then typically sent to the treasurer. The treasurer (or his representative) examines all of the documents. If he finds them in order, he initials the voucher (to show that final approval has been given) and signs the check. He then mails the check, and usually a remittance advice showing the details of payment, to the creditor. He then returns the voucher to the accounting department.

On receipt of the voucher the accounting department makes an entry in the check register showing the date paid, check number, voucher number, and amount paid. The date paid and check number are also inserted in the voucher register and on the voucher itself. The voucher is then filed in the paid voucher file.

Review of voucher system. The basic features of the voucher system may be summarized as follows:

1. Vouchers are prepared for all transactions that will require a general cash disbursement, whether payment is immediate or delayed.
2. All vouchers are entered in the voucher register at the time a transaction takes place by debits to the proper accounts and credits to Vouchers Payable.
3. All checks are entered in the check register as debits to Vouchers Payable and credits to Cash at the time of issuance.
4. The subsidiary accounts payable ledger is replaced by a file of unpaid vouchers.

Indicate whether each of the following statements is true or false.

_______ 1. Entries in the voucher register are based only on vouchers.

_______ 2. No check may be issued unless it is authorized by an approved voucher.

_______ 3. The file of unpaid vouchers constitutes the subsidiary accounts payable ledger.

_______ 4. The voucher provides an effective means of controlling all cash flows.

Now turn to Answer Frame 12[8] on page 198 to check your answers.

Frame 13[8]

MISCELLANEOUS MATTERS

Posting directly from documents. In order to maintain an efficient flow of paper work through an office, entries may be posted to the subsidiary ledger accounts directly from the primary evidences of transactions. For example, credits to the individual subsidiary accounts payable accounts may be made from the approved purchase invoices before they are entered in the purchases journal. Since the purchases journal is usually posted at the end of the month, there is no day-to-day need for immediate entry in the purchases journal. This permits the employees to schedule their time and work loads more effectively and still keeps each vendor's account up to date.

The use of documentary ledgers. In many cases of processing financial data, subsidiary ledgers are maintained in principle even though formal accounts are not used. The source documents, or copies thereof, take the place of the subsidiary accounts. To illustrate, as soon as invoices are recorded in the purchases journal, they are placed in an unpaid invoices file according to the date they are due for payment. Placing an invoice in such a file is the equivalent of a credit to a subsidiary ledger account payable. When the invoice is paid and an entry made in the cash disbursements journal, the invoice is removed from the unpaid file and transferred to the paid invoices file where it is filed alphabetically by vendor name. Removal of the invoice from the unpaid file is the equivalent of a debit to an accounts payable subsidiary ledger account. At the end of the month, after the general ledger accounts are posted, the balance in the Accounts Payable controlling account should equal the sum of the invoices in the unpaid invoice file.

The principle is equally applicable when the data are processed electronically. Through the medium of cards or paper tape, the individual receivables may be "debited" to a file of magnetic tape which can be read by a tape drive attached to an electronic computer. Also, through the use of cards or paper tape, the collections may be "credited" to the file of magnetic tape by the process of electronic collation of the data. Concurrently, the electronic computer can cause a tape to be prepared which contains a schedule of the outstanding receivables in the subsidiary file. A printed report can then be prepared from the tape.

Journals and ledgers recorded simultaneously. Traditionally, entry in the journal precedes the transcribing or posting of the data to ledger accounts. But machines have been developed by which data can be entered in a journal and posted to a ledger account simultaneously. For example, with suitably designed accounting machines and forms it is feasible to enter transactions for credit sales in the subsidiary accounts receivable ledger and in a sales journal concurrently. The need to transcribe data from the journal to the accounts is eliminated. Thus, the sorting function of the journal no longer exists.

The accounting functions performed with a computer system are not unlike those found in pen-and-ink and machine accounting systems. But the use of the computer will change the form of accounting records. Journals and ledgers appearing in the form illustrated in this chapter

Answer frame 12[8]

1. True. This is the system's main feature as regards the source of entries.
2. True. This is the typical procedure followed to control cash disbursements.
3. True. To the extent that information is desired relative to the amounts owed individual creditors, it normally can be obtained only from the unpaid vouchers file.
4. False. It is a system of control over cash disbursements; it has nothing to do with controlling cash receipts, which requires far different procedures.

If you answered incorrectly, review Frame 12[8] and then continue on in Frame 13[8] on page 197.

Frame 13[8] continued

will no longer be used as a means of recording and accumulating information, although the computer print-out may be in a form similar to the special journals illustrated.

Indicate whether each of the following statements is true or false.

_____ 1. Subsidiary ledger accounts, such as for accounts receivable, can be maintained on magnetic tape and processed by means of a computer.

_____ 2. Postings to subsidiary ledger accounts need not necessarily be made from a journal.

_____ 3. Source documents can, in some cases, serve effectively as subsidiary ledger accounts.

_____ 4. Entry in the journal must precede entry of the same data in ledger accounts.

Now check your answers by turning to Answer Frame 13[8] on page 200.

SUMMARY

Because of the large volume of similar transactions, most companies use several special journals rather than one general journal in order to secure a more efficient and accurate accounting for business data.

The special journals illustrated are only representative of ones that may be used and include the sales, purchases, cash receipts, cash disbursements, and payroll journals.

The sales journal generally is used only for sales on account, and may vary considerably in its design from company to company, as may all special journals.

The cash receipts journal is used to record all cash receipts from whatever source.

The cash receipts and sales journals can be combined into one journal, with a resultant saving of some effort as far as posting is concerned. But having separate sales and cash receipts journals does allow more persons to work with the data in the journals at the same time.

The purchases journal is used to record all purchases of merchandise on account. And most firms record purchases as if made on a credit basis even if the length of delay in payment is only the time necessary to write a check. Control is facilitated by paying all bills by check. The payment is recorded in a cash disbursements journal, wherein all cash disbursements are recorded.

The purchases and cash disbursements journals could be combined into a single journal, but this would limit division of labor.

A payroll journal may be used to summarize data pertaining to payroll accounting. Postings may be made from it or it may only serve as a memorandum record, with formal recording in other journals.

Every transaction that will not fit conveniently in a special journal is entered in the general journal.

The proper combination of journals in a particular company is a function of the volume of transactions, the types of transactions, management's information needs, and the number of persons having to work with the data at the same time. By using special journals time is saved in journalizing and posting, detail is eliminated from the general ledger accounts, division of labor is promoted, and the use of accounting machines is facilitated.

The voucher system provides an effective means of control over cash disbursements, provides for an orderly processing of bills for payment, does away with the subsidiary accounts payable ledger, and results in a paid voucher file which serves as a permanent and convenient reference for checking the details of a transaction.

When a voucher system is used, the voucher register and check register replace the purchases and cash disbursements journals.

Properly filed source documents are sometimes used in lieu of subsidiary ledgers made up of formal accounts. When electronic computers are used, the traditional journals and ledgers are not even used. The data are stored on punched cards or tape, or on magnetic drums or tape. The use of this type of accounting system is expanding rapidly.

The basic objectives of all accounting systems are the same. These are to provide useful information on a timely and economical basis to interested parties and to provide an historical record of financial activities.

You have completed the programmed portion of Chapter 8. Study the terms in the Glossary which follows and then go on to the Student Review Quiz as a self-administered test of your comprehension of the material in this chapter.

GLOSSARY

Accounts payable invoice file–an unpaid bill file in which invoices are filed according to due date. As invoices are paid they are removed from the file and are usually placed in alphabetical order in a paid invoice file. The accounts payable invoice file often serves as a subsidiary ledger.

Accounts receivable file–copies of sales invoices filed alphabetically (or in some other logical manner) in lieu of maintaining a subsidiary accounts receivable ledger. As payment is received the sales invoices are removed from the file and retained in alphabetical order in a permanent file.

Cash disbursements journal–a special journal in which all outflows of cash are recorded.

Cash receipts journal–a special journal in which all inflows of cash are recorded.

Check register–a special journal in which all checks written are recorded in numerical sequence; generally has one column entitled Vouchers Payable Dr. and Cash Cr. (especially when used in a voucher system).

Controlling account–an account in the general ledger that is supported by a detailed classification of accounting information in a subsidiary record.

Direct posting–a procedure under which postings are made to the accounts directly from the primary source documents.

Documentary ledgers–the filing of source documents, or copies thereof, to take the place of subsidiary accounts.

Notes receivable file–the place where notes receivable are filed after they have been recorded in a journal; usually filed either by due date or by name of maker; may serve as a subsidiary ledger of the documentary type.

Paid voucher file–a permanent file where vouchers which have been paid are filed in numerical sequence.

Payroll journal–a special journal used to record data concerning a company's payroll.

Purchases journal–a special journal in which all purchases on account of merchandise for resale are recorded.

Sales journal–a special journal in which all sales of merchandise on account are recorded.

Source documents–documents such as invoices, sales tickets, and cash register tapes which serve as the basis for recording financial transactions in the journal.

Subsidiary ledger–a group of related accounts showing the details of the balance of a controlling account in the general ledger.

Answer frame 13[8]

1. True. In large companies, this is where it is most likely to be maintained simply because of the efficiency of the computer.
2. True. Posting to subsidiary ledgers can take place from source documents.
3. True. For example, unpaid invoices can serve as the accounts payable subsidiary ledger.
4. False. Machines have been developed by which data can be entered in a journal and posted to a ledger simultaneously. In a computerized system, journals and ledgers as described in this chapter are not even used.

If you missed any of the above, reread Frame 13[8] before turning to the Summary on page 198.

GLOSSARY continued

Sundry accounts–miscellaneous accounts; usually the heading given a column in a special journal that is used to enter debits or credits to a variety of accounts with all entries posted individually and the column total not posted.

Tickler file–another name for an unpaid voucher file when the vouchers are arranged by the date upon which the discount period terminates or payment is due.

Unpaid voucher file–place where unpaid vouchers are filed according to their due dates; also serves as a subsidiary accounts payable ledger.

Voucher–a form with spaces provided for data concerning the liability being recorded (such as invoice number, invoice date, creditor's name and address, terms, description of goods or services, amount due, and accounts charged); also has spaces for approval signatures, the date of the check used for payment, and the check number.

Voucher per creditor per month–the voucher system used when the terms of discount run from the end of the month; all invoices from a given creditor are grouped and entered on one voucher, since one check paying all of the invoices for that month will be written.

Voucher register–a special journal in which prenumbered vouchers are recorded in numerical sequence. In addition to a credit column for Vouchers Payable, it normally has various columns for debits such as Purchases, Salaries Expense, and Transportation-In.

Voucher system–a procedure used to ensure tight internal control over all cash disbursement whereby all liabilities requiring cash payment are recorded on a voucher and in a voucher register prior to payment.

Vouchers Payable–an account title often substituted for Accounts Payable in the ledger when a voucher system is used.

STUDENT REVIEW QUIZ

1. Information relative to certain aspects of a business is processed through an accounting system so that–
   a. The results of operations can be determined.
   b. A degree of control can be exercised over operations.
   c. The financial position of the firm can be determined.
   d. Required governmental reports can be filed on time.
   e. All of the above.
2. Source documents serve which of the following purposes?
   a. As a record of completed transactions.
   b. As a means of communicating the results of operations for a period of time.
   c. As a means of communicating data about transactions.
   d. As a source of data for management reports.
   e. As a means of revealing the details of the system of internal control.
3. Which of the following statements is *false?* The use of special journals–
   a. Facilitates the division of labor in journalizing and posting.
   b. Systematizes the original recording of the major recurring transactions.
   c. Saves time in journalizing and posting.

d. Makes the adaption of the accounting process to accounting machines more difficult.
e. Eliminates considerable detail from certain accounts in the general ledger.

4. When special journals are used, adjusting and closing entries are generally recorded in the—
a. Cash disbursements journal.
b. Cash receipts journal.
c. General journal.
d. Sales journal.
e. Purchases journal.
f. Payroll journal.

5. The entry to record the conversion of an account receivable to a note receivable would probably be made in the—
a. Cash disbursements journal.
b. Cash receipts journal.
c. General journal.
d. Purchases journal.
e. Sales journal.

6. Match each transaction in column A with the appropriate journal in which it would be recorded in column B. Assume each of the journals listed is a book of original entry and is designed as illustrated in the chapter.

Column A	*Column B*
1. Acquired merchandise on account.	*a.* Sales journal.
2. Recorded the estimated bad debts for the period.	*b.* Cash receipts journal.
3. Recorded the payment of wages.	*c.* Purchases journal.
4. Sold merchandise on account.	*d.* Cash disbursements journal.
5. Sold merchandise for cash.	*e.* General journal.
6. Collected cash on account.	*f.* Payroll journal.
7. Gave a note to a trade creditor in settlement of his account.	
8. Received and paid a bill for advertising.	
9. Received a cash dividend.	
10. Sold land and received a note in payment.	
11. Paid rent for the month.	
12. Received a credit memo from a vendor.	
13. Sent a purchase order to a vendor.	
14. Paid a trade creditor's account late, thereby missing the discount offered.	
15. Recorded the payroll for the month.	

7. The form of the journals used by the individual firms in an industry (select the best answer)—
a. Will be identical to those used by other firms in the industry.
b. Is closely related to the design and flow of source documents in the individual firm.
c. Will be specifically designed to meet most efficiently the specific needs of, and to cope with the specific circumstances encountered in, the individual firm.
d. None of the above.
e. Is stated in (*b*) and (*c*).

8. When using a sales journal—
a. Sales must always be classified by departments.
b. Sales may be classified by department, sales territory, product line, and so.
c. Cash sales of merchandise will generally be recorded in the cash receipts journal.
d. Sales discounts taken by customers will be recorded in the sales journal.
e. Both (*b*) and (*c*) are correct.

9. Of the following, choose the *incorrect* statement.
a. An account in the general ledger that is supported by a detailed classification of accounting data in a subsidiary ledger or record is known as a controlling account.
b. As a general rule, the individual accounts supporting a general ledger account appear in the general ledger.
c. Individual accounts receivable accounts are likely to provide vital information to firms which extend credit with the result that it is quite essential that these accounts be kept up to date as to charges, payments, and balances.
d. More than one controlling account may appear in the statement of financial position.

e. A controlling account balance may be reported in an earnings statement.

10. Subsidiary ledgers are—
 a. Standardized for all firms.
 b. May be used by a company for accounts receivable only if it uses one for accounts payable.
 c. Are not even used by some small businesses.
 d. Are of no value to a service type business.
 e. Must contain formal accounts.

11. Which of the following figures would not be posted to a ledger account?
 a. The cash credit column total in the cash disbursements journal.
 b. The sundry debit column total in the cash disbursements journal.
 c. The purchases debit column total in the purchases journal.
 d. The accounts receivable debit column total in the sales journal.
 e. The vouchers payable credit column total in a voucher register.

12. Choose the correct statement among the following.
 a. Using a file of copies of sales invoices as a subsidiary accounts receivable ledger is an excellent example of direct posting.
 b. The sale of a plant asset should not be recorded in the sales journal.
 c. Postings to subsidiary ledger accounts are generally made monthly.
 d. If a firm makes a large number of credit sales each day and the dollar amount of each sale is small, it is advisable to enter these sales individually in the sales journal.

13. A documentary ledger is:
 a. A file of legal documents such as contracts, insurance policies, and so on.
 b. The use of source documents (or copies thereof) in place of a subsidiary ledger of accounts.
 c. Generally used as a supplement to the traditional subsidiary ledger.
 d. Used only with electronic processing of data.
 e. The use of source documents in place of general ledger accounts.

14. A voucher system is used in connection with transactions that involve only—
 a. The receipt of cash.
 b. The payment of cash.
 c. The purchase of merchandise.
 d. The sale of merchandise.
 e. The recording of revenue and expense.

15. Which of the following statements is not correct? A file of unpaid vouchers—
 a. May be used to replace the accounts payable subsidiary ledger.
 b. Is controlled by the Vouchers Payable account in the general ledger.
 c. Shows during the year the total amount of all recorded outstanding liabilities for goods and services.
 d. Shows only the total amount of outstanding liabilities for merchandise purchased.
 e. Frequently shows the net discounted amounts due on individual invoices payable.

16. The voucher is prepared and filed in the unpaid voucher file—
 a. As soon as the goods are requisitioned by a department.
 b. As soon as the purchase order for the goods is sent out.
 c. As soon as the invoice covering the goods is received.
 d. After receipt of the goods, the invoice, and after prices and extensions have been verified.
 e. When payment is made.

17. Use of the Discounts Lost account in a voucher system—
 a. Helps in implementing the principle of management by exception.
 b. Requires the processing of a second separate voucher each time a payment is not made in time to take advantage of the discount offered.
 c. Shows the same information as the Purchase Discounts account would show.
 d. Does all of the above.
 e. Does (*a*) and (*b*) of the above.

SOLUTIONS TO STUDENT REVIEW QUIZZES

Following are the solutions to the Student Review Quizzes presented at the end of each chapter. It is assumed that before you check the solutions for a particular chapter you will have already answered all of the questions in the quiz.

CHAPTER 1

1. (*e*) Since Assets = Liabilities + Stockholders' Equity, it must also be true that Stockholders' Equity is equal to Assets less Liabilities as shown below:

   $$A = L + SE, \text{ so } A - L = SE.$$

2. (*c*) Delivery equipment is an asset. Therefore, assets would be increased by $4,000. Since no payment has been made yet, liabilities are also increased by $4,000. There is no effect on stockholders' equity.
3. (*a*) Revenue is properly defined as the total flow of products or services delivered to or performed for customers by an entity. The difference between selling price and cost is called the margin or markup. Revenue represents an element which tends to increase stockholders' equity. Net earnings are calculated by deducting expenses from revenues.
4. (*b*) The advertising services were received during the month and were used in attracting customers to the firm with the objective of having those customers pay assets into the firm for goods and services provided. Since the advertising services were not paid for, a liability must be increased for the debt owed. Since the services were used up during the month, their cost should be shown as an expense. And expenses tend to offset the increase in retained earnings brought about by the recording of revenues as increases in retained earnings. Actually, it is only the excess of revenues over expenses which increases retained earnings.
5. (*c*) Collecting accounts receivable reduces the amount of these accounts still outstanding. Cash is increased by the same amount as the decrease in accounts receivable. Since both of these are assets, response (*c*) correctly describes the effect.
6. (*e*) The changes in assets and liabilities which occurred during the period of operation would have to be determined by comparing the statements of financial position prepared at the beginning and end of the period. The earnings statement would not give this information.
7. (*b*) The earnings for 1976 would be included in the total shown for retained earnings on the statement of financial position dated December 31, 1976. Also included in the total would be the cumulative earnings in past years less amounts paid out in dividends during the life of the firm.
8. (*f*) Net earnings appear as the last figure on the earnings statement. They also appear as an addition to beginning retained earnings (in arriving at ending retained earnings) on the statement of retained earnings. The Retained Earnings account appears on the statement of financial position, and its balance is the last figure on the statement of retained earnings.
9. (*c*) Although such activity may be undertaken by a CPA as part of his management advisory services, executive recruitment is not an accounting function. All of the others

listed involve financial information and are regularly engaged in by accountants.

10. (*c*) Generally, the right to express an opinion attesting to the fairness of published financial information is restricted by law to CPAs (and a few other public accountants in some states). All of the other indicated activities are regularly undertaken by accountants and others who are not CPAs. Many individuals offer their services in preparing tax returns; management consulting firms render management advisory services; many large companies have internal audit staffs; and the preparation of budgets is regularly undertaken by non-CPA accountants in private business.

11. (*d*) Cash, and other assets that will be converted into cash, and other assets that will be consumed or used up in the course of normal operations within one year or one operating cycle, whichever is longer, are classified in the statement of financial position as current assets. The concept of an operating cycle is also used in the classification of certain liabilities as current liabilities.

12. (*e*) Since all of the statements are true, this is the best answer.

13. (*e*) Since all of the statements are true, this is the best answer.

14. (*a*) Since financial accounting information generally relates to the entity as a whole and is historical in nature, it is not likely to be useful or relevant in this type of decision. Note that all of the other types of decisions listed require information relating to an entity as a whole.

CHAPTER 2

1. (*b*) Debits are entries on the left side of an account. By convention, assets and expenses are increased by debits; liabilities, stockholders' equity, and revenues are decreased by debits since they are increased by credits in order to keep accounts with debit balances equal in total to accounts with credit balances.

2. (*e*) All of the statements regarding expenses are true. Recall from Chapter 1 that all expenses could be entered directly as deductions from retained earnings. Since expenses are increased by debit entries, they normally have debit balances. Both (*c*) and (*d*) are correct because expenses are assets that expired in the production of revenue and are usually measured at the cost of the asset that expired.

3. (*a*) Cash was received which means the balance in the Cash account must be increased. Assets are increased by debits, and Cash is an asset and must be debited. The credit must be to Capital Stock since this is what was exchanged for the cash. A credit to Capital Stock increases the account to show the additional stock issued. The credit in (*b*) to Retained Earnings is incorrect since the capital was invested or contributed by stockholders, not earned by operations. Answer (*e*) correctly identifies the class of accounting elements involved, but does not state the names of the specific accounts involved.

4. (*b*) Answer (*e*) correctly identifies the classes of accounting elements involved, while (*b*) correctly identifies the exact accounts involved. An asset must be debited since the company has a right to receive cash in the future, but it does not have a written promise to pay as of a specific date. Consequently, a debit to Cash or Notes Receivable would be incorrect. Rights to receive amounts from customers are called Accounts Receivable, and this account should be debited.

   The credit should be to the revenue account, Service Revenue. This indicates that revenue has been earned by serving customers, and revenues are increased by credits.

5. (*a*) The receipt of the bill (or invoice as it is often called) indicates that the recipient owes the vendor for something already delivered or for a service performed. Since the service performed in the past week was advertising, an expense has been incurred and an expense account should be increased,

debited, and a suitable title for the account is Advertising Expense.

Since the bill has not been paid, the liability for future payment must be recognized and recorded. The Accounts Payable account is typically used for such debts. To increase a liability account, a credit must be entered.

6. (*c*) Answer (*b*) correctly analyzes the transaction as consisting of the receipt of one type of asset upon the surrender of another, but does not name the specific accounts involved. Customers are paying amounts they owe, which have been carried as accounts receivable. Since cash was received, the Cash account must be increased (debited). Since the amounts owed by customers has been decreased, Accounts Receivable must be decreased (credited).

7. (*d*) Answer (*e*) once again correctly identifies the classes of accounting elements involved but not the specific accounts. Since two types of assets have been purchased, two types of asset accounts are increased (debited). Since the items were purchased on open account, the liability account, Accounts Payable, must be increased (credited).

8. (*b*) Once again, answer (*a*) identifies the class of accounting elements involved but not the specific accounts. Since cash was received, the Cash account must be increased (debited). The providing of services to customers is an act of the earning of revenue, meaning that a revenue account must be increased (credited).

9. (*e*) In this transaction the incurrence and immediate payment of an expense are to be recognized. Since cash was paid out, the account, Cash, must be decreased (credited). Since the employee services have been received and used in producing revenue, an expense, in this case for salaries, must be increased (debited).

10. (*c*) A trial balance that does not balance always means that an error has been made. But the reverse is not true. A trial balance may be in balance and serious accounting errors may still exist—such as debiting an expense to an asset account. Total debits would still equal total credits, but both the assets and the expenses would be incorrectly stated.

11. (*e*) A ledger is a collection of all of the accounts in an accounting system, not just the statement of financial position accounts or the earnings statement accounts. Response (*a*) more nearly describes a journal which is covered in the next chapter. Response (*d*) describes a trial balance.

12. (*d*) All of the other statements listed are typically published and sent to owners and possibly other outsiders. But the trial balance is prepared by the accountant for his own personal use. It has very little, if any, information content to either insiders or outsiders.

CHAPTER 3

1. (*d*) For every entry that is made, the debits must equal the credits. Unless this is done, the ledger, the trial balance, and the statement of financial position will be out of balance. The double-entry system is based on an equality of debits and credits.

2. (*d*) Cross-indexing accomplishes all of these things (*a, b,* and *c*). In the journal it shows the account to which an amount was posted. In the ledger it shows the journal source of all amounts entered. This provides a link between the journal and the ledger accounts, facilitates the finding of errors, and reduces the likelihood of errors in posting.

3. (*a*) The trial balance shows whether total debits equal total credits in the ledger. The posting of an amount to the wrong expense account will not affect the equality of debits and credits. Items (*b*), (*c*), and (*d*) would affect the equality of debits and credits as shown in the trial balance and, therefore, would be detected.

4. (*b*) Both response (*a*) and (*c*) would result in a difference in the columns of $1,800 assuming no other errors had been made. Response (*b*) is one of several possibilities that could cause the difference. For in-

stance, a credit of $7,600 could have been posted as a credit of $6,700. Alternatively, a debit of $6,700 could have been posted as a debit of $7,600.

5. (*d*) A post-closing trial balance is taken *after* all expense and revenue accounts have been closed into the Expense and Revenue Summary account (which in turn is closed into Retained Earnings). Therefore, all expense and revenue accounts would have zero balances and would not appear in a post-closing trial balance.

6. (*c*) Expenses are closed by debiting the Expense and Revenue Summary account and crediting the expense account (Rent Expense in this instance). Items (*b*), (*d*), and (*e*) are all statement of financial position accounts and are not closed. Item (*a*) is a revenue account and is closed by *crediting* the Expense and Revenue Summary account and debiting Service Revenue.

7. (*c*) If net earnings for the period are $700, the account, Expense and Revenue Summary, would have a $700 credit balance after all expense and revenue accounts had been closed to it. Therefore, in order to close the account, a $700 debit would have to be made to the Expense and Revenue Summary account and a $700 credit would have to be made to the account, Retained Earnings.

8. (*b*) The Expense and Revenue Summary account receives amounts which are closed into it from the revenue and expense accounts. It is, therefore, a summary of these accounts. The balance in the Expense and Revenue Summary account at that point represents the net earnings (if a credit balance) or a net loss (if a debit balance). After all accounts requiring closing have been closed, the Expense and Revenue Summary account itself has a zero balance since it has been closed into Retained Earnings. The account does not summarize changes in assets and liabilities. The Retained Earnings account, response (*d*), is never closed because it is a statement of financial position account.

9. (*d*) Statement of financial position accounts are *never* closed (although it is possible that they may have zero balances for other reasons). As a result of closing, all expense and revenue accounts and the Expense and Revenue Summary account always are reduced to zero balances.

10. (*c*) Posting is the act of recording amounts in the ledger accounts as indicated in the journal. It is sometimes referred to as a transfer of amounts from the journal to the ledger. Response (*e*) would be correct if it said "from the *journal* to the *ledger*."

11. (*c*) The totals of all the debits and all the credits in the journal will be greater than the total debit and credit balances in the ledger if any account in the ledger has both a debit and a credit. For instance, if the Cash account had a debit of $10,000 and a credit of $8,000, it would have a debit balance of only $2,000 since the credit is offset against the debit. In the journal the $10,000 debit would be included in total debits and the $8,000 credit would be included in total credits.

12. (*b*) In response (*a*), the second and third steps should be reversed. In responses (*c*) and (*d*), the third step should be first.

CHAPTER 4

1. (*e*) An example of each situation would be:

a. Insurance Expense (an expense)
    Unexpired Insurance (an asset)
  To transfer the expired portion of the asset, unexpired insurance, from the asset account to an expense account.

b. Wages Expense (an expense)
    Accrued Salaries Payable (a liability)
  To record wages earned by employees but not yet paid. The expense and liability accounts are both increased.

c. Rental Payments Received in Advance (a liability)
    Rent Revenue (a revenue)
  To transfer the portion of rent which has been earned from a liability account to a revenue account.

d. Accrued Interest Receivable (an asset)
    Interest Revenue (a revenue)
  To record interest that has been earned but not yet received. The asset and revenue accounts are both increased.

2. (*b*) The information given tells you that 1 percent of the credit sales are estimated to be uncollectible. Thus, the amount of the entry is $170 (1 percent of $17,000). The amount must be charged to an expense account, but it can only be credited to an Allowance for Doubtful Accounts since it is not known at this time which of the accounts receivable will be uncollectible. In this manner, an expense is recognized and an asset reduced.
3. (*b*) A debit to the Bad Debts Expense account is incorrect. The company makes an entry at the end of *each* accounting year as follows:

   Bad Debts Expense (an expense)
       Allowance for Doubtful Accounts (a contra account to Accounts Receivable)

   By making this entry, the company has already indicated that it expects some of the accounts to become uncollectible and has charged the year of sale with this expense.

   When an account actually becomes uncollectible, it would be double counting to again debit the Bad Debts Expense account. The correct entry is to reduce the asset contra account, Allowance for Doubtful Accounts, as indicated in response (*b*).
4. (*c*) Two things are missing from the accounts—they do not show the asset, the right to receive interest to be received later, and the revenue earned, the interest. Assets are increased by debits and revenues are increased by credits. Thus, entry (*c*) is correct.
5. (*e*) The correct entry is:

Bad Debts Expense	130	
Allowance for Doubtful Accounts		130

   The goal is to build the balance of the account, Allowance for Doubtful Accounts, up to its required balance of 1 percent of $14,500, or $145. It already has a balance of $15. Therefore, a credit of $130 is needed.

   Entry (*d*) has the correct dollar amount but has the debit and credit reversed.
6. (*a*) The policy is for three years and cost $900. The expense applicable to each year is one third of the $900, or $300. Since only one half of the first year of the policy falls within the current accounting year of the company, the amount of the entry is $150.

   The entry must transfer $150 of the asset, unexpired insurance, to the expense, insurance expense. To do so, the expense must be debited and the asset credited as in response (*a*).
7. (*a*) The percentage estimate of bad debts must be *flexible* rather than constant. As the firm's experience on bad debts changes over time, the percentage estimate to use in future years must change if the estimate is to be relatively accurate.
8. (*a*) An expense and a liability must be increased. Both responses (*a*) and (*d*) accomplish this. The liability increased in (*d*) is accounts payable which is usually used to show only amounts owed to trade creditors. Since the liability increased is for amounts owed to employees, response (*a*) is preferable.
9. (*d*) Computation of amount:

Cost	$3,400
Less salvage value	200
Amount to be depreciated	$3,200

$$\text{Depreciation per Year} = \frac{\$3{,}200}{4} = \$800.$$

   October 1 to December 31 is only one fourth of a year so the current amount of the entry is $800/4, or $200.

   An expense account, Depreciation Expense—Office Furniture, must be debited (increased) and the contra asset account, Allowance for Depreciation—Office Equipment, must also be increased (credited). The latter account will be shown on the statement of financial position as a deduction from the asset, Office Equipment. Response (*e*) has the debit and credit reversed.
10. (*d*) The liability, accrued wages payable, would be understated because of the

failure to include the debt owed to employees. The stockholders' equity of the company would be overstated because retained earnings would be overstated (as the result of an understatement of wages expense).

11. (*c*) Adjusting entries are necessary only before financial statements are to be prepared. Only if financial statements are to be prepared each month would response (*a*) be correct. Only if the company's accounting year-end were December 31 and if statements were to be prepared at that time would response (*b*) be correct.

   Adjusting entries are made for continuous activity so that accounts will have their proper balances before financial statements are prepared. If they are not made, the statements will be inaccurate.

CHAPTER 5

1. (*a*) The list price is often the price to the ultimate consumer. The price to the trade customer is the list price less the trade (but not the cash) discounts:

List price	$1,000
	0.75
	$ 750
	0.80
	$ 600
	0.90
Gross invoice price	$ 540

2. The correct entry is:

Accounts Payable	540.00	
Cash		529.20
Merchandise Inventory		10.80
To record payment of invoice.		

Gross invoice price	$540.00
Purchase discount ($540 × 0.02)	10.80
Net Amount Due	$529.20

3. (*c*) The list price less the trade and quantity discounts is called the gross invoice price since this is the gross amount at which the goods are sold. The transportation charges do not change this billed price, so the discount is on this billed price.

4. *Dollar difference:*

   Amount of discount:

   $\$5,000 \times 3\% = \$150.00$

   Amount of interest on the loan:

   $\$4,850 \times 0.06 \times \frac{20}{360} = 16.17$

   Savings $133.83

   Equivalent rate of interest:

   A 3 percent charge for the use of the $5,000 for an additional 20 days is equivalent to an annual rate of 54 percent computed as follows:

   $$\frac{20}{360} = \frac{3\%}{X\%}$$
   $$20X = 1,080$$
   $$X = 54\%$$

   (In this type of computation it is customary to use a 360-day year and to assume there are 30 days in each month.)

5. (*a*) The cash discount is based only on the gross invoice price of $4,000 since the seller is selling only the goods, not the goods and the transportation services.

6. (*a*) Cash discounts, not trade discounts, are used to encourage prompt payment of an invoice.

7. (*d*) Sales discounts are shown as deductions from sales revenue because they represent a reduction in the amount of revenue actually produced by the sales.

8. (*c*) Since the freight terms were f.o.b. shipping point, the purchaser is responsible for the charges. Under perpetual inventory procedure the Merchandise Inventory account is increased by the amount of the freight costs.

9. September 25 (*c*) September 26 (*b*). September 25 is the last day of the discount period. If the invoice is paid on this day, a discount of $1,200 × 0.03 = $36 is allowed and this is credited directly to the Merchandise Inventory account. If the invoice is paid after September 25, no discount may be taken, and the amount due is the gross invoice price.

10. Allowance granted (*b*). Return allowed (*c*). If an allowance is granted, only an

entry recording the allowance and reducing the receivable is required. If goods are returned, however, two entries are required: one at selling price and one at cost.

CHAPTER 6

1. (*d*) Purchase discounts are considered to be direct reductions of the cost of purchases. Since purchases are assets and normally are recorded as debits, the purchase discounts, to be reductions, must be shown as credits.

2. (*d*) The net cost of purchases is determined as follows:

Purchases		$9,000
Add: Transportation-in		700
		$9,700
Less:		
Purchase returns and allowances	$400	
Purchase discounts	200	600
Net Purchases		$9,100

Cost of goods available for sale is determined as follows:

Beginning inventory	$ 5,000
Add: Net purchases (see above)	9,100
Cost of Goods Available for Sale	$14,100

Cost of goods sold is determined as follows:

Cost of goods available for sale (above)	$14,100
Less: Ending inventory	3,000
	$11,100

3. Under periodic procedure:
   pre-closing trial balance (*a*) and (*c*);
   post-closing trial balance (*b*).
   Under perpetual procedure:
   pre-closing and post-closing trial balances (*b*).

   When periodic inventory procedure is used, the beginning inventory and purchases amounts appear as debits in the pre-closing trial balance. Credits of equal amounts are entered in the credit column of the Adjustments columns opposite these items, and Cost of Goods Sold is debited for the total. The ending inventory is debited in the debit column of the Adjustments columns, and the amount is carried to the *debit* column of the Statement of Financial Position columns. Cost of Goods Sold is credited for the amount of the ending inventory. The net debit balance in Cost of Goods Sold is then transferred to the debit column of the Earnings Statement columns. The Statement of Financial Postion columns are similar to the columns in a post-closing trial balance (assuming closing entries have been journalized and posted correctly and the account balances have been determined properly).

   Under perpetual procedure the cost of goods sold and inventory changes are recorded throughout the period. At the end of the period, the amount shown in the Inventory account represents the ending book balance. This amount appears in both the pre-closing and post-closing trial balances. There are no Purchases or related accounts when perpetual procedure is used; all net purchases are recorded directly in the Inventory account.

4. (*c*) Response (*c*) correctly uses a revenue reduction account, Sales Returns and Allowances, as a debit for the retail price of the goods returned. It also shows that the customer now owes $150 less than before returning the goods.

   There is no need to use the Merchandise Inventory or Cost of Goods Sold accounts since periodic inventory procedure is used.

5. (*b*) Responses (*c*) and (*d*) are far from being correct. Equipment has not been purchased, response (*c*), and a liability account must be credited to be increased rather than debited as in response (*d*).

   When periodic inventory procedure is used, all merchandise purchases are debited to the account, Purchases.

   If perpetual inventory procedure were being used, response (*a*) would be correct.

6. (*d*) Response (*d*) correctly shows that the liability of $1,000 no longer exists and that only $980 in cash was paid (since payment was made within the discount period). The Purchase Discounts accounts shows the amount by which the debit to the Purchases account exceeds the actual outlay for the merchandise.

7. (*b*) The company is entitled to take the discount since 3/10 E.O.M. means that if

the bill is paid within 10 days after the end of the month in which the invoice is dated the discount may be taken. In the example given, the discount could be taken any time through August 10.

The liability is reduced by $800; and since the discount was taken, only $776 in cash was paid. The difference of $24 once again shows the amount to be deducted from purchases to arrive at their net cost.

8. (*d*) When periodic procedure is used, the related costs such as transportation and receiving usually are debited to separate accounts rather than the Purchases account. Response (*d*) is a typical treatment.

9. Perpetual (*a*). Periodic (*c*). When merchandise is sold under perpetual inventory procedure, it is necessary to debit the Cost of Goods Sold account and credit the Merchandise Inventory account for the cost of the merchandise. Throughout the period, an effort is made to keep an accurate account of the merchandise inventory still on hand. The portion that has been sold is charged to expense as the cost of the merchandise sold. The entry is not necessary under periodic procedure since no attempt is made to keep an accurate account of inventory on hand throughout the period (at least in the formal accounting ledger). Instead, the correct amount is determined by physical count at the end of the period.

The entry debiting the Accounts Receivable account and crediting Sales for the retail price is necessary under both methods.

10. (*a*) Ending inventory is a deduction from total goods available for sale to arrive at the cost of goods sold. If it is overstated, cost of goods sold will be understated.

Cost of goods sold is a deduction from revenues in arriving at new earnings. If it is understated, net earnings will be overstated.

In reference to response (*e*), gross margin is equal to sales revenues less cost of goods sold. If cost of goods sold is understated, gross margin will be overstated rather than understated.

11. (*d*) Response (*a*) would be correct if it had indicated that transportation-in was added rather than subtracted.

Response (*b*) is incorrect for two reasons. Transportation-in should be added rather than deducted. Ending inventory should be deducted rather than added.

Response (*c*) is incorrect because purchase returns and allowances should be deducted rather than added in determining the cost of goods sold.

CHAPTER 7

1. (*e*) The work sheet is an informal schedule. The accounting process could (although not as easily) be completed without preparing a work sheet. The work sheet may contain as many columns as the accountant wishes to use. The more conventional ones contain 8 or 10 columns depending on whether they include or exclude columns entitled, Adjusted Trial Balance. It would be *helpful* to include explanations of each adjustment at the bottom of the work sheet but it is not *required*.

2. (*b*) The depreciation *per year* is computed as follows:

$$\frac{\text{Cost} - \text{Salvage Value}}{\text{Years of Estimated Usefulness}} = \frac{\$2{,}700}{9} = \$300$$

Since only one month of the asset's life has expired, the amount of depreciation recorded is $25 which is computed by dividing $300 by 12 months.

3. (*d*) When depreciation is recorded the entry is:

Depreciation Expense	400	
Allowance for Depreciation—Store Fixtures		400

Notice that the credit is to the allowance account rather than to the Store Fixtures account. The store fixtures *gross* amount shown will remain at $4,000 throughout the period. As the allowance account is continually increased during the life of the asset, the *net* book value of store fixtures decreases even though the amount appearing in the Statement of Financial Position debit column opposite store fixtures remains at $4,000. On the statement of financial position itself the store fixtures and allowance for depreciation appear as follows after the first year:

Store fixtures	$4,000	
Less: Allowance for Depreciation	400	
Net undepreciated amount		$3,600

4. (*a*) The Supplies on Hand account is an asset. The adjustment for the supplies used during the month would be as follows:

Supplies Expense	290	
Supplies on Hand		290

The original debit balance of $315 less the credit of $290 leaves a balance of $25 in the Statement of Financial Position debit column.

5. (*c*) When earnings are realized for a particular year, the total of the Earnings Statement credit column exceeds the total of the Earnings Statement debit column (before the net earnings amount is included). To make the two columns balance, the net earnings amount must be entered in the Earnings Statement debit column. The amount is then carried to the Statement of Financial Position credit column since earnings increase the balance in the Retained Earnings account (which normally has a credit balance).

6. (*a*) Adjusting and closing journal entries are still necessary. The work sheet only helps in identifying the adjusting and closing entries which must be made. It does not take the place of these entries.

7. (*b*) The allowance for depreciation account is a special subdivision of the credit side of a plant asset account. As such, it is called a contra account. The credit balance in the allowance account is deducted from the debit balance in the plant asset account on the statement of financial position to arrive at the net undepreciated balance of the plant asset.

8. (*a*) The remaining balance in the Unexpired Insurance account is $400 which represents one third of the original coverage. Therefore, the original premium must have been $1,200.

The original entry must have been:

Unexpired Insurance	1,200	
Accounts Payable		1,200

9. (*d*) and (*f*) The beginning inventory must be credited in the Adjustments credit column in order to transfer it to the Cost of Goods Sold expense account. The ending inventory is entered in the Adjustments debit column since it is credited to the Cost of Goods Sold expense account. The ending inventory must also appear in the Statement of Financial Position debit column since it is an asset.

10. (*b*) The debits and credits of the adjusting entries must be equal. Had the statement been—"If the Earnings Statement credit column total exceeds the total of the Earnings Statement debit column (before the net earnings figure is entered), this indicates that the company has realized earnings"—it would have been true.

Each of the other statements is true.

CHAPTER 8

1. (*e*) The first four statements are all correct. Other purposes are also conceivable, such as seeing that bills are paid on time and that orders received are filled and shipped on time.

2. (*a*), (*c*), and (*d*) are correct. (*b*) is accomplished by the earnings statement, while (*e*) is not formally recorded in any source document but is part of the management structure and the duties associated with various positions of employment within the firm.

3. (*d*) The use of specialized journals facilitates the use of accounting machines.

4. (*c*) The general journal is used to record all entries which are not suited to the other journals and adjusting and closing entries do not fit well in any of the special journals.

5. (*c*) Special journals typically are not designed to handle this type of transaction simply because it is not a recurring transaction for most firms.

6. 1. (*c*)
   2. (*e*)
   3. (*d*)
   4. (*a*)
   5. (*b*)
   6. (*b*)
   7. (*e*)
   8. (*d*)
   9. (*b*)
   10. (*e*)
   11. (*d*)
   12. (*e*)
   13. No entry
   14. (*d*)
   15. (*f*) or (*e*)
7. (*e*) since both (*b*) and (*c*) are correct.
8. (*e*) since both (*b*) and (*c*) are correct—sales may be classified, and cash sales are recorded in the cash receipts journal.
9. (*b*) The details supporting a general ledger account usually appear in some subsidiary accounts or records. Although not covered specifically controlling accounts can be established for any type of account for which there are frequently recorded transactions. Thus, there could be a selling expense control account which would be reported in the earnings statement.
10. (*c*) Subsidiary ledgers or records are only necessary where the details of a general ledger account are so numerous as to complicate the acount and the trial balance. It is conceivable that some firms will not have such circumstances and, therefore, not find it necessary to use subsidiary ledgers or records.
11. (*b*) There is no ledger account entitled "sundry accounts" and, consequently, the total of this column cannot be posted to a ledger account.
12. (*b*) The sales journal is used only to record the sale of merchandise by a firm to its customers and not for miscellaneous sales of other types of assets. Such sales would have to be recorded either in the cash receipts journal, if sale was for cash, or in the general journal if on a credit basis.
13. (*b*) A documentary ledger takes the place of a subsidiary ledger.
14. (*b*) The voucher system is designed to provide tight control over cash disbursements.
15. (*d*) It shows more than the total amount of outstanding liabilities for merchandise purchased. All liabilities which will require the payment of cash will be included at some time before payment is made. Various types of liabilities may be included at any point in time (for example, the principal payment on long-term bonds).
16. (*d*) Only after the quantity and quality of goods have been verified and the arithmetic checked is the voucher authorizing payment prepared and filed.
17. (*e*) Attention is focused only on the discounts lost rather than on the discounts taken. When a discount is missed, a new voucher must be prepared because the original voucher is for a smaller amount than would actually be due. The necessity for preparing a new voucher and the use of the Discounts Lost account bring to the attention of management those discounts which were missed—which, in a well-managed company, should be the exception rather than the rule.

INDEX